Vision From a Little Known Country
A Boisen Reader

Edited by
Glenn H. Asquith, Jr.

Journal of Pastoral Care Publications, Inc.

VISION FROM A LITTLE
KNOWN COUNTRY

©1992
Journal of Pastoral Care Publications, Inc.

Cover design: Darwin Melnyk
Floral sketch: William Ridley

Library of Congress Cataloging-in Publication Data

Vision from a little known country : a Boisen reader / edited by Glenn
  H. Asquith.
       p.   cm.
  Includes bibliographical references and index.
  Contents: pt. l. Articles by Anton T. Boisen. 1923-1961 -- pt.
  2. A critique of Boisen's life and work.
  ISBN 0-929670-05-1 : $22.50
     1. Pastoral psychology--Study and teaching--United States-
-History--20th century. 2. Boisen, Anton T. (Anton Theophilus),
1876-1965. 3. Psychiatry and religion--History--20th century.
I. Boisen, Anton T. (Anton Theophilus), 1876-1965. II. Asquith.
Glenn H., 1946-   .
BV4012.V57 1991
253.5'2--dc20   91-40744
                                                        CIP

Printed in the United States of America
on acid-free paper

To My Parents
Glenn H. Asquith, Sr.
and
Helen U. Asquith

and

To My Sisters
Nancy Ann Asquith
and
Helen Jean Lawrence

Photo of Anton T. Boisen provided by the Rev. Emil M. Hartl, who reports that this photo was distributed at the conference of the Institute of Pastoral Care in Plymouth Massachusetts honoring the 25th anniversary of CPE, at which Anton T. Boisen was present.

CONTENTS

PART II
A CRITIQUE OF BOISEN'S LIFE AND WORK

ACKNOWLEDGMENTS

Grateful acknowledgments is made to the following publishers for permission to reprint articles from their journals: The Christian Association for Psychological Studies' *Journal of Psychology and Christianity*; Colgate Rochester Divinity School's *Crozer Quarterly*; Human Sciences Press' *Journal of Religion and Health* and *Pastoral Psychology*; the Journal of Pastoral Care Publications' *The Journal of Pastoral Care*; the University of Chicago's *Journal of Religion*; and the Religious Education Association's *Religious Education*.

The Editor thanks the following persons: J. Thomas Minor, Director of Reeves Library at Moravian College the Theological Seminary, and staff members Linda LaPointe and Debra Gaspar for their assistance in locating many of the older article reproduced in this volume; Mickey Ortiz and other staff of the Word Processing Center of Moravian College for their meticulous and efficient job of producing the first draft of the manuscript; and Nena Asquith, Editorial Assistant in the Department of Publications, Moravian Church in America, for her help in printing the final draft of the manuscript.

—G.H.A.

INTRODUCTION

Glenn H. Asquith, Jr.

Anton T. Boisen (1876-1965) has been regarded as the founder of Clinical Pastoral Education (CPE). In 1925 he recruited four students for his first summer program of clinical training at Worcester State Hospital in Massachusetts. Although William S. Keller, M.D., preceded Boisen by two years in providing clinical exposure to theological students, Boisen was the first ordained clergy to supervise such an experience as a full-time chaplain of an institution.

Boisen believed firmly that a first-hand study of human experience—what he called a reading of the "living human documents"—was a necessary supplement to classroom training in theological education. He focused on the experience of the mentally ill, because he believed that some forms of mental illness serve a curative, problem-solving function for the individual. As such, he believed that these forms of mental illness have a religious dimension which is worthy of study by persons interested in the spiritual life.

Boisen, a Presbyterian minister who later served the Congregational church, arrived at these beliefs as a result of the first of several psychotic episodes which he experienced in his own life. Following his release from the hospital, he continued his education and affiliated with a group of physicians, theologians, and other professionals who helped him to channel his interests in the direction of clinical training for theological students. During the balance of his career, in spite of several more psychotic relapses, he published five books and scores of articles in professional journals concerning the religious dimensions of human experience. One of his books, *The Exploration of the Inner World* (1936), is still considered to be a major contribution to the psychology of religion. His autobiography, *Out of the Depths* (1960), gives a detailed account of his experience and is a primary illustration of his method of studying human experience. He refers to it as "my own case record."[1] It also gives a rich account of his involvement in the development of clinical pastoral education.

Boisen has been criticized because much of his work throughout the second half of his life was "intensely autobiographical,"[2] representing a constant attempt to validate his interpretation of the meaning of his own experience. Edward Thornton suggests that he did not initiate clinical pastoral education simply because of its benefit for theological inquiry; he was also looking for colleagues in research.[3] Having experienced his own inner world, he wished to explore systematically the inner world of others.

Indeed, the intensity of Boisen's own experience gave him a personal "cause" which also, however, had a very pastoral dimension. Through the structure of clinical pastoral education, Boisen sought to hear in detail the stories of other mentally ill persons with an eye toward helping them and others reinterpret the meaning of their experience. Having experienced psychiatric care in the 1920s, he developed an important hypothesis which was written in a letter in November of 1920, just about six weeks after his committal to Boston Psychopathic Hospital.

> In [one class of insanity] there is no organic difficulty. . . . The difficulty is rather in the *disorganization of the patient's world.* Something has happened which has upset the foundations upon which his ordinary reasoning is based. Death or disappointment or sense of failure may have compelled a reconstruction of the patient's world view from the bottom up, and the mind becomes dominated by the one idea which he has been trying to put in its proper place. That, I think, has been my trouble and I think it is the trouble with many others also.[4]

Thus, because of the vision which Boisen received in what he termed in his autobiography as "A Little-Known Country," he began an exploration which not only led to the formation of clinical pastoral education but also to extensive research and writing in the psychology of religion. In addition to this work, which is still considered relevant and even prophetic in contemporary experience, his clinical method also inspired the contemporary definition and development of the field of

---

1. Anton T. Boisen, *Out of the Depths: An Autobiographical Study of Mental Disorder and Religious Experience* (New York: Harper & Brothers, 1960), 9.

2. Paul W. Pruyser, "Anton T. Boisen and the Psychology of Religion," *The Journal of Pastoral Care* 21:4 (December, 1967), 209.

3. Edward E. Thornton, *Professional Education for Ministry* (Nashville: Abingdon Press, 1970), 56, 58.

4. Anton T. Boisen, *The Exploration of the Inner World: A Study of Mental Disorder and Religious Experience* (Philadelphia: University of Pennsylvania Press, 1971 [1936]), 11.

pastoral theology.[5] The purpose of this book is to provide a renewed understanding and appreciation of Boisen's important contributions to these various fields.

Personal History

In light of the above introduction, it can be seen that no inquiry into Boisen's professional contributions can be made without understanding several significant factors in his history which were formative to his work. These include his family history and education, his relationship with Alice Batchelder, and his experiences during and immediately after his first hospitalization.

Family History and Education

Boisen came from a family of educators and religious leaders. His father migrated from Germany to America before completing his doctoral work and became a professor of modern languages at Indiana University at Bloomington. His maternal great-grandfather was a Reformed Presbyterian minister who organized a theological school and then became professor of languages at the University of Pennsylvania. His maternal grandfather (from whom he received his middle name, Theophilus, which means lover of God) was a professor of natural sciences at Indiana University for forty-six years and pastor of a Reformed Presbyterian church in Bloomington for thirty of those years. His mother was the first woman to enroll at Indiana University and taught for one year at the University of Missouri before returning to Bloomington to marry Hermann Boisen. Anton, their first child, was born in 1876. His father was an energetic but very impulsive man who died of a heart attack when Anton was only seven years old. Nevertheless, he still had a major impact on Anton's development, for from him Anton gained an early interest in scientific inquiry as well as a great love for nature. Hermann spent much of his leisure time teaching Anton to distinguish the different varieties of trees. Shortly before his death, he took Anton and several other boys on a long hike in search of trailing arbutus, a rare mountain flower that became an important symbol in Anton's later life, especially in his relationship with Alice Batchelder.[6]

After Hermann's death, the family lived with Anton's grandfather, Theophilus Wylie. Thus he was raised in the rigid morality and practice of Reformed Presbyterianism.[7] All through adolescence, he felt shame and guilt for his inability

5. See Glenn H. Asquith, Jr., "An Experiential Theology" in Leroy Aden and J. Harold Ellens (eds.), *Turning Points in Pastoral Care: The Legacy of Anton Boisen and Seward Hiltner* (Grand Rapids, MI: Baker Book House, 1990), 19-31.

6. Boisen, *Out of the Depths*, 26.

7. See Glenn H. Asquith, Jr., "Anton T. Boisen and the Study of 'Living Human Documents'," *Journal of Presbyterian History* 60 (Fall, 1982), 244-265 for a description of

to control sexual feelings. In his autobiography he reports the first indication of later difficulties when, on Easter of 1898 at the age of twenty-two, he became severely depressed over his sexual feelings. He finally found great relief when he was able to confess those feelings first to his mother and then to his favorite college professor. The professor, Dr. William L. Bryan, reinforced Boisen's need to control his feelings and said that his salvation from this struggle would come both from Christ and from "some good woman."[8] In spite of this questionable advice, Bryan, who taught philosophy and psychology, had an important influence on Boisen by introducing him to the theory and method of William James and by guiding his reading of James' *Principles of Psychology.*

After graduation from college and after a brief period of high school teaching, Boisen decided to become a forester. The decision grew out of loyalty to his father's memory and also "stood for the idea of adventure, of exploration, of cutting loose from the beaten path and starting forth into unknown territory."[9] He studied at Yale Forest School and then engaged in various surveys for the U.S. Forest Service and became affiliated with Raphael Zon, a well-known scientist who taught him the fine points of scientific inquiry. It was during this time that he experienced a call to ministry.

In the fall of 1908, Boisen entered Union Theological Seminary in New York with the desire to study further the psychology of religion as interpreted by George Albert Coe, including a seminar on the psychology of mysticism. While Coe had a major influence on him, there were at least two points on which they disagreed. James' work enabled Boisen to interpret the meaning of major turning points in his life, such as the Easter crisis of 1898 which was described above. He referred to this type of crisis in one's life as a mystical experience and with James believed that such experiences were real and self-authenticating. In distinction, Coe had never had such an experience himself, and therefore he rejected the reality of mystical experiences as merely part of the excesses of revivalism.[10] Coe also believed that all psychotic experiences were due to organic factors; he did not accept James' notion that the "sick soul" could also play a role in mental illness, a central concept in Boisen's theory. Nevertheless, Coe, like James, was a champion of the empirical study of religious experience. James' theory and its application by Coe is evident throughout Boisen's works. In 1953, he mourned the fact that clinical pastoral education was

---

Boisen's religious history; Boisen's article in this anthology entitled "Divided Protestantism in a Midwest County" also gives a comprehensive cultural and religious analysis of the religion of his youth.

8. Boisen, *Out of the Depths,* 47.
9. Ibid., 51.
10. Ibid., 62.

not taking the challenges and implications of James' *Varieties of Religious Experience* more seriously.[11]

Alice Batchelder

Any serious inquiry into Boisen's life and work must consider his relationship with Alice Batchelder, the woman he refers to as "The Guiding Hand" in his life.[12] He met Alice in 1902 at the age of twenty-six when she came to Indiana University to speak on behalf of the Y.W.C.A. He reports that he fell in love with her immediately, but he also confesses that it was doomed to be a one-sided affair from the outset. Whenever he expressed his love for her, she would request that their relationship cease entirely.[13] Boisen blamed himself continually for the fact that they were never married, and his psychotic episodes were triggered whenever he was confronted with another failure in their relationship. Nevertheless, all of his major career choices, from his call to the ministry to his movement into clinical training, were influenced by this relationship. Driven by an obsession for her, he sought continually to place himself in a professional position that would be "good enough" for Alice, so that she would consent to marry him.

A Purpose and Theory Revealed

In 1920, at the age of forty-four, Boisen came up against a serious personal and professional bind. Following his graduation from seminary and his ordination by the Presbyterian church, he participated in several religious surveys for the Presbyterian Board of Home Missions. He then had a mediocre career in several small pastorates in the Congregational church. After returning from service with the Overseas Y.M.C.A. during World War I, he was determined to find a good pastoral position so that he could propose to Alice, because he would have both a vocation that she approved and a solid financial basis for marriage. Unfortunately, when none of this materialized, he became more frantic and desperate in his search for a solution.

It was while he was rewriting his Statement of Faith for the New York Presbytery (with the hopes of being reassigned to a Presbyterian church) that he became obsessed with the "family of four" delusional system. The system told him that he would have to give up Alice to someone else, because he was not good enough for her. As he became more preoccupied and agitated with these thoughts, his behavior became more bizarre. His family had him committed to Boston Psychopathic Hospital. In the three weeks that followed (during which he was

---

11. Anton T. Boisen, "The Present Status of William James' Psychology of Religion," *The Journal of Pastoral Care* 7:3 (Fall, 1953), 157. This article is reprinted in Part I of this book.
12. Boisen, *Out of the Depths*, 209-210.
13. Ibid., 52.

transferred to Westboro State Hospital), Boisen experienced a severe psychosis marked by violent delirium, hallucinations, and delusions. It was during this time that he had the vision that he had "broken an opening in the wall which separated medicine and religion."[14] He also became obsessed with the meaning of seeing the moon centered in a cross (which stood for suffering) until he realized that he was viewing the moon through wire screening on the porch of the hospital.[15]

This realization contributed to his recovery; he suddenly came out of the acute disturbance much as one awakens from a bad dream. It was then, as he began to reflect on the meaning of his experience, that he found a new purpose in life and formed a new understanding of mental illness. In a letter to a friend, Fred Eastman, written very shortly after this disturbance, he observed that his cure was found "in the faithful carrying through of the delusion itself."[16] He also noted that the doctors who treated him were "not fitted to deal with religious problems" and that "if they succeed in their aims, the patient is shorn of the faith in which lies his hope of cure."[17]

It was during this time of reflection that Fred Eastman sent Boisen a copy of Freud's *Introductory Lectures*. It was his first introduction to Freud, and he was "very excited" to find much that supported his own views.[18] Reinforced and encouraged, Boisen wrote the following letter on February 14, 1921, which declared his intention to engage in a pastoral exploration once he was released from the hospital.

> My present purpose is to take as my problem the one with which I am now confronted, the service of these unfortunates with whom I am surrounded. I feel that many forms of insanity are religious rather than medical problems and that they cannot be successfully treated until they are so recognized. The problem seems to me one of great importance not only because of the large number who are now suffering from mental ailments but also because of its religious and psychological and philosophical aspects. I am very sure that if I can make to it any contribution whatsoever it will be worth the cost.[19]

In summary, Boisen's ideation contained religious symbolism. Finding out the meaning of these symbols led to a new purpose in life and to his eventual recovery and discharge from the hospital. He saw the experience as a religious one because of its positive result, and he believed that persons with theological training needed to be present in psychiatric hospitals along with the doctors to work with those having similar experiences. His desire to involve theological students in this vision, while

---

14. Ibid., 91.
15. Ibid., 101; c.f. *The Exploration of the Inner World*, 4.
16. Boisen, *Out of the Depths*, 101.
17. Ibid., 102.
18. Ibid., 103.
19. Boisen, *The Exploration of the Inner World*, 7.

having a strong personal dimension, was also based on his intent to provide a much-needed ministry to the mentally ill.

Finding a Place

In January, 1922, after fifteen months at Westboro State Hospital, and while still an outpatient there, Boisen moved his residence to Episcopal Theological School in Cambridge, Massachusetts, and enrolled as a special student at Andover Theological Seminary, which was affiliated with Harvard Divinity School. He took several courses: abnormal psychology with William McDougall, the psychology of belief with Macfie Campbell, and social ethics with Richard C. Cabot, M.D.

Cabot became an important ally in the formation of CPE; he shared with Boisen the vision of including a clinical year as part of theological study.[20] Having been professor of clinical medicine at Harvard Medical School, Cabot returned from World War I with a concern for the larger problems of humanity. He moved from medicine to Harvard's chair of Social Ethics and then became professor of Sociology and Applied Christianity at Andover Theological School. He was instrumental in the incorporation of the Council for the Clinical Training of Theological Students in 1930 and served as its president until 1935.

Boisen was influenced by Cabot's emphasis on making an accurate diagnosis of a patient's problems on the basis of known facts as well as his seminar on the preparation of case records for teaching purposes. While continuing to study part time with Cabot in the year 1923-24, Boisen went to work in the Social Service Department of Boston Psychopathic Hospital. His exposure to the methodology of the social worker reinforced his concern for making a careful study of all aspects of a person's situation, including his or her religious experiences.[21]

Through association with Cabot, Boisen learned of an opportunity for which he had been waiting. Dr. William A. Bryan, Superintendent of Worcester State Hospital, announced that he was willing to try a chaplain at his institution. The CPE movement owes a debt to Dr. Bryan for his courageous and innovative decision. When he was criticized for the decision by his peers, he said "he would be perfectly willing to bring in a horse doctor if he thought there was any chance of his being able to help the patients!"[22]

On July 1, 1924, Boisen began his work as chaplain at Worcester State Hospital with the understanding that he would also spend part of his time at Chicago Theological Seminary. He became involved at the seminary through

---

20. Richard C. Cabot, "Adventures on the Borderland of Ethics: A Plea for a Clinical Year in the Course of Theological Study," *The Survey* Graphic Number 55:5 (December 1, 1925), 275-277, 315-317.

21. Boisen, *Out of the Depths*, 148-49.

22. Boisen, *The Exploration of the Inner World*, 9.

Arthur Holt, who expressed great interest in having theological students study how the church could address the problems of the mentally ill. Boisen continued this dual service until 1930, spending the fall quarter of each year in Chicago. During this time, support for the CPE movement grew, and Boisen participated in the incorporation of the Council for the Clinical Training of Theological Students— the first formal organization of the movement—on January 21, 1930.

In June of that year, Boisen's mother died and in November he was once again hospitalized with an acute psychotic episode. He had become preoccupied again with the "family of four" ideation. Although his disturbed condition lasted less than three weeks, the event precipitated Cabot's withdrawal of support of Boisen. Cabot had always disagreed with Boisen's interpretation of mental illness, but now he decreed that Boisen should have nothing more to do with the program of clinical instruction.[23]

Motivated by his desire to be near Alice (who was then employed in Chicago) and by his ties with Chicago Theological Seminary, Boisen became chaplain at Elgin State Hospital in Illinois on April 1, 1932. He immediately organized a Chicago Council for the Clinical Training of Theological Students and continued the development of CPE at Elgin. One of his first students at Elgin in the summer of 1932 was Seward Hiltner, a student at Chicago Theological Seminary.

Boisen suffered a third major psychosis in November of 1935 after receiving word that Alice was terminally ill with cancer. He was hospitalized until two weeks after Alice died on December 2, 1935.

From 1938 to 1942, Boisen served full-time on the faculty of Chicago Theological Seminary. During this time he published many articles and engaged in several team teaching experiences with other faculty at the seminary. He returned as chaplain to Elgin in 1942. Beginning in 1945, and for the rest of his career, he visited clinical training centers as an educational consultant to the Council for Clinical Training of Theological Students. He offered help and materials to the centers and had an opportunity to observe the progress of the movement. He found that many centers were digressing from the type of training that he had envisioned. He was especially critical of those centers that focused heavily on psychoanalytic theory, group dynamics, or techniques of counseling as opposed to the in-depth study and understanding of human experience. He was also troubled by the fact that clinical training was not being accepted as a component of seminary curricula.[24]

---

23. Boisen, *Out of the Depths*, 171.
24. Ibid., 185-87.

Contemporary Relevance

While the contemporary world is facing issues different than in the time of Boisen, the theological and religious questions regarding suffering and conflict, illness, and social movements remain the same. Boisen focused on the religious meaning of individual suffering (especially as manifested in mental illness), and (as will be seen in this book) he was also very interested in the "social conditions" which surrounded human suffering. Thus, while this material reflects the vision of one man which began over seventy years ago, it can be argued that this vision not only has contemporary relevance but also speaks with a prophetic voice to the future.

This collection of articles enables the reader to return to the roots of modern pastoral theology and examine the foundational role which Boisen played in the development of the field. From Boisen's pastoral ministry-in-depth to the mentally ill, modern pastoral theology was born; his basic thesis inspired Seward Hiltner's landmark definition of the field in 1958.[25] One takes the experience of the mentally ill and reflects in depth upon it in light of one's reading of classical theology; from this exercise a new, integrated theology is borne which is relevant to human experience and which continues to inform the work of the pastor. As Charles Gerkin has pointed out, Boisen wanted to read those human documents with the same reverence, respect, and depth with which one using modern hermeneutical method reads biblical texts.[26]

Empirical theology and the dialogue between religion and psychology would have proceeded without Boisen because, historically and culturally, the time was right for such developments. However, Boisen's "vision from a little known country" was a new vision which swam against the main stream of these movements, and pastoral theology and the pastoral care and counseling movement would not have proceeded the way it did without his work. Boisen's approach to empirical theology and the psychology of religion had a distinctively clinical, pastoral, and educational perspective which indeed made him the "Father of the Clinical Pastoral Movement."[27]

Boisen's article, "Theological Education Via the Clinic" (found in this collection) is evidence of the uniqueness of this vision. It indicates that, while Richard Cabot was indeed interested in involving theological students in the clinic, he did not see any value in focusing on the experiences of the mentally ill. Cabot held the majority view of the medical community in the mid-1920's that mental illness was

---

25. Seward Hiltner, *Preface to Pastoral Theology* (Nashville: Abingdon Press, 1958).

26. Charles V. Gerkin, *The Living Human Document: Re-Visioning Pastoral Counseling in a Hermeneutical Mode* (Nashville: Abingdon Press, 1984), 39.

27. Fred Eastman, "Father of the Clinical Pastoral Movement," *The Journal of Pastoral Care* 5:1 (Spring, 1951), 3-7 (reprinted in Part I of this book).

organic and that theological students were wasting their time trying to discern any religious or theological meaning in it. However, Boisen had a deeply existential reason for believing that some forms of mental illness *did* have religious meaning because they led to a new perspective and purpose in life for him and for others.

In this way, Boisen's vision differed from Cabot, Russell Dicks, and other early leaders of CPE. Cabot and Dicks were primarily interested in improving the pastor's *skill* in ministry in personal crisis, whereas Boisen and Hiltner developed a vision of ministry in depth with theological reflection which led more fully to the development of modern pastoral theology. Boisen's call to read the "living human documents" led to a new way to apprehend and construct theology;[28] as a result, the clinical method of learning has since been included in the curricula of most theological seminaries in the United States.

This leads to an "autobiographical" dimension of my own interest in Anton Boisen. As a beginning, 23-year-old theology student, I recall having great difficulty with a systematic theology course which required me to write a five-page paper on my own views of several major Christian doctrines, including God, Christology, the Holy Spirit, and the Church. I later realized that I struggled to write even five pages on these huge topics because I had not had sufficient life experience to build any substantial understanding of them. It was only later, as I found myself in ministry to dying persons who were raising hard questions about life and faith, that basic Christian doctrines developed both vital importance and substance in my own conception. The "living human documents" completed my theological education in exactly the way in which Boisen intended, though I did not realize this until I first read *The Exploration of the Inner World.* This discovery began my own journey of exploration of this interesting and unique concept.

A second autobiographical element has to do with my own call to ministry. During the very month in which Boisen died (October, 1965), I found myself for the very first time in the ward of a state psychiatric hospital visiting someone close to me who had attempted suicide. I was overwhelmed by the curious and frightening specter of mental illness and impressed with how much seemed yet to be done in understanding it. Because I was at the point of needing to declare a college major, I opted for psychology and dedicated my life to this understanding, which later led me to the specialized ministry of pastoral care and counseling. Boisen's work, represented in the following articles, was a milestone in this understanding. Hence, the document of my own experience and pilgrimage intersects with his. Though I never met the man, he became a spiritual mentor as I lived among his files, papers, and copious writings.

---

28. See Glenn H. Asquith, Jr., "The Clinical Method of Theological Inquiry of Anton T. Boisen," (unpublished doctoral dissertation, The Southern Baptist Theological Seminary, 1976) for a full analysis of this method and its results.

A Sample and Critique of the Vision

The articles in this collection are divided into two parts. The first is a chronological selection of Boisen's articles from professional journals which represent his views on a variety of subjects: the formation of clinical pastoral education, his theory of mental illness, his interest in the social context of religion as well as the individual, examples of his method of reading the "living human documents," his critique of CPE as it developed, his pastoral interest in music and worship relevant to the mentally ill, and his theological views. Certain ideas are repeated in several articles, such as reference to the religious experience of major religious leaders; these repetitions indicate central themes which Boisen wished to address in a variety of contexts.

The second part is a selection of critical articles about Boisen and his work written by leaders in the field from a variety of perspectives, primarily after Boisen's death in 1965. These deal with his pioneering role in CPE, his continuing contributions to theological education and the psychology of religion, his case study method, and some more recent thoughts on his psychiatric diagnosis. In both parts, each article is introduced with a paragraph discussing its particular significance and contribution.

Throughout the reprinted material it will be noted that the language used, especially in Boisen's articles, is clearly dated and not gender inclusive. This is a real concern because of its potential for alienating many readers. However, it has generally been the policy in writing and publishing that changes in language use are not made in material directly quoted in its historical context. To do so in this material would require massive and frequently awkward changes which would alter the basic integrity of the author's style. Therefore an editorial decision was made to let the material stand as written, with the hope that the language use will not detract from the basic message and intent of the writing.

A Vision Renewed

The following words by Thomas W. Klink were written enroute from Elgin, Illinois on October 6, 1965. As CPE had gained wide acceptance and plans were being made to form a national organization, this always-distant and sometimes-crazy man who died quietly in a state hospital was nearly forgotten except for the faithful few mentioned by Klink. The last paragraph, in particular, provides a summary for the purpose of this book.

Anton T. Boisen, 1876-1965: A remembrance of
the committal of his ashes, October 6, 1965

The Elgin State Hospital cemetery lies halfway between the "back hospital" and the Farm Colony. It is reached by a gravel track around the water tower, past rusting piles of old-issue hospital beds, and two raw gravel pits. On the low hillside a bulldozer labored without pause; over the ridge a pile of burning refuse billowed dark smoke. The burying ground itself is neat, almost inconspicuous. There is a low, pleasant carpet of native grass. There is a fence, a hedgerow to the north, a gentle slope and rows of plain grave markers. The filled space occupies only a bit more than half of the enclosed plot. This is unspectacular waste ground and the hospital seems to use it as repository for that which has lived out its usefulness.

The scene was not spectacular, today. The weather was modestly autumnal and the sky just ordinarily overcast. Except for the cluster of awkward mourners—forty or fifty persons including Chaplain Charles Sullivan, Professor Victor Obenhaus (who, respectively, read the requested service and the obituary), a few patients, a handful of friends, a few hospital staff, a little group of ex-students—it was an unremarkable state hospital burial.

There were no tears.

There was little conversation, little drama.

But, because he lived and suffered and imposed his always-distant urgency on others, some of the living seem less likely to be scattered as burned-out ashes "back of the hospital," over the fallow waste ground.[29]

As Henri Nouwen observed in 1968, "perhaps there is need for time and distance to be able to see the full stature of the man whose obvious weaknesses obstruct a clearer view of him."[30] On the eve of the 25th anniversary of the formation of ACPE, this book is a statement that the time has now come for a renewed appreciation of Anton Boisen's vision from "a little-known country."

29. Thomas W. Klink, "Anton T. Boisen: 1876-1965: A Remembrance of the Committal of His Ashes, October 6, 1965," *The Journal of Pastoral Care* 19:4 (Winter, 1965), 230.

30. Henri J. M. Nouwen, "Anton T. Boisen and Theology Through Living Human Documents," *Pastoral Psychology* 19:186 (September, 1968), 63. (This article is reprinted in Part II of this book.)

Part I

JOURNAL ARTICLES BY ANTON T. BOISEN
− 1923-1961 −

CONCERNING THE RELATIONSHIP BETWEEN RELIGIOUS EXPERIENCE AND MENTAL DISORDERS

Anton T. Boisen

[This is Boisen's first published article on mental disorder, written while he was a graduate student at Harvard University. Published in *Mental Hygiene* in April, 1923, it calls for a cooperative relationship between religion and medicine in treating the mentally ill, in an era when medical science had been elevated to such a place that (as Boisen observed) the clergy were considered irrelevant or unnecessary in this treatment. While stressing the unique identity and contribution of the religious worker, Boisen also notes that training is needed for this task, which will apply to both the specialist and parish clergy.]

While looking over the books in a psychiatric library some months ago, I was surprised—in fact, startled—to find a four-volume treatise entitled *The Insanity of Jesus (La Folie de Jesus)* by a professor of psychiatry in the University of Paris. It had never before occurred to me that any man could take such a serious view of the mental condition of Jesus as to use up four sizeable volumes upon it, much less that there was sufficient evidence in regard to it to occupy so much space. A glance at the contents told me at once more about the writer than it did about Jesus. He is entirely hostile to religion in any form. Not only was Jesus a degenerate paranoiac and a weakling, but Paul, Augustine, Ezekiel, and other religious geniuses were all afflicted with "*paranoia theomanique*," and if they were living today, would very properly be confined in hospitals for mental disease. The author is intemperate and violent in his tone, he is lacking in any sense of value or proportion, and he is wholly uncritical in his use of sources. He is not, therefore, to be taken over-seriously.

This book has, however, drawn my attention to a problem of great importance concerning which I find a growing body of literature. Not only Dr. Binet-Sangle, but also a Dr. Hirsch and a Dr. Lomer have made psychiatric studies of Jesus and contend that he was a paranoiac. A Danish authority named Rasmussen is of the opinion that he was an epileptic. Meanwhile psychiatric studies of other great religious geniuses are appearing by the score, not merely from the pens of over-rash Freudians, but also from adherents of the more orthodox schools. The theologian, on the other hand, if he is not serenely oblivious to these psychiatric ventures, is very indignant at what he considers assaults upon the heroes of the faith. He is even apt to resent Professor James' sympathetic *Varieties of Religious Experience*, because it dares to suggest that there is a connection between experiences that to him are sacred and a supreme value and experiences that have in them many elements of the morbid and pathological.

The suggestion that I would offer is that the psychiatrist is right in drawing attention to the common characteristics in the experiences of individuals whom we regard as religious geniuses and those of patients in our hospital for mental disease, but that he has failed to recognize with sufficient clearness the sharp contrast and the real line of demarcation between them. I would offer the further suggestion that the common characteristics are due to certain common causative factors and that therefore study of the one type in the light of the other may be of real value in solving the problem of effective treatment for those who are suffering from mental difficulties, both in their incipient and in their more developed stages.

In making this suggestion I am of course assuming that many mental disorders are of mental rather than physical origin, and that in such cases a conflict is proba-bly at the root of the difficulty. Such conflicts, as I view them, are in themselves neither good nor bad. They often represent an intermediate stage through which certain individuals must pass if they are ever to reach a level of development at which their interest, instead of being devoted exclusively to baseball and jazz music and matters that savor of the pornographic, or perhaps being bound up in some hope that cannot be realized, become genuinely attached to things that have endur-ing value both for the individuals themselves and for the race. Such conflicts are found in all those experiences which the religious worker calls conversions. Not infrequently such conversion experiences are accompanied by voices and visions and other automatisms which the psychiatrist regards as pathological. But the conver-sion experience has this characteristic: it results or tends to result in a reintegration of the personality around what the individual regards as the purpose of life. The conversion experience, in other words, tends to bring the individual into harmony with himself and with his environment.

But conflicts do not always result happily. Sometimes they result in defeat or demoralization or more or less permanent cleavage. This, as I see it, is the explanation of some psychoses. But between these two end states of clear-cut victory and unification and clear-cut defeat and demoralization there may also be a condition of acute conflict or of unstable equilibrium. This unstable equilibrium I regard as the explanation of many cases of "psychoneurosis" and perhaps of some "manic-depressive" types of mental trouble.

According to this view, the significant thing about Jesus or Paul or Augustine is not the presence or absence of certain pathological phenomena, which may have been incidental to some severe conflict through which they had passed and the consequent sensitizing of their minds; the significant thing is the end attained in terms of character and social helpfulness, in the breadth of their sympathies, in the unification of their interests around a great and socially useful purpose, and in the serenity and beauty and strength of the resulting personality. It is, therefore, of the greatest importance, in the treatment of any case of mental difficulty, to take into account the character of the conflicting forces and the general direction in which the personality is tending. Medical workers are, I think, beginning to see this and there is significance in the fact that specialists in mental disorders are entering the domain of philosophy and ethics and religion, and are speaking with an authority that the philosopher and the theologian, who start with abstract ideas or traditional dogmas, no longer possess. The physician, as a result of his empirical method and his careful, systematic study of living men and women, has thus in very truth become a physician of souls, while the traditional "physician of souls," clinging to his traditional methods, has become merely the custodian of the faith.

This raises the question of the relationship between the medical and the religious worker and the need of cooperation between them. The view may be taken that the medical worker has the field and that the religious worker has now become unnecessary so far as treatment of mental disorders is concerned. My own view is that the religious worker, with all his limitations and with his waning influence, has yet in his keeping three things that are of fundamental importance in dealing with this problem.

1. A message with regard to the ultimate realities of life that has brought comfort and hope and strength to many a sufferer. Inasmuch as a sense of being out of adjustment with what they conceive to be the purpose of life is characteristic of many sufferers from mental disorders, the guidance of a wise religious teacher should be of great value.

2. An effective means of reeducation through suggestion in prayer. The religious man who is true to the teachings of Christianity has all that M. Coue can give him and much more.

3. A group of socially minded people of whom the religious worker is the chosen leader and through whom he can greatly multiply his own effectiveness. Such a group can be utilized to provide a wholesome environment for the man in distress.

The task of most religious workers is and must always be to deal with these problems before they reach the advanced or acute stages that we meet with in the hospital for mental disease. But to be able to do this effectively, religious workers must have a far better understanding of such problems than they have today. To this end there should be specialists in this field who would have much the same relationship to the average pastor that the medical specialist has had to the old-time general practitioner. Such specialists, working in cooperation with medical workers, can bring to bear upon certain acute and difficult cases such insight and experience as the group of religious workers may possess. They can also serve as "liaison officers" between medical workers in psychiatry, with their already advanced knowledge, and religious workers at large. Such a plan, by using machinery already in existence, could without additional expense to the state greatly increase the effectiveness of psychiatric work, not merely in the way of prevention, but in the matter of more sympathetic oversight of discharged patients. I do not mean by this to imply that the medical profession does not already possess facilities for this work, but I do say that the problem is one of such magnitude that the church can help. This applies not merely to local communities, but to hospitals as well. Those who have had any experience in hospitals for mental disease know that, except in the expensive private sanitaria, the physicians are so busy with their routine duties that conferences with the patients, even though recognized as desirable, are almost out of the question.

In suggesting this plan I am under no illusion as to the present equipment of the average pastor for such work. His academic preparation has not included the consideration of such problems. He finds himself quite at a loss when he meets them in actual life. The one chief piece of machinery that the Protestant Church has worked out for dealing with the man who is sick of soul is the "revival meeting," and it is an open question whether this method in practice does not do almost as much harm as good. What I do see is the potential power of the church to contribute to the solution of this problem. I also see the influence upon the church of a new method which will lead the trained religious worker to study the human personality and the forces that operate upon it as medical workers have studied the human body and its behavior.

THE CHALLENGE TO OUR SEMINARIES

Anton T. Boisen

[This article first appeared in *Christian Work*, January 23, 1926, after Boisen had become Chaplain at Worcester State Hospital and was also Research Associate in the Department of Social Ethics at Chicago Theological Seminary. In the midst of the "Fundamentalist-Modernist Controversy" in the U. S. at that time, Boisen points out the bankruptcy of both traditions in caring for the mentally ill. He holds the theological seminaries primarily responsible for this deficiency, noting that their curricula are oriented toward the traditional disciplines with no attention to understanding the human personality. He goes on to suggest that seminaries offer advanced degrees with minimum residency requirements which require research in the candidate's own parish—a prophetic recommendation of what has become the Doctor of Ministry degree in many seminaries. With such attention to human experience, seminaries will help to construct a "new theology"—a pastoral theology—which will enrich the church's ministry.]

As a chaplain in a hospital for mental disorders and as research worker in a theological seminary, I have been much interested in the articles by Justin Wroe Nixon on "Theological Education at the Crossroads," and that by Richard C. Cabot on a "Clinical Year for Theological Students," so ably reviewed by Mr. Eastman in *Christian Work*. These articles call attention to what seems to me the great weakness in present-day theological education and point the way to the line of developments next in order. If I have any criticism it would be that they do not go far enough. Dr. Cabot thus stops short of the crucially important proposition that in mental disorders we are dealing with a problem which is essentially spiritual. He counts himself among the large group of physicians who look upon mental disorders as due to physiological causes. If with the new and rapidly growing group of psychiatrists—among whom in this country Dr. Adolph Meyer, Dr. Macfie Campbell, Dr. W. A. White, and Dr. Thomas W. Salmon are leaders—he accepted the "psychogenic" explanation he would recognize in the field of mental disorders a problem of even greater significance to the theologian. It should be just as important for a religious worker to spend a "clinical year" in such a hospital as ours as it is for a physician to serve his time in a general hospital before he goes out into general practice.

In support of this assertion let me point out that at least two-thirds of the cases which come each year to our hospital are without discoverable physical explanation. Neither are they to be explained in terms of intelligence or reason. As measured by the intelligence tests, of which we hear so much today, our patients will average just about as high as the people outside. The difficulty is rather one of attitude and belief, and is rooted in a sense of personal failure. It is important to bear in mind that in a large proportion of our cases religious ideas figure prominently. At a staff meeting in almost any hospital for mental disorders one will hear about as many religious terms as he will at a gathering of ministers. One of the very common questions which is asked of a patient is, "Have you ever heard God talking to you?" If the patient answers "yes," the presumption is that he is hallucinated and therefore committable. Those psychiatrists who accept the "psychogenic" interpretation of the functional mental disorders find the explanation in a conflict of wishes or desires. Such an explanation is by no means new. It was expressed a great many years ago by the Apostle Paul, who found "a law in his members" which warred against the law that he had accepted as his own and who proclaimed the good news of a means of escape from the situation. It is however new to have such a conflict thus recognized as the explanation of mental disorders.

It would follow, then, that functional mental disorders and religious conversion experience may have a relationship which is at once very close and very far apart. They may each be solutions of a common situation, a conflict within the personality. But one is a happy solution and the other an unhappy solution or else no solution at all, but a condition of unstable equilibrium with the issue still in the balance. If this be true, then it follows that we can understand the one only in the light of the other, that mental disorders concern the religious quite as much as they do the medical worker, and that religious experiences are quite likely to have pathological elements.

But of any such possibility the Church is utterly oblivious. She takes no interest in cases of pronounced mental disorder. While she is active in caring for the sick, and, according to the Interchurch Survey of 1919, 381 hospitals are supported and are controlled by the Protestant churches of America, only three of these hospitals, so far as I have been able to discover, are especially concerned with the problem of mental disorders, and even in these three the approach is almost wholly medical. The large and rapidly increasing group of sufferers from mental disorders, aggregating more than a quarter of a million inmates of institutions, are therefore cared for almost entirely in our state hospitals for the insane. Here they are left practically without Protestant religious ministration. We have therefore this truly remarkable situation—a Church which has always been interested in the care of the sick, confining her efforts to the types of cases in which religion has least concern and least to contribute, while in those types in which it is impossible to tell where the domain of the medical workers leaves off and that of the religious worker begins, there the Church is doing nothing.

Nor is that all. The church's efforts to deal with those conflicts which make for mental disorder, and to do so before they reach the advanced stages which we encounter in our hospitals for the insane, are at present without scientific basis or intelligent direction. The conservative evangelical churches are, it is true, still concerned with the problem of the sick soul. If one asks a minister of the "Fundamentalist" persuasion what he is trying to do, a question which I have asked many times in the survey work which I have done, he will usually answer, "We are trying to save souls." Their message is indeed a message of salvation. To them man is innately bad. To be saved he needs to be born anew. To carry the message of salvation they have the revival meeting. Undoubtedly they are doing some good, for their methods are rooted in the experience of centuries. To many a sufferer the traditional message has brought a new hope and a new purpose in life which makes it worthwhile for him to go on living. It gives him in prayer all that suggestion and auto-suggestion can accomplish as a means of re-education, and far more besides. And it surrounds him with the fellowship of the believers. But it is treatment without diagnosis. And it has no clear idea of what salvation means, nor of what people need to be saved from. Its hell is a future affair and it has been blind to the hell which was right before its eyes.

My liberal friends, however, supply neither treatment nor diagnosis. If Billy Sunday comes to town they do not co-operate or else they co-operate with reservations and exceeding discomfort. But they have nothing to substitute for Billy Sunday's message nor for his methods. For the soul that is sick they have no gospel of salvation. They are all too ready to turn him over to the doctors and then forget about him. They are chiefly concerned in the attempt to interpret the ancient tenets in terms of modern thought, and their practical emphasis is placed upon programs of social reform and religious education. And even in the task of religious education it may be questioned whether the real dangers and the real objectives are as clearly understood as they ought to be.

For this situation in the Church at large, the theological seminaries must take their share of the blame. I am not sure but they, upon whom the task of training the Church's leaders is placed, may not be chiefly responsible for the situation. I have in recent months examined carefully the catalogs of a number of theological schools and I have discovered that most of them are still concerned chiefly with the traditional disciplines—the Scriptural languages and literature, Church history, systematic theology, the philosophy of religion, and sermon making. With few exceptions it is still possible for a student to go through the theological seminary and receive the stamp of approval without ever having studied the human personality either in health or in sickness, or the social forces that affect it.

Such are my reasons for believing that the problem of mental disorders presents a peculiar challenge to the Church. I see here a field which from our standpoint is almost unexplored and a task which promises much, not merely in the help which it may be possible to give to a very large group of sufferers, but one which promises much in the insight which it may afford into the spiritual forces with which the Church has always been primarily concerned and into the laws which govern these forces; a task which promises much, also, in the new meaning which it should give to the Church's message of salvation. When we remember that what we know today about the human body has come very largely through the study of diseased conditions, is it any wonder that a Church which has so completely ignored the problem of the soul that is sick, is able to speak with so little authority concerning the laws of the spiritual world or even to prove that there is such a thing as the soul at all?

And such, also, are my reasons for approving of the suggestion of a clinical year for theological students. In fact I have for more than a year been trying to recruit theological students to serve as attendants in our hospital because of my profound belief in the importance of confronting them with the problem with which we are dealing. For we have here a problem which must be studied from real life and not from books. It is, moreover, absolutely essential to have the co-operation of medical men, for here the provinces of religious and medical workers overlap, and the medical workers is not in possession of the field. The religious worker is a mere beginner, and he must be very careful not to embark in any half-baked attempt at "soul-healing."

In addition to the clinical year I should favor some plan for encouraging high-grade research work on the part of pastors in the field, comparable to that which medical men are now doing. If we are to make progress in our understanding of this problem and in the methods of dealing with it, some of the important research work must be done by them. No inquisitive investigator dares to trespass upon the sacred domain of the individual personality, unless the individual be in captivity. But the wise pastor stands in a peculiar relationship with his people. He is admitted to their homes. He is their trusted friend and guide. They come to him often with their problems and perplexities. It should be possible for him without violation of confidence to contribute much toward the understanding of the problem. The ordinary parish may thus become the laboratory of the new religious psychology and the opportunity for really worthwhile study and research greatest after the young minister leaves the seminary. With the view of encouraging such research I should favor the offering of higher degrees which might be earned with a minimum requirement of a residence at the seminary and a maximum of patient, careful, thorough work in the candidate's own parish.

With the inauguration of such a program no miracle need be looked for. Results are not going to come all at once. The problem of the human personality and of the laws and forces which are concerned therein is entirely too difficult and too baffling. Neither are we to expect any radically new message. Rather are we likely to find confirmation of the old message of Jesus and of Paul and new insight into the value of the work which the Church is actually doing or which it may do.

What is involved is a thoroughgoing shift of attention and a new method of attack and then, in the end, a new authority, grounded not in tradition but in experience. Theological education of the past and of the present is entirely too much after the order of the "culture" which I once heard defined before a woman's club as "something which you get from books or from a college and bring to the people." The theological training of the future will be a continuous affair, with the parish as the laboratory, and the person in difficulty as the main concern, and the seminary as the clearing house of information and the supervisor of methods. The attention will be shifted from the past to the present; from books to the raw material of life. Experience will no longer be fitted to the system but system to experience. History will not be neglected but the present will be our starting point. Through the study of the present we shall be able to understand the past and the past may then throw light upon the problems of the present and of the future. Studying the human personality in health and in disease, in prosperity and in disaster, seeking patiently and systematically and reverently to discover the motive forces and the machinery which are involved and to formulate the laws which govern them, we may be able to lay the foundations of a new theology. And through the cooperation of many men working together over a long period of time, the Church may once more come into its own and speak no longer as the scribes and Pharisees and interpreters of traditions but with the authority of the knowledge of the laws of the life that is eternal.

THEOLOGICAL EDUCATION
VIA THE CLINIC

Anton T. Boisen

[This historic article, which announces the incorporation of the Council for Clinical
Training, appeared in the March, 1930 issue of *Religious Education*. It is essentially a
"promotional piece" in which Boisen was seeking both financial and philosophical support for the new clinical training movement. The growing differences between Boisen
and Cabot on ministry to the mentally ill are evident in this article—differences which
resulted in a complete split between the two later in the same year. Nevertheless, Boisen
convincingly expresses his vision of the value of reading the "human documents" and
its application to "dealing with the problems and difficulties of ordinary people."]

On the the twenty-first day of January in the year 1930 there was incorporated in
the State of Massachusetts a new organization, the Council for the Clinical
Training of Theological Students.

This council is in part the outgrowth of an experiment which for the past six
years has been under way at the Worcester State Hospital in providing to students
of theology clinical experience in dealing with the maladies of personality. It is also
the outgrowth of the "Plea for a Clinical Year for Theological Students" made by
Dr. Richard C. Cabot in the *Survey Graphic* for September, 1925. Dr. Cabot is
himself the chairman of the new organization. The other members include
Reverend Henry Wise Hobson and Dr. William A. Bryan of Worcester and Dr.
William Healy, Reverend Ashley Day Leavitt and Reverend Samuel A. Eliot of
Boston. The staff includes in addition to myself Reverend Donald C. Beatty of the
Pittsburgh City Home and Hospital at Mayview, Pennsylvania, Reverend

Alexander D. Dodd of the Rhode Island State Hospital and Reverend Philip Guiles, the field secretary, three men who have served two years in this hospital and are now seeking to extend this undertaking to new fields.

It will thus be seen that from the beginning this undertaking has had to do with the service and the understanding of the mentally ill. It has been my view that the functional group of mental disorders are of peculiar interest to the religious worker. According to this view, they are disorders of emotion and volition, of belief and attitude, rooted not in cerebral disease nor in the breaking down of the reasoning processes but for the most part in the age-old conflict which the Apostle Paul so vividly describes, the conflict between the law that is in our minds and that which is in our members. Such conflicts, when they result happily, as in the case of Augustine, George Fox and John Bunyan, we recognize as religious experience. When they result unhappily, we sent the sufferer to a hospital for the mentally ill and speak of him as insane. As chaplain in such an institution, I have felt that the religious worker might do well to take account of the unhappy solutions of the inner conflict and that he might with profit learn from the medical profession the importance of the study of the pathological as an approach to the understanding of the normal. I have also been impressed with the methods of instruction used by my medical friends. I have watched with interest the medical interns who came to the hospital to do work under guidance as part of their medical education. I have seen how real and how vital such instruction became as they and their teachers dealt together with the actual raw material of life, and I have become convinced that the theological student might well spend less time with his books and more time with the human documents in such a hospital as ours. I have become convinced that clinical experience should be just as important to the man who is to be charged with the cure of souls as it is to the man who is to care for the bodies of men.

With this view of mine Dr. Cabot has never fully agreed. He has indeed from the beginning been my advisor and helper in this undertaking, but in mental disorder he sees nothing of any peculiar interest to the religious worker. In his judgment all the thoroughgoing insanities have an organic basis and psychotherapy can be little more than palliative. He believes that the physically ill, the handicapped, the disabled, the aged, the feeble-minded and the delinquent have just as much claim upon the attention of the religious worker as have the mentally disordered, and his plea for a clinical year in the course of theological study had reference to bringing the student into close contact with concentrated human misery in all its forms. For this reason we have made the name of our organization sufficiently broad to permit of its extension to other kinds of institutions. And we plan in the not far distant future to explore the possibilities of some of these other fields of human distress. But for the present I can speak only of the work among the mentally ill, and the reader must take warning that I write with the inevitable bias of the specialist and from a point of view which is challenged by other medical men besides Dr. Cabot.

The opportunity to try out my plan was not easy to secure. Most hospital superintendents, as I have good reason to know, look somewhat askance at religious work among their patients. Even though with Freud or with Adolph Meyer, they may recognize the "mental factors" in the genesis of the disorders of the mind, as Dr. Cabot does not, they do not recognize the religious aspects of mental disorder or the religious implications of the psychogenic interpretation. Church services on Sunday they generally accept in accordance with hoary tradition as part of the hospital routine. They even pay a small honorarium for these services. But they call in ministers from neighboring churches who know little or nothing of the special problems of the hospital inmates, and these ministers receive little encouragement to visit the patients or to try to understand the nature of their difficulties. In my own case, after spending a year and a half in graduate study of psychiatry at Harvard, I had to wait a whole year before in the Worcester State Hospital I found the chance for which I was looking. This hospital, under the able leadership of its superintendent, Dr. William A. Bryan, takes the position that the problems of mental disorder are very complex and must be approached from many angles. It is even willing to admit that the religious worker may have something to contribute as well as something to learn. This position is not due to any ecclesiastical bias. Dr. Bryan, unlike some of the other superintendents to whom I applied, is not a churchman. He is, however, much interested in his patients. When criticized for the rank innovation of bringing in a chaplain on full time, he is said to have remarked that he would not hesitate to bring in a horse doctor if he thought there was any chance that he might help his patients. And not only did he consent to bring in a chaplain, but he also consented to let the chaplain enlist some theological students to serve in the hospital during their vacation periods under conditions which permit them to learn something of the problems with which the students were dealing.

This experiment in theological education began in a small way. At first the students worked ten hours a day on the wards as ordinary attendants. There were not many of them the first summer—only three. The plan was only moderately successful, but we were encouraged to try it again with some modifications the following year. This time two men were secured to take charge of a recreational program for the benefit of the patients. For each of these men the hospital furnished maintenance, and salaries of fifty dollars a month were paid from contributed funds. In addition, two students who applied later on and were anxious to come were given positions as ward attendants. The following year we had seven students and the next year ten. Under the present plan, each student serves five hours a day as an attendant on the wards and three hours a day under the direction of the chaplain's department in the conduct of a recreational program. In addition, each student is required to do special case work, to attend conferences and staff meetings and to do a certain amount of reading. Two students thus do the work of one attendant on the wards. In consideration of this fact, the hospital pays one of the men. The other is paid from contributed funds. In addition to those who have come for the summer, three men have spent an entire year with us and one man two years, each one of these doing some special service.

It is to be noted that this plan calls for a definite program of service to the patients and that it is made possible through contributed funds. We seek to contribute as much and ask as little of the hospital as possible. We feel that it is time that the church and those interested in religion were paying some attention to the group of sufferers found in our mental hospitals. It seems a truly astounding situation that a group of sufferers larger than is to be found in all other hospitals put together, a group whose difficulties seem to lie in the realm of character or personality rather than in organic disease, should be almost entirely neglected by the church. Notwithstanding the fact that the church has always been interested in caring for the sick and that the Protestant churches of America are today supporting some 380 hospitals, scarcely any attention is given to the maladies of the mind. Only three of these hospitals, so far as I have been able to discover, are concerned particularly with that problem and the 375,000 mental sufferers are cared for almost entirely in state institutions. And there they are left almost without Protestant religious ministration. It seems not inaccurate to say that if a man has a broken leg he can be cared for by the church in a church institution. But if he has a broken heart he is turned over to the state, there to be forgotten by the church. We feel, therefore, no hesitation in appealing for assistance in behalf of our patients and in behalf of those students of religion who are seeking to understand their difficulties.

Of all the work done by our students, the most important both from the standpoint of the hospital and of the students themselves is undoubtedly the work on the wards. From the standpoint of the hospital it is of great importance to have the wards manned with efficient and intelligent attendants. There is probably no one in the employ of the hospital upon whom the welfare of the patient is more dependent than the attendant or nurse who is with him on the ward all day long. But to secure such attendants is no easy matter. There are indeed devoted men and women whose faithful service on the wards cannot be too gratefully recognized, but the fact remains that the average new attendant is a man with a mental age of about thirteen years who has no interest in the patients or in the problems which they present. He is generally a floater who has previously worked in some other hospital, who stays about three and a half months and is then either discharged for inefficiency or brutality or drunkenness, or else he leaves without notice. And the limitation in pay and the fact that the position carries with it no promise of a career and no encouragement to home-making makes the situation difficult to rectify. Under such conditions the hospital can easily make use of a group of intelligent and willing college graduates who are keenly interested in the patients and their problems. From the standpoint of the student, the work on the ward has the advantage that it brings him into close contact with the patients. He sees them day in and day out. He is able to observe what they do with their leisure time, what attitude they take toward their work and toward other people and how they meet the irritations, the disappointments, the successes, the set-backs and other critical situations which because they are genuine furnish the really reliable tests of character. He is thus able to obtain an insight into the mind of the patient which is possible in no other way. The notes which our students have thus been able to get have proved of value to the physicians in their efforts to understand the patients' difficulties.

The recreational program, which constitutes the other major contribution to the welfare of the hospital inmates, is of varied character. Intramural baseball, baseball games with other institutions, volleyball, hikes, play festivals and carnivals, choral singing and entertainments and the publication with the aid of mimeograph and bulletin boards of a semi-weekly news sheet and of a weekly pictorial have thus far been the chief activities. Toward this program, the student is required to give three hours a day.

By thus cutting the required routine work to eight hours a day, the student has left sufficient time and strength to do the special case work, to write up his notes, to do the reading and attend the ward walks and staff meetings and the special conferences which are held twice each week for the benefit of this group, all of which are essential if the student is himself to profit by his experience. In the special conferences, members of the medical staff have contributed generously of their time and interest and the student has the great advantage of seeing the same case approached at once from different angles. We are especially fortunate in being able to profit by the very thoroughgoing research work on the endocrine factors in dementia praecox, which is now being carried on at the Worcester State Hospital under the direction of Dr. Roy G. Hoskins, Director of the Memorial Foundation for Neuro-Endocrine Research. We also seek to give each student some part in the research work which has now been going on for six years in the religious and social factors in mental disorders.

The plan seems to be working out to the satisfaction both of the hospital and of the students. The attitude of the hospital authorities is sufficiently indicated by the steady increase in the number of student workers which has been authorized and that of the students by their enthusiastic response and by the increasing number and quality of the applicants.

Of the thirty-five students who have served in the hospital during the first five years of this undertaking two are planning to devote themselves to psychiatry by way of the regular medical course. Three others, as already indicated, after two years of training at this hospital, are now serving as specialists in other hospitals. Eight are either teaching or preparing themselves to teach. One is studying to be a medical missionary. Twenty-one have gone or are preparing to go into the regular pastorate. It will thus be noted that five out of the thirty-five have been sufficiently interested in the problem with which they have been confronted to devote themselves to it as specialists. I should have been much disappointed if this had not been the case. We are greatly in need of specialists. Trained psychiatrists who have any insight into the religious aspects of the cases with which they are dealing are at present none too common, while the supply of trained religious workers thoroughly grounded in psychiatry who are ready to give themselves to the large group of sufferers who inhabit our hospitals has been totally lacking. But the great majority of the theological students who have taken advantage of this opportunity are going into the pastorate, there to apply to the ordinary problems of the ordinary parish such psychiatric understanding and technique as they may have gained. It is particularly to be noted that the students are all following the established channels of service. We have not been encouraging them to set up as psychotherapists or to start church clinics. It is our conviction that psychotherapeutic work can often best be done, without any advertising of the fact, by anyone who has the necessary understanding and technique. We are furthermore convinced that, in the disorders of the mind as well as in the disorders of the body, the study of the pathological is one of the best approaches to the understanding of the normal and that the main application of the hospital experience should be in dealing with the problems and difficulties of ordinary people. We know of no one who has greater need for such understanding or who has it more fully in his power to do effective work in the prevention of mental difficulties than the adequately trained representative of that profession which for hundreds of years has been chiefly concerned with the inner adjustments of individuals.

Let there be no misunderstanding. We are laboring under no illusion in regard to the adequacy of the present-day understanding of the disorders of the mind or the sufficiency of three months of training, no matter how thorough, to place at the student's disposal the understanding and the tools now available. We recognize that we are as yet but touching the fringes of this most difficult of difficult problems and we have too much respect for the human personality to suppose for an instant that after one summer at our hospital a student is equipped to deal successfully with the delicate and baffling inner difficulties of his people. We only hope that we may have been able to start something. We hope that we may have awakened in the student an interest in the personal experience of individuals and that we may have acquainted him with methods of observation and generalization which will lead him on into life-long devotion to patient, accurate, reverent exploration in all its range of that inner world with which religion is concerned. We hope that it may lead to a new insight into the issues of life and death, which may be at stake in the lives of even the apparently commonplace, which will pervade and determine the minister's religious message and give to it increasingly the authority of truth and the power to inspire confidence. And we hope that he may gain constantly in that insight and wisdom which shall make him for the man in distress a safe counsellor and guide. More than this, we hope that this attempt at providing for students of theology clinical experience in dealing with the maladies of the personality may contribute toward the development of a body of workers who, through patient and painstaking cooperative effort over a long period of time, may arrive at a new understanding of these disorders of the mind and of the laws and forces therein involved which shall reinterpret and revitalize the enduring elements in the religion of their fathers and lead onward toward the realization of the new and better types of personality and the new and better social order.

DIVIDED PROSTESTANTISM IN A MIDWEST COUNTY: A STUDY IN THE NATURAL HISTORY OF ORGANIZED RELIGION

Anton T. Boisen

[This article from the October, 1940 issue of the *Journal of Religion* is a prime example of Boisen's interest in applying his empirical method to studying the "social conditions" of human experience as well as individual narratives. It is especially revealing of the Reformed Presbyterian tradition in which he grew up in Bloomington, Indiana, which stressed individual morality and emphasized the intellect at the expense of the affective side of religious experience. Boisen uses H. Richard Niebuhr's analysis to discuss the function of organized religion at different points in the collective history of groups. Portions of this article later appeared in abbreviated and disguised form in chapters 2 and 4 of Boisen's book, *Religion in Crisis and Custom* (Harper & Brothers, 1955), which is devoted to expressions of religion at times of social crisis.]

Sociology and history are commonly distinguished one from the other on the basis that history is the record of temporal sequences which are not likely to be repeated, whereas sociology is the attempt to discover relationships which are recurrent and universal. It follows that sociology must in many cases turn to history for its data and that history may find in sociology a valuable ally in the interpretation of its findings. This paper is an attempt to study the history of a particular middle western county with special reference to a pattern which appears to be recurrent in the development of organized religion and the forces which are operative in determining this pattern.

I

The county in question was selected from among a number of sample areas which I have studied because it is the one I know best. More than that, the data are unusually full and the situation revealed presents some unusually interesting features. This county is located in southern Indiana about fifty miles southwest of Indianapolis and about ninety miles northwest of Louisville. It was first opened for settlement in 1818. In 1820 it was designated as the seat of the state university— Indiana Seminary, as it was called originally. The early settlers were of the Scotch-Irish and English stock which came swarming over the mountains and down the Ohio Valley in the early part of the sixteenth century.

Within the general stream of migration were certain more selected groups. Some of these were drawn to Bloomington, the county seat of Monroe County, by the presence of the college. A group of Presbyterians who came from Virginia by way of Kentucky had an important part in the launching of the college and for many years a large proportion of the faculty were Presbyterians and the Presbyterian church was closely identified with the college.

Another such group was the psalm-singing Presbyterians whose advance guard made its appearance in Monroe County in 1820. They also were drawn to Bloomington because of its promised college. While of the same Scotch-Irish stock as most of the early settlers, they were a much more compact group. Even though they were considerably divided among themselves, they had come from the same part of northern Ireland, and they had kept together throughout their peregrinations in America. Most of them came to Bloomington from the Chester County district in South Carolina.[1] Later on there was another, though smaller, stream of migration from southwestern Pennsylvania. Since these Scotch-Irish psalm-singers are of especial interest from the standpoint of this study, some remarks are in order concerning their church organizations.

---

1. Professor Woodburn in his monograph on the Scotch-Irish Presbyterians in Monroe County, Indiana ("Indiana Historical Society Publication," IV, No. 8, 452-55) includes some correspondence between the captain of a Chester County rifle company and his own grandfather in Bloomington. These letters were written in 1831-34. They express great pride in the marksmanship of his riflemen, a very warlike attitude toward the slave-holders and nullificationists, and profound discouragement with reference to the religious and economic conditions in his state. "Folks here," he says, "are getting more and more anxious to leave this State of sin and misery. Money is harder to get here than you ever knew it and the price of labor is lower than in Indiana. Heavy debts and ruin to many families will, I fear, be the consequence of the present depressed state of business." In 1834 he was able to sell his farm for six dollars an acre, and with his family of ten children he joined the South Carolina colony in Bloomington.

There were at that time other Chester County colonies in Xenia, Ohio; Madison and Princeton, Indiana; and Sparta, Monmouth, and Paxton, Illinois.

The Scotch-Irish, when they began to come to this country in large numbers in the middle of the eighteenth century, brought with them their own churches. Among these were two dissenting bodies which had been more or less persecuted in the old country. These were known as "Reformed Presbyterians" (or "Covenanters") and "Associate Presbyterians" (or "Antiburghers"). Both of them held rigidly to the view that church music should be confined to the use of the Psalms of David. Human hymns and instruments of music were sternly forbidden in their services of worship, and Sabbath-keeping and church attendance were regarded as imperative.

In the year 1782 the leaders of these two bodies became convinced that it was inexpedient to maintain two separate organizations. They therefore united to form the "Associate-Reformed Presbyterian Church"; but as so often happens there were those who refused to agree. The result was the continuance of the Associate Presbyterians as a smaller and much more conservative group known popularly as the "Seceders" along side of the larger and relatively liberal body. A smaller group of Reformed Presbyterians also refused to unite.

After some years the Reformed Presbyterians again made their appearance as an organized church. The Scotch-Irish had continued to arrive in large numbers from the old country, and among them were many Reformed Presbyterians who could not be reconciled to the nonexistence of their own church. In 1798 a Reformed Presbyterian presbytery was organized in New York City.[2] This body grew rapidly through the arrival in this country of others of the same faith.

In 1832 there came a split in the new church. The attitude toward civil authority which the Covenanters as staunch "come-outers" had held in the old country was carried with them to the new. This took the form of criticism of the Constitution of the United States because it contained no explicit recognition of God. There were those who held that until this was rectified Covenanters should not vote or sit on juries or swear to support the Constitution. The issue fought out at a meeting of the General Synod which was held at the old First Reformed Presbyterian Church in Philadelphia.[3] The two Scotch-Irish psalm-singing churches had now become four in the process of being transplanted to America.

When in 1837 my grandfather came out to Bloomington as a member of the faculty of Indiana College, he found all four of these churches represented in this town of perhaps fifteen hundred inhabitants. All four of them had been organized

---

2. Among the organizers was my great-grandfather, Samuel Brown Wylie, at that time a ministerial student from the University of Glasgow. His *Life of Alexander McLeod* (New York: Charles Scribner, 1855) is the source of much of the information here given.

3. Now the Chambers-Wylie Memorial Presbyterian Church on Broad Street near Spruce. Samuel Brown Wylie, the pastor of this church and vice-provost of the University of Pennsylvania, was at this time the leader of those who upheld the right to vote even at the cost of splitting the organization.

and led by men who came from the neighborhood of Chester, South Carolina. In addition there were four others—the Presbyterians, the Methodists, the Disciples (originally a Stoneite group), and the Baptists. Just what churches there were at this time outside of Bloomington I have not been able to determine, but within a relatively short period we hear of two Cumberland Presbyterian churches and a number of Methodist, Disciples, and Baptist churches. The latter included four varieties—the Separate, the Regular, the Primitive, and the Missionary Baptists. Before long the Disciples were split into two groups over the issues of instrumental music and missionary activity. Within Bloomington itself a "New School Presbyterian" was added in 1851, and in 1841 an Episcopal church was organized by the president of the University,[4] after he had withdrawn from the Presbyterian ministry.

We have then in this early period in Monroe County three groups of churches. (1) There was, in the first place, a more or less liberal group consisting of the two Presbyterian churches and the Episcopal church. These were composed chiefly of college people and of those who wished to be identified with college people. (2) There was a very conservative group consisting of the four psalm-singing Presbyterian churches. These where characterized by great loyalty to family and clan, by their emphasis upon Old Testament morality, and by their requirement of an educated ministry. Their services were long, their sermons doctrinal and dry,[5]

---

4. Andrew Wylie, the first president of Indiana University, during his presidency of Jefferson College had become much concerned over the divisions in the church. This concern he shared with his neighbors, Thomas and Alexander Campbell. He was thus led to advocate union with Washington College, another Presbyterian school seven miles distant. He was thereupon ousted from the presidency of Jefferson College but was soon after elected to the presidency of Washington College. His lengthiest publication, issued in 1840, is entitled *Sectarianism Is Heresy.* It indicates that his break with the Presbyterian church grew out of the quarrel of 1837, which had led to the division into the New School and Old School bodies. Andrew Wylie had held with the New School group for interdenominational cooperation. When the Indiana Synod and the Vincennes Presbytery declared in favor of the Old School, he withdrew and later united with the Episcopal Church.

5. In my grandfather's diary I find the following entry:
"SABBATH, AUGUST 12th, 1838. This morning about ten o'clock I started in company with Dr. Hamill to go to the Seceder Church, where the sacrament was to be held; got there about eleven o'clock [the church was a few miles east of town]. The psalm had already been explained. Mr. Hall preached from the words 'And they crucified Jesus.' The sermon was good, nothing extraordinary however. After an intermission of a few minutes the exercises were continued by a Mr. G. He began to exhort to the duty of self-examination. He debarred [excluded from the communion table] all who would sing any human compositions in worship or who would learn to sing by using verses of hymns. His general remarks and observations on the particular sins to which they were to direct their attention occupied *about two hours and a half.* It was the most tedious piece of work I have ever listened to. After a very abrupt termination the tables were filled, the blessing asked, the words of the institution

and church attendance was compulsory on the part of all members of the family. Family "worship" was held every day, often morning and evening. There was among them no appeal to the emotions and no attempt to win converts. Their growth came through birth and immigration. (3) There were the churches which represented the new revivalistic movement which was sweeping the Ohio Valley. Of these the Methodists, the Disciples,[6] the Baptists, and the Cumberland Presbyterians were represented in Monroe County. From the standpoint of our inquiry it is important to recognize that in contrast to the liberal and conservative groups this group sprang out of the spontaneous religious fervor of the common people. Instead of appealing to the desire for culture or status, instead of clinging tenaciously to the symbols of an inherited culture, these groups were attempting to meet pioneer conditions and to grapple with the moral problems of pioneer men. They brought people together in great numbers at their camp meetings, and there under the spell of vigorous singing, of stirring testimony, of exhortations by able, but often poorly educated, preachers strong emotions were often aroused. Many individuals felt themselves released from a burdening sense of sin and received the "baptism of the Spirit." Such individuals often became zealous missionaries, serving as lay leaders or being ordained as ministers to serve a group of struggling churches under the circuit-rider plan. It was through such men that Methodist, Disciples, and Baptist churches were planted throughout Monroe County, while the Presbyterians remained under the shelter of the county seat.

II

For many years the situation remained essentially unchanged. The six Presbyterian churches were, however, in time reduced to three. In 1858 the Associate and the Associate Reformed bodies merged to form the "United Presbyterian Church." The national union was marked by the characteristic "come-outer" reaction on the part of minority groups, so that the union resulted in three

---

read but not explained, and the words to the communicants spun out about half an hour long, neither good nor bad. After that I left. I got home about six o'clock."

6. In classing the Disciples with the revivalistic group, I am guided by the fact that they represented a popular movement, that they did not require college or seminary training for their ministers, that they sought to make converts, and that they made extensive use of the protracted meeting. It should be noted, however, that although under Barton W. Stone they had begun with a powerful revivalistic impulse characterized by all sorts of abnormal manifestations, Alexander Campbell's interest was more intellectualistic and practical. As against the radical mysticism of the Methodists he stressed reason and the good life; as against the divisiveness of the Presbyterians he stressed church unity; as against the centralization of the Methodists he stressed local autonomy. He had thus talking points which he and his followers used tellingly in their many disputations (cf. A. W. Fortune, "The Disciples in Kentucky," *Proceedings of the Convention of the Christian Churches in Kentucky, 1932*).

churches where only two had been before. Locally, however, there was agreement, as Professor Woodburn puts it, that the only differences between them were that one sang the Psalms of David and the other David's Psalms. Late in the sixties the New School and the Old School Bodies succeeded in resolving their differences. In 1868 the New Side Convenanters disbanded, most of their families joining the United Presbyterian, the rest the Presbyterian Church. Here again the local action was the result of national developments, which are not without significance from the standpoint of this inquiry.

From the beginning of its existence in this country the Covenanter church had been strongly opposed to slave-holding. When in 1800 Alexander McLeod received a call from the First Reformed Presbyterian Church in New York City, he made it a condition of his acceptance that the church must be free from all slave-holding.[7] In 1802 he and Samuel Brown Wylie were commissioned to visit the Carolinas and take counsel with their brethren there regarding the sin of slave-holding.[8] In 1806 the church formally declared itself against slave-holding. Apparently, therefore, the opposition to slavery, which had had not a little to do with the migration from the Carolinas, was not motivated entirely by economic considerations. In any case, the Bloomington Covenanters were active in the Underground Railroad before the Civil War, and they even received Negroes into their fellowship. When war was declared, they gave vigorous support to the Union side. Among the Covenanters who took a prominent part was George H. Stuart, the leading layman of the First Church in Philadelphia. He served as national president of the Christian Commission, an organization which corresponded somewhat to the Y.M.C.A. of the World War. It thus became his duty to visit other churches. This was all right so long as the war lasted, but after it was over he was admonished by the Synod regarding the sin of "occasional hearing" and especially regarding the practice of singing hymns of non-Davidic origin. When he refused to heed the Synod's admonitions, he was excluded from membership. The First Church thereupon severed its connection with the General Synod, and the Bloomington Church, in accordance with my grandfather's advice, did likewise.[9]

---

7. Wylie, *op. cit.*, chap. iv.

8. *Remarks of Samule B. Wylie on the Occasion of the Fiftieth Anniversary of His Arrival in Philadelphia, Published at the Time of His Death in 1852.*

9. The First Church in Philadelphia seems to have been growing somewhat liberalized. This is indicated by the fact that its leadership included not only such a distinguished citizen of Philadelphia as Mr. Stuart but also the University of Pennsylvania's first professor of sociology, Robert Ellis Thompson. My grandfather's action in withdrawing with them was determined by the close ties which bound him to the Philadelphia church. His father had been its pastor for forty-nine years, and his brother, who succeeded him, was co-pastor and pastor for fifty-five years. But churches which had no such strong ties also withdrew. It is to be noted that no attempt was now made to maintain a separate organization. They identified themselves, instead, with other

In my own early years in Bloomington at a time when the population was about five thousand and the university enrollment about five hundred we had, therefore, three different brands of Presbyterian churches. As David Starr Jordan used to put it, we had the United Presbyterians, the Reformed Presbyterians, and the Presbyterians who were neither united nor reformed. There was also a strong Methodist church, a strong Disciples church, a Baptist church, a Church of Christ (known locally as the "Sassafras Church"), a weak Episcopal and a small Catholic church. The general grouping was much the same as in the 1840's. The Presbyterian church had become mildly evangelistic in its emphasis, but this church and the Episcopal church were still made up chiefly of college people, and of those who associated with college people. The United and the Reformed Presbyterians were still very conservative in their practices, even though the former was under very able and enlightened leadership. Both of them still made exclusive use of the Psalms of David in their services of worship, while the Reformed Presbyterians still refused to allow instrumental music, and they still forbade their members to vote. The Methodists, the Disciples, and the Baptists were still dominant among the rank and file of the population, while in the county at large their sway was undisputed except for two Cumberland Presbyterian churches, a few Churches of Christ and an occasional Separate, Regular, and Primitive Baptist organization. These churches were still evangelistic in their emphasis. They were concerned with the task of "saving souls," and they held that a man must be "converted" in order to be saved. They had their annual revival meetings, and they still encouraged or tolerated emotional expression on the part of their people. Young people from the more sedate communions would frequently attend these revivals to see the fun.

Going back after many years, I find some striking changes. The town has now eighteen thousand inhabitants, and the university six thousand students. The churches also have grown. More than that, there have been some changes of type. The Methodists today worship in a large and costly building. The older people with their "Amens" have long since passed away. There is now a stately service which appeals to college people. And the old efforts to induce the conversion experience have been discontinued. What is true of the First Methodist Church is true also of the Disciples of Christ, of the First Baptist Church, and also of the fine new Methodist church on the other side of the tracks. Among all these, conversion experiences of the old type are now very rare.

---

bodies already existing. The First Church in Philadelphia, after remaining independent for a number of years, thus united with the General Assembly of the Presbyterian Church.

The New Side Covenanters still exist, but since 1868 they have been a steadily diminishing body. In 1926 they reported 13 churches and 1,900 members. In the same year the Old Side Covenanters had 89 churches and 7,000 members, the Seceders 11 churches and 320 members, and the Associate Reformed 143 churches and 20,000 members.

But I find also a number of churches of which I had never heard in the 1890's. Among the thirty-two churches within Bloomington's city limits are three Pentecostal Assemblies of Jesus Christ, two Nazarene churches, an Assembly of God, a Wesleyan Methodist, a Free Methodist, and a Church of God. In these new churches I find somewhat the same type of service and somewhat[10] the same message which I used to hear in the Methodist church years ago. They are interested in saving souls, and they believe that men need to be converted in order to be saved. They emphasize the reality of sin and guilt, and they proclaim deliverance through the wonder-working power of the Blood of the Lamb. Like the Methodists and Baptists of the days gone by, they have sprung from the spontaneous religious fervor of the common people, and they are propagated through the missionary zeal of those who feel that they have found the greatest of all blessings. Their membership is made up of working-class people, who have been drawn in from the surrounding countryside to man the mills and the quarries and who, since the beginning of the depression, have had tough going.

In the county at large, outside of Bloomington, there are now sixty-two churches, some of which, however, are rather feeble. Of this number fourteen are Methodist (three of these having been Methodist Protestant); ten, Baptist; two, Separate Baptist; one, regular Baptist; one, Primitive Baptist; nine, Disciples of Christ ; eight, Church of Christ; while four are union chapels. The newer churches include one Nazarene, one Assembly of God, seven Pentecostal Assemblies of Jesus Christ, and four Trinity Pentecostal. Of the latter at least two are off-shoots of the Assembly of God in Bloomington.

Therefore, we still have today the same three groups of churches—the conservative churches, which persist by reason of their great resistance to change; the churches composed of college people and of those who accept the standards of college people; and the churches which spring out of the common soil of human nature. The alignment is, however, different today. The Methodists, the Disciples, and the Baptists have taken their place alongside of the Presbyterians and Episcopalians as respectable, middle-class churches, and a new group of churches has sprung up to meet the needs which formerly they had met.

III

The situation in Monroe County is by no means an average one. Its significance is rather to be found precisely in the unusually clear relief with which certain factors, which are, I think, operative in all organized religion, stand out. Let me call attention to the following considerations: (1) the coexistence throughout the one

---

10. The Bloomington Methodists of the eighties and nineties were already on their way toward respectability; hence the "somewhat."

hundred and twenty years of Monore County's history of the beginning, of the middle, and of the terminal stages of institutional religion, the types thus represented being constant as regards their general characteristics but shifting as regards the identity of the constituent bodies; (2) the presence throughout this period of a group of churches characterized by a strong clan loyalty and by a marked tendency toward splitting over relatively trivial issues; (3) the existence, especially during the early and the later years, of a considerable body of economically distressed folk, nearly all Protestants of English and Scotch-Irish descent, among whom the emotional cults have found their greatest following; and (4) the presence of an important university, which, especially in recent years, has accentuated the cultural differences and has speeded up the processes of liberalization and secularization within the larger churches.

Notice first of all that we have in this county a fine exemplification of Professor H. Richard Niebuhr's thesis regarding the life-history of organized religion.[11] According to that thesis, the religious denomination begins usually among the underprivileged with a group of believers banded together on the basis of some vivid religious experience and the new vision which accompanies it. As time goes on, these believers' groups develop in accordance with a fairly definite pattern. They become more prosperous, and the original believers are replaced by their children. The process of institutionalization then sets in. The children accept the faith of their parents without sharing their experience. Short-cuts and protective devices are introduced. The sacraments become means of grace rather than symbols of belief. The creeds become standards of doctrine rather than confessions of faith. Even religious experience itself tends to become standardized in the form of patterns of behavior, which have to be induced by artificial devices. In general, the process is one of leveling. The prophetic forward movements are leveled down and conventionalized. The eccentric and regressive manifestations are leveled up and become respectable. This process is exemplified most strikingly in the Methodists, the Disciples, and the Baptists of Bloomington. They began under the impulse of a vital religious movement. They were believers' groups, characterized by strong emotion, insisting upon first-hand religious experience, and propagated spontaneously through the missionary zeal of their converts. They have now taken their place among the respectable. The newer cults represent the period of spontaneity and creativity. In the course of time they, likewise, will become respectable middle-class churches. And the Presbyterians? Their period of spontaneity and creativity lay in the time of John Knox three hundred years ago. They are merely a little further along in the process which characterizes any vital religious movement. In their psalm-singing offshoots we already see the terminal stages of institutional religion.

---

11. *The Social Sources of Denominationalism* (New York: Henry Holt & Co., 1929).

These Scotch-Irish psalm-singers, who are so unusually well represented in Bloomington, are worthy of careful consideration. In any attempt to understand them and the tragedies of loyalty presented by their much subdividing, we may begin by recognizing that a church is first of all a fellowship. It is a group banded together on the basis of a loyalty which is accepted as supreme. Doctrine and ritual are of secondary importance. These are taken over from those who represent authority and are thus functions of the social relationships, particularly to the parents and early guides.[12] The persistence of these groups is due to that principle. If a great and beloved president of the university throughout his long period of service has remained a leader in the united Presbyterian Church in Bloomington, it is not due to any conviction on his part regarding the unique claims of the Psalms of David. So also the dean of the school of education in the university, who is equally active in the Old Side Covenanter Church, has no determining views regarding instrumental music in the church. Neither is he opposed to voting. Both these men are guided rather by considerations of loyalty. They have felt it a point of honor to be true to the church of their fathers. They have stayed with it, not because of doctrine but in spite of it.

Loyalty to family and clan is, in fact, so important in these churches that they may be said to represent tribal religion. The maintenance of group integrity in the face of changing conditions and against the onslaughts of an alien culture is with them a primary concern, and for this reason obedience and conformity to established patterns are required. The past rather than the future is the focus of attention. The German and the Scandinavian Lutherans in this country are examples. They are struggling to maintain their group identity and integrity, and in so doing they have become more conservative than their kindred in the old country. Religion of this type is especially likely to appear where the group has been subjected to pressure or to persecution. The ecclesiastical zeal of the Irish Catholics as compared with the Italians may thus be accounted for; so also the rigid attitudes of the various religious groups in Asia Minor and the legalism of the ancient Pharisees. The Scotch-Irish psalm-singers were just such a group. They had been solidified by persecution in the old country. In this country they were facing the disintegrating forces of impoverishment and disheartenment, which changed so many of their fellow countrymen into the "poor-white" or "hill-billy" type. They therefore stuck together throughout their wanderings. They clung to a faith in education. They retained a pride of race and clan.

The divisive tendencies which we find among them may be explained by the removal of external pressure and persecution and by the attempt to maintain loyalty, not through reason and love but through force and fear and arbitrary

---

12. A. T. Boisen, "The Problem of Values in the Light of Psychopathology," *American Journal of Sociology*, Vol. XXXVIII (July, 1932).

authority. The children who grow up under such conditions are likely to feel strong resentment, which sometimes takes the form of open rebellion and the disowning of the loyalty. More frequently, however, love is mingled with fear, loyalty with resentment. The individual may then accept the faith of his father, but the repressed hostility may be ready to seize upon some trivial doctrinal or ritualistic pretext in order to express itself. Divisions in the church then result, not from real issues of belief and practice but from unrecognized antagonistic social attitudes.

No consideration of these psalm-singing Presbyterians should fail to do justice to their sturdy character. They are a fine lot—strong, honest, neighborly, thrifty. Nonetheless, it must be recognized that their loyalty to race and clan is too often divorced from clear objectives. There is, in consequence, confusion as to what is important and what is unimportant in the principles emphasized and in the means employed. Therefore, their religion becomes static. There is fear of deviating even in the slightest from what is already established, and the confusion is accentuated by lurking antagonisms which are ready to find expression in church quarrels.

IV

The astonishingly rapid growth of new cults of the Holiness and Pentecostal types cannot be explained in terms of any one factor. The fact that this growth has taken place among the economically distressed factory and quarry workers and has been especially rapid since the depression is, however, significant.[13] This is true not merely in Bloomington but in the country at large. It has also been true of other periods of economic distress. It brings to our attention the fact that the mystical experiences out of which such movements arise are most likely to occur in periods of stress and crisis. Under normal conditions the individual is busy with his customary pursuits, and his reflections upon matters philosophical and religious are generally in terms of an accepted currency of ideas. His personality may, in fact, be regarded as a reflection of the social organization and as the subjective aspect of his particular culture.[14] His attitudes, his beliefs, his standards of value are taken over from his environment without much thought on his part. They are functions of his social relationships, particularly to those whom he admires and whose authority he accepts. In time of crisis, however, the individual finds himself face to face with the ultimate issues of life, and as his mind is stirred through strong emotion, ideas come flooding in as from an outside source. These ideas he is likely to attribute to a divine or to a demonic origin. In so far as he does come to feel himself in contact with a superhuman world there will be for him a new social frame of reference. The

13. A. T. Boisen, "Economic Distress and Religious Experience," *Psychiatry*, Vol. II, No. 2 (May, 1939).

14. G. H. Mead, *Mind, Self, and Society* (Chicago: University of Chicago Press, 1935).

accepted bases of judgment and reasoning no longer apply. There is a transvaluation of values—a break with the culture pattern of his particular time and race. Face to face with what he regards as ultimate reality, philosophy and theology become for such an individual no mere matters of academic concern but matters of life and death. Under such conditions meaning and emotion outstrip symbol. Instead of beginning with words and concepts according to the common practice, he is forced to seek new words to express the new ideas which come thronging in upon him. Such experiences may open the eyes to a larger universe and give insights which are new and creative. Again they may give new life and meaning to traditions and concepts which before had been stale and profitless. Frequently, they leave the individual cut loose from his moorings—perplexed, bewildered, sure only that things are not what they seem. They may thus be either constructive or destructive. They may be associated with mental disorder of the type, however, which should be recognized as an expression of nature's power to heal. They are likewise to be looked upon as wellsprings of religion. Even the unlettered laborer who passes triumphantly through such an experience may, like John Buynan, emerge a poet and theologian of no mean order.[15]

The danger of mental unbalance is at a minimum where the strain is shared by a group; it is at a maximum where the experience is a solitary one. Studies which have been made of the effect of the economic depression upon the mental health of our people[16] thus show that there has been no demonstrable increase in the incidence of mental disorder. The explanation is to be found in the fact that economic distress tends to increase the sense of fellowship and forces people to think together about the things that matter most. It thus tends to lessen the sense of isolation and guilt which is the primary evil in the functional types of mental illness.

The revivalism of the early nineteenth century would thus be related to the impoverishment and disheartenment of those who had been forced to seek new homes in the wilderness. Its reappearance today in this college town is to be explained in large part by the suffering and privation to which working-class families have been subjected by reason of the hard times in the stone industry. It is religion of the type which tends to appear spontaneously wherever men are grappling desperately with the issues of spiritual life and death. Such religion is rooted in the creative forces latent in struggling humanity. It is a manifestation of nature's power to heal in the face of overwhelming difficulties. Its primary concern is release from the sense of sin and guilt. It finds the solution in the acceptance of

---

15. An extended consideration of the interrelationship of religious experience and mental disorder will be found in my *Exploration of the Inner World* (Chicago: Willett, Clark & Co., 1936), esp. chaps. i and ii.

16. Paul O. Komora and Mary A. Clark, "Mental Disease in the Crisis," *Mental Hygiene*, XIX (1935), 289-330.

personal responsibility and emotional identification with a fellowship conceived as universal and abiding. The individual who has that experience is thereby given a role in a great world-drama. He finds a new purpose in life and goes forth with a contagious enthusiasm which communicates itself to other individuals. The group is thus formed on the basis of a shared experience, and it grows of itself through the zeal of its converts.

It is characteristic of this type of religion that it tends to break down old culture patterns and to create new social alignments. In a recent study of the Holy Roller cults[17] I have reported the case of an intelligent, well-educated, economically well-to-do white man who received the "baptism of the spirit" and identified himself with a Negro Holy Roller group. This is not an isolated case. Whites are not infrequently found in Negro Holy Roller meetings, and sometimes Negroes are welcomed in white groups of the Pentecostal variety. Apparently, the mystical experience means a new social identification, which tends to create new values and to break across the lines of class and caste, even lines so fixed as those which separate the Negroes from the whites. We may therefore say that the revivalism of the early part of the nineteenth century served as a solvent to many old social formations and that it was instrumental in creating a new culture suited to the pioneer conditions of the Middle West.

Religion of this type has of course its dangers and its limitations. One grave danger lies in the overvaluation of the abnormal. Because the vivid sense of fellowship with God comes so frequently in time of stress and crisis and is attended by abnormal manifestations, the mistake is made of trying to gain this sense of fellowship with God through artificially induced abnormal manifestations such as speaking with tongues, jerking, dancing, and the like. The accidental is thus mistaken for the essential.

Another danger lies in the tendency to stop short of a satisfactory adjustment to the external world. The mystical experience, in so far as it results in a genuine reorganization of the personality, means an "orientation in time." The Pentecostal convert thus thinks in terms of a life beyond. This hope for the future becomes for him a source of strength, and it enables him to bear up under the trials and discouragements of the present. Too often, however, his attitude is one of passive endurance rather than active endeavor. Too often he makes no effort to correct the glaring social evils responsible for his original distress but leaves these for the Lord when he returns in glory.

The tendency to stop short of a satisfactory adjustment to the external world is seen also in the common failure to achieve any true perspective. The Pentecostal convert tends to get rather "chummy" with God. He is apt to bring the divine

---

17. "Economic Distress and Religious Experience," op.cit.

down close to his own level. He is likely, moreover, to be lacking in deference toward the beliefs and feelings of other men and toward the findings of scholars and scientists. His universe may thus be only a little larger than the private world of the psychotic patient. It may be merely the world of a very small segment of society—a world too diminutive to include what science is telling us about stars and atoms and plants and men.

In spite of their weaknesses and shortcomings we still seem justified in saying that even the more primitive Holy Rollers represent the period of spontaneity and creativity in organized religion and that when in the course of time they take their place in the ranks of respectability, the earnestness and sincerity of their adherents will find its reward in the raising of the social and economic standards of themselves and their families.

V

The fact that such a surprising development of emotional cults has taken place in a university town calls attention to the relationship of religion and higher education and raises the question of why it is that those church bodies which have insisted most upon an educated ministry have failed most signally in meeting the needs of the rank and file of the people. Our findings suggest the following considerations.

We may notice first the important part which the churches have had in the development of higher education in America. Not only have they founded and supported great universities like Harvard and Yale and Princeton and Chicago and colleges like Dartmouth, Williams, Amherst, Oberlin, and Grinnell, but they had much to do with the beginnings of our state institutions for higher learning. Even the Methodists and the Baptists and the Disciples of the early nineteenth century have been zealous in the founding of colleges. So also are the Holy Rollers of today. Faith in higher education has characterized Protestant Christianity. It has believed in the gospel of enlightenment.

It is equally clear that the college which began under the fostering care of the church has now outgrown its allegiance to the church. Even though many members of the university faculty are active in the churches of the town, there is a growing attitude of indifference and of skepticism regarding the claims of Christianity. The church no longer enjoys the authority and prestige which belonged to it in the early days. This is true not merely of the university in Bloomington, it is true, in general, not only of the secular institutions but even of those which have been founded and supported by the church. This is particularly true in precisely those sections of the country in which the church's work has been most efficient.[18] This is a situation which calls for careful consideration. To those who believe that the hope of this sick and suffering world lies in a new religious orientation and quickening it must be evident that the solution is not to be found in a tribal religion which tends to undergird strife and thus increase the dangers which are threatening to destroy our civilization. Neither is it to be found in a religion of personal salvation which makes no effort to cope with the perils which now confront our great human family. It must be found in a forward-looking and enlightened religion. What then is the explanation of liberal Christianity's loss of influence?

First of all, we may say that no little part of the difficulty is to be attributed to the institutions of higher learning themselves. They have not yet accomplished the task which the church has entrusted to them. They are still in the process of learning. One of the growing points lies in the development of specialization. During the early days at Indiana University the members of the faculty were distinguished by the comprehensiveness of their knowledge. When my grandfather[19] was appointed to the chair of "mixed mathematics," that term—which he quickly changed—was used to include physics and chemistry and geology and astronomy. During his fifty years' tenure at the university he also at one time or another taught Latin and Greek, algebra, plane, solid, and analytic geometry, conic sections, and calculus. On Sundays he preached in the little Covenanter church. He was perhaps an extreme instance, but many of his colleagues also occupied rather broad settees in place of a chair. In 1885 under the presidency of David Starr Jordan the curriculum was drastically changed. Specialization was introduced. The students now elected their courses. At the same time the number of courses was greatly increased. Great gains were thereby achieved. This process continuing for more than half a century in our institutions for higher learning has resulted in the mastery over many important fields of human experience, but it has also been attended by certain losses. Too often the specialists have become mere technicians. They have not achieved any larger perspective. To add to the difficulty, those who have devoted themselves to the study of human nature have rather generally disclaimed any concern with the problem of motives and values—the dynamic forces of human life. The tendency has been to allow their problems to be determined by their methodology, while their methodology has been taken over from the exact sciences and is not suited either to the material they have to work with or to the yardsticks at their disposal.

The result has been that, while science has made magnificent progress in understanding and controlling the material world, it has made little progress in the

18. Boisen, "Factors in the Decline of the Country Church," *American Journal of Sociology*, XXII (1916), 177-92.

19. Theophilus Adam Wylie, not to be confused with his cousin Andrew Wylie, the first president.

understanding and control of human nature. Humanity today seems much like a child of three at the wheel of a high-powered motorcar. The power which has been placed in our hands through the achievements of science has become a source of terrible danger.

We are, however, beginning to see the light. There is today increasing recognition of the fact that human nature cannot be studied piecemeal. Specialization has come to stay, but the specialist is discovering that he cannot be sufficient unto himself. He must cooperate with other specialists and learn to see his particular specialty in its large setting. We are, furthermore, beginning to recognize the significance of the wishes, the attitudes, and the value judgments as the driving and guiding forces of human life.

The conclusion follows that, in so far as our institutions for higher learning begin to concern themselves with the problems of motives and values and with the comprehensive view, they are likely to make a contribution to the understanding of the laws of the spiritual life which will give new vision and new power to the forces of religion.

Far more important than any failure of our scientists to penetrate into the field of religion is the failure of the professional servants of the church to keep pace with the institutions of higher learning. They have as yet done little in the way of exploring the field which is peculiarly their own. Their attention has remained centered upon the traditional disciplines of biblical languages and literature, church history, systematic theology, and homiletics. It is still possible for a student to go through almost any of our theological schools and get his degree without ever having made any firsthand studies of the human personality either in health or in sickness or of the social forces which so largely determine it. The liberal church has not in its own domain taken any considerable part in that cooperative enterprise to which we give the name of "science." It has made little use of the methods of empirical observation to build up a body of tested knowledge regarding the forces of the spiritual life and the laws according to which they operate.[20] For this reason its position is apologetic. It is trying to explain the ancient tenets in terms of modern thought. It speaks not with authority but as the scribes and interpreters of traditions.

Perhaps this fact may help to explain why those churches which have insisted upon an educated ministry have failed to attract and hold the common people. We need not assume that the standards are to be let down but rather that something is wrong with the kind of education we have been giving.

---

20. Some important work has been done in the fields of the psychology and sociology of religion and of religious education, but, as far as most theological schools are concerned, these disciplines are not yet a basic part of their educational structure. What is more to the point, the spirit and method of cooperative inquiry have not as yet penetrated to the ministers who man our churches.

It still remains to be seen what will happen when the servants of the church begin to apply the methods of cooperative inquiry to the problems of living men, seeking not only to help but also to understand. It seems not too much to hope that as they learn to ask the significant questions and to verify and reverify the answers there may come new insights regarding the end and meaning of life and the way to individual and social salvation. Among the fields which need to be explored there seems to be none of greater importance than that inner realm of aspiration and conflict out of which the mystical cults arise. It is perhaps inevitable that a religion which springs out of the desperate struggle for personal salvation should not concern itself with social evils. This follows from the fact that constructive solutions of inner conflicts require the acceptance of personal responsibility, not its projection. The fault must be found in one's self rather than in others. The Pentecostal convert must, therefore, take a more or less passive attitude toward the social evils around him. This is assuredly more wholesome than the attitude of the man who tries to reform the social order as an escape from the need of reforming himself; but when these personal problems are approached by someone other than the man who is himself in desperate need, when they are treated with sympathetic understanding and are made the subject of cooperative study, then it may be possible to see things in true perspective. Then also it may be possible to bring the driving power of vital religion in its creative stages under the control of the best intelligence of the day. When this time comes, it should no longer be necessary for those upon whom the pressure falls most heavily to seek help outside of the church in the vagaries of the ecstatic cults, and the way of individual salvation may become one with the task of bringing in the world that ought to be.

THEOLOGY IN THE LIGHT OF PSYCHIATRIC EXPERIENCE

Anton T. Boisen

[This article was in the January, 1941 issue of *The Crozer Quarterly*, a scholarly journal of liberal Protestantism published by Crozer Theological Seminary. It is perhaps the most complete published example of Boisen's use of his case method to yield theological discussion and conclusions. It is the case of Oscar O., "A Devoted Husband," which Boisen used many times in his teaching and writing—probably because of its parallels to his own case. In the extensive quotation of the patient's report, one can see the patient's response to the many questions in Boisen's case study forms, cited in Asquith, "The Case Study Method of Anton T. Boisen" (in Part II of this book). The "General Principles" at the end of the article are representative of the fruit of Boisen's pastoral theological method—the result of his cumulative reading of the "human documents."]

The idea of God and the laws of the spiritual life are derivatives of the social nature of man. Such in brief is the thesis of this paper. I shall try to show that the idea of God is the symbol of that which is supreme in the individual and social system of loyalties and that explicitly or implicitly it is operative in the lives of all men. It thus represents that fellowship with which man as a social being seeks identification and of which his system of values is merely a function. To feel oneself estranged from that fellowship is the essence of the sense of guilt, and constitutes the primary evil in the functional types of mental illness. Restoration to mental health (salvation) requires release from this sense of estrangement and reestablishment of right relationship. In psychotherapeutic practice the needed forgiveness is mediated by the physician, and no results are achieved except as the patient comes to trust the physician. In those spontaneous cures known as "conversion experiences" there is characteristically the sense of being forgiven directly by God. Such experiences have a profound emotional effect which passes in an unbroken series from the mild mysticism of the recognized conversion experience to the turmoil of acute mental disorder. The emotional impact of the mystical experience is due to the shift in social reference which is involved in the changed concept of the self and the new role in a cosmic drama.

Methodology

The thesis proposed has been derived from twenty years' experience as a student of religion among the mentally ill. It will be considered in the light of a particular case. The use of a case has the following advantages:

1. It is an aid to clear thinking. It will enable us to proceed with some assurance that we are talking about the same things without waiting to agree on definitions.

2. It introduces us at once to the primary sources for the understanding of human nature.

3. It lends itself to the pooling of insights on the part of different specialized workers.

The case which we are using has been selected out of a large number as a *type*. By that is meant a case which presents a certain constellation of tendencies which statistical studies have shown to be related and which moreover presents them freed so far as possible from complicating features. The basis on which this particular case was chosen is a certain set of ideas and attitudes. This patient gave unusually striking expression to a group of ideas which we have found to be characteristic of the acute functional disorders. He was, moreover, unusually free from the malignant attitudes of suspicion and hostility and from overt eroticism. It will therefore serve admirably to raise the problem of the relationship of the mystical and of the pathological.

The Test: A Case Record

The patient chosen for consideration was brought to the hospital because of an attempt at suicide. He had been found in his home with the gas turned on and both wrists cut. According to the commitment papers the motive was self-sacrifice. He wanted to relieve the world of its sins. The onset of the illness, according to the patient, was "quite long—it was a whole week!" The wife states that she had not noticed anything out of the way until two days before. There had been a previous commitment thirteen years back. Then also the onset had been sudden, the disturbance severe, and the duration brief.

In appearance he was a short, stocky man of fifty-three with barrel chest and heavy muscles. When first seen, the disturbed condition had already passed. For one who had just emerged from so searching an ordeal he showed a surprising degree of quiet self-assurance. He talked frankly of his experience in a sensible and matter-of-fact manner. There was no hesitation and no push of speech.

According to his account he was of good middle-class Swedish stock and was second in a family of nine, of whom seven were boys. All of the children lived to maturity and have given good accounts of themselves. The father as a young man had served several years as steward on a sailing vessel. After he was married he was employed in a flour mill. The patient describes him as a home-loving man who together with the mother became quite religious in their later years. He, however, from his fourth to his twelfth year had lived in his grandmother's home.

He considers himself to have been a fairly normal boy. He went through seven grades of school. He did not repeat any grades, but his scholastic standing was only fair and he hated school. In a fight, however, he was not so dumb. He could lick any boy in his room. After leaving school he served an apprenticeship; then at the age of twenty-one he went to sea. After seven years of roving he settled down in the United States and at the age of thirty-one he married. His vocational record is good. He had no difficulty in holding jobs and made good wages, $66 a week being his regular scale. His trade, however, is a highly specialized one and jobs are scarce, those that do come being portioned out by the Union. For this reason he has been idle a good part of the time.

Of his sex adjustments he talks frankly and without apparent attempts at concealment. There had been the usual difficulty with masturbation in the adolescent period, but he thinks it was not excessive. At least he had never worried over it. At sixteen a girl older than himself attempted to initiate him into the mysteries of sex but his response was unsatisfactory. There were no further hetero-sexual relationships until he went to sea. In this period he went with his mates to houses of prostitution in some of the ports they visited, but he never contracted any venereal disease and apparently he kept within the limits of respectability as judged by his particular group. His wife at the time he met her was working in a restaurant. He became interested in her and then discovered that she came from his native town in Sweden. According to him the marital adjustments have been happy on both sides. The wife also admits no irregularities. One gets the impression that the home is something of a matriarchy. The wife is a quick, attractive, business-like person, accustomed apparently to having her own way. She says of him, "He always says anything I say is all right." He says of himself that he has good will power and that whenever he wanted anything he did not hesitate to assert himself. One gets the impression, however, that he did not choose to assert himself very often.

The patient and his wife were both brought up in the Lutheran Church. Of his early training he says that his grandmother used to drag him off to church and Sunday school and that he hated it. He "never did grab anything in religion." He claims to be something of a free-thinker. In politics he inclines toward socialism. In religion he comes from Missouri. He wants proof before he is ready to believe. Neither he nor his wife has ever been active in the church.

According to his wife the first indication that anything was wrong was an increasing self-absorption and loss of sleep. She noticed this first on Friday. By Sunday he had become extremely agitated. He kept pacing the floor, moaning and lost in thought. When spoken to he was irritable, especially toward her. He asked her to go away and leave him alone. This she finally did. The suicidal attempt came during her absence. She explains the difficulty as due to lack of work. For three years he had worked only fourth time and for the past three months he had not worked more than ten days. Of course it was not his fault. He had to be content with what the Union assigned to him, but it meant that she and the older daughter had been obliged to become the chief support of the home.

The patient was quite ready to tell of his experience and allowed me to get it down pretty much word for word. Here is his report.

> I must give it to you in order. You can't understand unless we go back to the beginning thirteen years ago. You must know how the whole thing started, how I made a sort of bet with God. I was at a socialist meeting one night. A man there spoke of Jesus and of his giving his life for others. He asked if there were not many other men who would be willing to do that.
>
> That night I was thinking about what the socialist speaker said and that I would gladly give my life for my family alone. In the night I was waked up and a voice said, "You must be put to the test to see if you will really give up your life." And it seemed as though God were right in front of me and the voice seemed to be God's voice and words from the Bible came into my head. I began to feel very nervous. It seemed as though something were getting into me. I did not tell my wife. I felt she would not understand. I got up and ran out in the street in my underwear. Of course that was a very strange thing to do, but it was just like the old Greek who found out how to weigh a ship. He was in his bathtub at the time the idea came to him and he got so excited that he jumped up and ran out without anything on. You get an idea so big it just carries you away. But a policeman brought me back and I slept until eight or nine o'clock in the morning.
>
> I think it was the same night that blood came into my mouth and something said it took almost two thousand years to produce a man like me. I had lived for two thousand years. It was just like I had gone through many generations. Sometimes I was born rich and sometimes I was born poor. . .

About a week after that I was sent to the hospital. After that dream I was nervous. I had a feeling like when they bind up your arm and give you a blood test. I was sort of filled up. It was a queer feeling—something you don't understand what it is. I had the feeling that there were two sides and that I had to go to one side or the other in order to get salvation. I was out in the park when it happened. I had my child on my arm and my wife was with me. I got up and started to go. I felt I had to. My wife, she looked at me and saw my eyes was bloodshot. She wanted me to go to the doctor, but I felt I would break my agreement with God if I did. Just then a policeman came along and my wife called him. He started to take the child away and I started to fight. Then other policemen came and they took me to the hospital.

In the hospital I was put in a straight-jacket. The first night I had a dream. I seemed to be crucified, and the whole room was full of devils. They were trying to hurt me, but I was full of power. You see I was in a delirium. I dreamed I was dead. I dreamed I was laying in the grave just like Jesus did.

In about three days my mind came back, and I was released at the end of three weeks. I got along very well after that. I had steady work and there was nothing to worry about. During the last three years work has been scarce and there has been plenty of time to think. No, I had not been thinking much about religion. My wife was told at the hospital that the trouble came from reading the Bible, so I put the Bible in the attic. I don't want to make her nervous. And I didn't go to church.

This last attack began when something told me to go and get the Bible. I had started then to pray to God. I had been feeling lonesome and I had it in my mind that there is a God. Then it came to me that I had a second instalment to pay. I had to finish paying my bet with God. I came then into a state of fear. Something said to me, "Are you willing to commit suicide?" And it was just like I had to do it. I turned on the gas. That was for my wife. Then I slashed my wrists, one for one daughter and the other for the other daughter. But everything I have done before came to a good end and I have the feeling that this will too. I just felt that I had to do it to keep my promise. I have the feeling now that I am a new man. All this is over. I have done my part.

No, I didn't hear anything. It's just like when you sit and think. Something comes to you. Sometimes it comes quick just like something talks to you. I suppose it comes from God. I can't see any other explanation. Yes, it came from the best part of myself. I never got any messages from the devil, though one time something did say to me that the devil is a part of God.

Yes, I did say that when this came on it was just like I hypnotized myself. When I talk with a doctor I talk about self-hypnotizing. A doctor understand that. He don't understand about religion.

Did I think of myself as Christ? Yes, I guess I did. That was before I understand. You get happy and you wake up and think you are it. It's just like reading a story and missing the last part. You get puzzled as to who you are.

My plans? I want to get to work as soon as possible and get along the same as before. I don't want to take any more of them fits. When this thing came on, I thought I was going to have to preach, but the voice said, "You was going right the way you was. I don't need you to preach. I have other men I can send to do that."

At the staff meeting the patient made a very good impression. He told his story clearly and showed remarkable insight. He went into considerable detail but without any push of speech. His answers were always to the point. On one occasion, when he was asked if he did not consider his experience something unusual, he replied, "No it's just like eggs in an incubator. First one cracks and then another." On another occasion he was asked what he thought of when he saw the sun. He replied, "I think of God. It's one of the things that makes me think there must be a God. I really think the earth is like an incubator and the sun gives the heat. I got that idea in a dream."

Points to Notice

1. *How the Disturbance Began*

The patient's own explanation of the onset was that he had an idea so big that it just carried him away. What that idea was is fairly clear. He thought that God was talking to him, that he was really a very different person from what he had supposed, and that he had a great responsibility resting upon him. Ideas of death, of rebirth, of previous incarnation, and of mission were also present. We have then clearly exemplified in this case the entire constellation of ideas which have been found to be characteristic of the acute functional disorders.[1] In all such cases the actual disorder seems to begin, just as in this case, with an experience interpreted as a manifestation of the superhuman.

2. *Nature's Power to Heal*

This case would be recognized by most psychiatrists as one that had a favorable prognosis. The onset was very sudden, the disturbance acute, and the attitudes free from such malignant tendencies as suspicion, hostility, and overt sexuality. According to my view, disorders of this type are not evils but attempts at re-organization, analogous to fever or inflammation in the body. They are manifestations of nature's power to heal, and, as such, they are closely related to those spontaneous constructive solutions of inner conflicts which we know as "conversions."[2]

3. *The Mystical and the Pathological*

Experiences such as that of our patient serve to dramatize life. They reveal problems which are present in ordinary life but which in ordinary life do not carry enough emotional charge to lift them into the field of attention. Under ordinary conditions the individual is busy with his customary pursuits, and his reflections on

---

1. Boisen, *Exploration of the Inner World*, Chicago, Willett, Clark & Co., 1936, chap. I.
2. *Op. cit.*, pp. 53ff.; also chap. II.

matters philosophical and religious are generally in terms of an accepted currency of ideas. He therefore indulges in a lot of mere verbalization. In time of crisis, however, he is confronted with the ultimate issues of life. Who am I? What is this world in which I live? What am I in this world for? Where am I now? How far have I succeeded or failed? are questions which become fraught with meaning. The individual feels himself face to face with reality. Philosophy and theology are no mere matters of academic concern but of life and death. Under such conditions meaning and emotion outstrip symbol. Instead of beginning with words and concepts one must seek words to express the new meanings which come thronging in. Under intense emotion the mind is stirred in ever-widening circles and at deeper levels. Ideas then come flooding in as from an outside source. The tendency is to attribute them to a divine or to a demonic origin. Such experiences may serve to give new life and meaning to traditions and concepts which before had been dry and meaningless. They may open the eyes to a larger universe and bring insights which are new and creative. Sometimes they result in a break with the past and with its particular culture patterns. Not infrequently they are definitely destructive, shattering the accepted foundations of judgment and reasoning. In any case they spring out of strong emotion and they produce intense emotion of terror or of joy. We may class them as *mystical* experiences in so far as they give the sense of identification with the larger fellowship presented by the idea of God. Such a sense of identification with God is common in mental disorder as well as in religious experience. Pathological features tend to appear in proportion as the experience is solitary, as it comes in the nature of a sudden release from the pressure of accumulated difficulties, when it is preceded by a prolonged period of dryness and sense of deprivation, and when there is a sense of condemnation by God or of danger from a hostile source.

4. The Idea of God

It is clear that our patient's two disturbed periods began with the idea that God was talking to him. The conditions leading up to this idea are, however, not clear in either of the two periods. We know that he had not been addicted to churchgoing and that at other times he had never shown any particular interest in religion. On the basis of our observation of other cases we can say that it is not necessary to find an explanation in terms of previous indoctrination but that ideas concerning the superhuman tend to appear spontaneously whenever an individual becomes absorbed in a problem which vitally affects his personal destiny. Under intense concentration and strong emotion the mental processes are quickened. Ideas darting into the mind then become so vivid that they are interpreted as coming from an outside source and are attributed to God or to the devil in accordance with the value judgments involved.

Such experiences always produce a profound emotional effect and, as in this case, may so upset the accepted norms of judgment and reasoning that mental disorder results. Where, as under certain types of religious influence, the experience takes place within a social matrix and follows certain accepted social patterns, and where God is thought of as approving, the result may be an accession of power.[3] Where, on the other hand, the experience takes place in isolation, especially where it involves the sense of condemnation and fear, the result is likely to be mental disorder. The present case was that of an isolated experience and involved ideas of death and world change. The sense of guilt and condemnation is not so clear. The profound emotional impact is to be explained by the shift in social reference and by the changed concept of the self.

The significance of the experience of feeling oneself face to face with God may be considered in the light of Mead's theory of the social basis of the personality.[4] According to that theory the personality is merely the subjective aspect of culture. It is the internalization within the individual of the organized social attitudes made possible through the use of language. Herein lies the difference between human social organization, but its basis is physiological (instinctive). The individual members of the beehive and of the anthill cooperate because of the way they are built. Reproduction is taken care of by one individual, the queen, with her enormously overdeveloped sex organs. The fighting is done by a group of soldiers who are good for nothing else. Another group takes care of the food-getting, the housing, and the care of the young. All cooperate automatically, and, if they need any special tool, such as flying apparatus, they grow it. In mammals we see another line of development, but even here the same distinction holds to some extent. Among all animals below man the sex drive is confined physiologically to certain rutting seasons. In man it is controlled by the *mores*. With the introduction of language the sex drive and other matters vital to the welfare of the race are governed by the internalization within the individual of the group attitudes. By means of language the individual is able to respond to certain common social symbols which call forth the same response in himself as they do in others. In this way he builds up within himself certain more or less consistent response to these symbols, and the particular organization of social attitudes which is developed in him is his character. The individual's system of values thus depends upon the group which he reflects or represents. His standards of value are, in other words, functions of his social relationships, particularly to those with whom he identifies himself.

A consequence of this view, which Mead did not develop but which seems to follow, is that the idea of God is the symbol under which loyalty to the group is raised to the level of the universal and abiding. It stands for that in his social experi-

---

3. Boisen, "Economic Distress and Religious Experience," *Psychiatry*, II, No. 2 (May, 1939).
4. G. H. Mead, *Mind, Self and Society*, University of Chicago Press, 1934.

ence which the individual most admires and loves, that to which he gives his allegiance and by which he judges himself. It represents, thus, a reality of vital importance to every living man whether he calls himself religious or not. To feel oneself brought face to face with God is, then, the experience of being brought into that fellowship which is for the individual all-important. And inasmuch as the entire personality is a social product and a reflection of a particular social group, the experience of feeling oneself identified with a superior fellowship means inevitably a new concept of the self. Moreover, the accepted standards and values no longer apply, because the individual has found that which seems to him infinitely greater.

5. *Spiritual Maturity and the Sovereignty of God*

In our consideration of this case we have been interested primarily in those aspects of our patient's experience which are typical and we have disregarded the particular personal problems with which he was grappling. We may, however, at this point call attention to what seems to be the centre of his personal problem. The key to that problem may be found in the beginning of his first disturbed period. He had gone to a socialist meeting, and the speaker asked if there were not other men beside Jesus who were willing to give their lives for others. That night, he tells us, he kept thinking about what the socialist speaker had said, and the question came to him, "Would you be willing to give your life for your wife and family?" And it came to him that he must be put to the test. We must, of course, be careful not to draw too many inferences from the immediate occasion of a disturbance. We know that especially in the acute disorders we have to do with an accumulation of inner stresses and that the upsetting experience may be the merest touch. Nonetheless we may assume that the upsetting factor must have some relationship to the central problem. We notice, therefore, that the question with which the disturbance began had to do with this man's relationship to his wife and family. Examining his story from this standpoint, what do we find? The picture seems fairly clear. Here was a reasonably steady, self-reliant individual who after serving his apprenticeship as a mechanic goes to sea. There are in this period some irregularities. At some of the ports he goes with his comrades to houses of prostitution, but these indulgences do not seem to have gone beyond the bounds of respectability as judged by his group. After several years of wandering he married a young woman from his native town in Sweden whom he meets in this country, an attractive person of considerable force of character. With his marriage his entire manner of life is changed. He becomes now a devoted husband and father. His evenings are spent at home, or at least in company with his wife and daughters. Aside from his labor union he belongs to no organizations. It is therefore clear that his wife was now supreme in his system of loyalties. His entire life was built around her, and his love for her was for him the equivalent of a religion. There is in this nothing unusual. Sex love, as Professor

Hocking points out,[5] is closely associated with religion; not that religion can be explained in terms of sex, but that sex love at its best approaches religion. Both seek somewhat the same thing—union with the idealized other-than-self. But it is also true that sex love seeks something beyond the finite love object and that it cannot be satisfied with the finite. It seems fair to assume that this law was operative in the case of this simple mechanic. It was not for him sufficient to have reorganized his life around his love for his wife. He had undoubtedly, after the manner of lovers, sworn to his readiness to give up everything for her sake; and his picture of himself was that of a devoted husband and father. But the actualities would sometimes become a bit trying. As a rugged, self-reliant male he found it not always easy to submit to her domination, and he probably became uncomfortably aware of attitudes within himself which were at variance with the undying devotion which he professed. The problem of his ultimate loyalty was thus pressing heavily upon him. We may therefore hazard the guess that the source of strain in this case was not so much the sense of guilt as the need of achieving a higher level of adjustment, the level represented by the psychoanalytic doctrine of autonomy and the Christian doctrine of the sovereignty of God.

At first thought these two doctrines may seem opposed one to the other. We submit, however, the proposition that they are really contributory to each other. Modern psychiatric experience tends to support the old Christian doctrine and to throw new light upon it. But ancient religious insight sees deeper. It recognizes the principle of autonomy. At the same time it recognizes the fact that no individual can be self-sufficient and it finds the solution in the idea of the sovereignty of God. By this is meant that true autonomy is achieved through finding one's role as a child of God and taking one's place in the larger universe. One's loyalty must thus be transferred from the finite to the infinite. Such dependence upon God is entirely consonant with self-reliance in that it makes the individual independent of the trials and vicissitudes of his temporal existence.

6. The Concept of the Self

With the idea that God was talking to him there came to our patient a new concept of himself. He was more important than he had ever before dreamed. It had taken two thousand years to produce a man like him. He had appeared in many forms. Sometimes he had been born rich. Sometimes he had been born poor. Questioning revealed that like many another acutely disturbed patient he had identified himself with Christ. This question of who one is appears characteristically in the acute psychoses. The disruption of the accepted idea of one's role in life is

---

5. *Human Nature and Its Remaking*, Yale University Press, 1923, chap. 42.

undoubtedly a factor of fundamental importance in the causation of the disturbance.

This confusion regarding one's identity as a factor in the acute psychoses gives support to the view that the concept of the self is the nucleus of the personality. The growth of the personality is thus dependent upon the discovery of relationships to some particular idea of ourselves and of our role. A fundamental change in the idea of the self therefore compels a thoroughgoing reorganization of the personality. We may furthermore suggest that this man's identification of himself with Christ, fantastic though it seems at first thought, is probably related to Paul's doctrine of the "indwelling Christ" and to Jesus' teaching regarding the fatherhood of God. The enlarged concept of the self is one of the eternally valid insights of religion. So also is its recognition of the individual's insignificance. It is characteristic of religion that it extends the horizon in both directions. Religion rejoices both in the microscope and in the telescope. Our patient's fantastic idea of himself is thus not without an element of truth.

7. *The Problem of Sin and Salvation*

The fact that our patient had no evident sense of guilt is unusual. It is possible that a sense of estrangement and condemnation had been present in the earlier stages of his two periods of disorder. We must not forget that on both occasions he came under observation only after God had spoken to him and he may already have had the feeling of being forgiven. It is therefore in order to point out that the functional mental disorders are rooted commonly in a sense of sin or guilt due to the presence of masses of experience and dynamic action patterns which the individual is neither able to control nor to acknowledge for fear of condemnation. The sense of guilt is thus the social judgment which the individual pronounces upon himself on the basis of the ethical standards which he has accepted as his own. But the standards themselves are merely functions of the social relationships to those with whom he wishes to be identified. The essence of the sense of guilt is therefore not so much the transgression of a code as the breach of trust which is involved. It is thus primarily a matter of social relationships, and salvation, or cure, consists in release from the sense of estrangement and restoration to the fellowship of the good, but fellowship which is symbolized by the idea of God.

Very striking in this case are the ideas of death and of rebirth. The test to which this patient felt himself subjected had to do with his willingness to give his life for others. This was true of both disturbed periods. Associated with this was the idea that he had lived in many previous incarnations. Ideas of death are characteristic of the acute disturbances generally and ideas of rebirth are frequent. There are those who hold that the idea of death such as we see in this case is an expression of the wish for rebirth and that in any case ideas of death and of renewal are closely associated.

Mental disorder of this type, together with the conversion experience to which it is closely related, exemplifies an important therapeutic principle. What it seeks is complete commitment to that which is supreme in the individual's hierarchy of loyalties. It is the desperate attempt in the face of an accumulation of difficulties to get rid of all that is alien to the accepted ideals and thus to make possible the needed reorganization or rebirth. From this standpoint the ideas of death and rebirth which recur so frequently are by no means accidental. They represent the exact meaning of the experience as a manifestation of nature's power to heal. This requirement of complete commitment, even to the point of self-sacrifice, is the essence of Jesus' doctrine of the cross. Jesus proclaimed repeatedly, in words whose meaning seems perfectly clear, that no man could be his disciple unless he was willing to give up all that he had and follow him. To Jesus himself the idea of his death clearly represented the last full measure of devotion to the Love that ruled the universe. It was his declaration of the principle that the redemption of the many is to be brought about through the sacrificial devotion of the few, and it summoned men to enlist in that sacrificial task. It was, therefore, his proclamation of the good news that in such devotion, rather than in conventional morality and success, lay the way of salvation. It represented thus a shift from a static to a dynamic morality which finds the good life not in outward correctness but in self-forgetful devotion to the best. To the man overwhelmed by his sins it brought thus the offer of a new chance. This same principle was central in Paul's gospel of deliverance.

It is a sad reflection upon the frailty of human nature that Jesus' own teaching regarding his death has been so largely misconstrued. Instead of a summons to the sacrificial way of life it has become the doctrine of a vicarious atonement, according to which, as commonly interpreted, Jesus gave his life to satisfy the demands of justice and thereby paid the price which enables those who believe in him to obtain salvation in a life hereafter. His commanding challenge to a life of adventurous devotion has thus all too often become just another means of evasion.

Psychoanalytic literature today has much to say about neurotic self-punishment. Alexander, for example, regards it as the "counterfeit coinage" by which unacceptable cravings are permitted to buy indulgence. This, he holds, comes about through the axiomatic assumption that by means of punishment and suffering one achieves not only absolution from sin but a justification for commiting it.[6] According to my view neurotic self-punishment stands for a valid principle. The difficulty is that most mental sufferers have not been able to pay the full price but have resorted to various compromises and concealment devices. That our patient is

---

6. Franz Alexander, *Psychoanalysis of the Total Personality*, Washington, Nervous and Mental Disease Publishing Co., 1930, p. 94.

now at home and apparently in good condition may be explained by the fact that he did stand the test.

8. *Organized Religion*

Our patient had the idea that he was going to have to preach, but a voice said to him, "You was going right the way you was. I don't need you to preach. I have other men whom I can send." The orders from above are not always so sensible among our acutely disturbed patients. The prophetic call is common among them. But however misguided it may be in particular cases, it stands nonetheless for a principle of fundamental importance. It seems to be of the very essence of religion that it must express itself socially. Religion has to do with the on-going process of the perpetuation and improvement of the race and with the establishing and making effective of loyalties that are universal. The prophetic call stands also for the principle that the new insights and the new vision which come through the crisis experiences of life must be made effective in the work-a-day world long after the emotional glow has passed. This is true both individually and socially. Institutionalization is thus part of the process by which moral achievements are passed one from one generation to another.

This patient after he had recovered from his first attack was told that the difficulty came from being too religious. He therefore put his Bible up in the attic. He thus side-stepped the problem with which he had been faced and later on he found that he had another "instalment" to pay. Just what he has done with his Bible since the last disturbance I do not know. He has now been for more than eight years outside the hospital, free apparently from further trouble. The outlook for the future seems most hopeful. We should, however, feel somewhat better satisfied if we knew that he were now consulting his Bible and if he belonged to some organized group which was helping to keep alive in him the very real insights which came to him through his disturbed periods.

Some General Principles

Generalizations derived from this and many other cases of mental illness during the past twenty years may be summarized as follows.

1. *Conscience* is not the rigid "super-ego" of the Freudians, which needs to be broken up or eradicated like a vermiform appendix, but the subjective aspect of culture; the internalization within the individual of the social organization which enables him to direct his own life without external compulsion. It is the artistic sense applied to the field of social living which lies on the growing edge of human

nature and tells the individual of his success or failure in maintaining his status and his growth.[7]

2. *Moral Standards* do not exist in a vacuum but are a function of our social relationships, particularly to those whom we count most worthy of love and honor.

3. *Religion* is not a means of escape from reality, but even in its cruder forms it is an attempt at orientation with reference to the ultimate issues of life which manifests itself spontaneously whenever those issues come to the fore. It is not a system of beliefs and values but the sense of fellowship raised to the level of the universal and abiding, with the idea of God as the symbol of that which is supreme in the hierarchy of loyalties.

4. *Sin or Guilt* is not so much infraction of moral law as breach of trust as regards the ultimate loyalties. The essential evil, which is seen strikingly in functional mental illness, is the sense of estrangement and isolation resulting from the presence in one life of that which one is afraid to tell for fear of condemnation.

5. *Repentance* is not an evil, even in its more morbid forms, but exactly what Christian theology has always held, the first step in the process of salvation. Emotional disturbances, even to the point of serious disorder, are frequently manifestations of nature's power to heal. Such types should be sharply distinguished from those which represent the end results of character difficulties. This distinction, now seldom made even by our best psychiatrists, is all-important in any understanding of mental illness in its relation to religious experience.

6. *Salvation, Cure, or Mental Health* is not dependent upon modification of the standards but upon reestablishment of right relationship with that which is supreme in the individual's system of loyalties. A breach of trust must be followed by the experience of reconciliation marked on the one side by acknowledgement of wrongdoing and on the other by the capacity to understand and the willingness to resume friendly relations.

7. *The Sovereignty of God* is not just an idea carried over from a monarchical period or a demand for weak submission to constituted authority, but the recognition that true maturity and autonomy on the part of the individual is achieved through the transfer of loyalty from the finite to the infinite and the progressive adjustment of his personal life to the moral order of the universe. Dependence upon God thus becomes a source of comfort and strength which makes the individual independent of the changes and dangers of life.

---

7. W. E. Hocking, *op. cit.*, p. 123.

THE PROBLEM OF SIN AND SALVATION IN
THE LIGHT OF PSYCHOPATHOLOGY

Anton T. Boisen

[This article from the July, 1942 issue of the *Journal of Religion* shows that Boisen had indeed "done his homework" in expressing his view of psychology and psychotherapy. He was influenced by major figures of his time in the psychoanalytic school of psychology, such as Freud, Rank, and Horney, who provided support for his thesis. He also turned to prominent theorists in the sociology and psychology of religion—Mead, Weber, James, Coe and Starbuck. Section IV provides an interesting glimpse at Boisen's view of psychotherapy; his primary goal was to achieve an empathic relationship, with "technique" being of secondary importance (c.f. "The Minister as Counselor").

The extended discussion in this case regarding the sex drive also parallels Boisen's own struggle with sex and its impact on his view of "sin and salvation." Because of this struggle he could heartily affirm, in the midst of a scholarly case analysis, that acute illness can lead one out of isolation through confession to restoration to the "Fellowship of the Best," i.e. salvation. This process is achieved "beyond any finite therapist."]

The problem of sin is represented in its extreme manifestations by two types—the delinquent and criminal, on the one hand, and the nonorganic mental patient, on the other. In the first are those who have rebelled against the loyalty to parents and to organized society, or, more commonly, those who have never learned to take it seriously. In the second are those who have taken that loyalty seriously but have not achieved inner unification on the basis of the accepted ideals. They are those who judge themselves, those whose policemen are within, whereas in the case of the delinquent and of the criminal the policemen are outside. The delinquent is thus in conflict with society. The mental patient is in conflict with himself.

This paper will be concerned with the second type. More than that, it will be limited to that type of mental illness which is essentially a desperate struggle for salvation, a manifestation of nature's power to heal which is analogous to fever or inflammation in the body. Those types which represent the reactions of drifting and of concealment show little religious concern and few cases of recovery.[1] They are important as a background but have no direct interest from the standpoint of the problem before us.

I

A case drawn from my hospital file is representative of the type. The interesting feature of this case is an episode in the patient's history which occurred some twenty-five years before he came to us. It was a conversion experience of the dramatic variety, preceded by a period of acute distress, which by the psychiatrist would be labeled "anxiety neurosis."

At the time he came to the hospital this man was forty-three years of age. He had just made an attempt at suicide. He had also some peculiar ideas. He thought that the Knights of Columbus were on his trail, that the Masons were trying to get him into their order, and that he had been chosen a subject for Edison's experimentation in the spirit realm—something which was going to "hasten his demise." No evidence of physical trouble was discovered. He was found to be well informed and of good intelligence.

He had been born in Germany of respectable, middle-class parents. His father he described as "very strict and ready to knock any foolishness out of his head." His mother was "kind-hearted and awfully soft." In later life she was quite religious. He himself went through grammar school, finishing at fourteen at the head of his class. His teacher wanted him to study for the teaching profession. He chose, however, the trade of wheelwright. At the age of sixteen he came to America.

It is clear that this boy was anything but the delinquent sort. He had not rebelled against the authority of his parents or of his teachers. Neither had he failed to take it seriously. He was definitely a good boy, well meaning and conscientious, perhaps to a fault. The first requirement in moral and religious education had thus been fulfilled, but the second was unachieved. He was having trouble with that drive which must somehow or other be brought under control before the boy can become a man. From his twelfth year on there had been difficulty. He told us that he had felt "unspeakable worry" over it, so that often he cried about it at night.

---

1. Anton T. Boisen, *The Exploration of the Inner World* (Chicago: Willett, Clark & Co., 1936), chap. i.

About a year after his arrival in this country the problem became so acute that he was driven to consult a physician. The latter, after listening to his story, advised him to try religion.

He had at the time become rather shaky in his religious faith and had wandered far from the admonitions of his pious mother, but he now determined to investigate. It so happened that a series of revival meetings was under way in Boston, and he attended them. His account of what happened is as follows:

> One day while Mr. Moody was preaching and I had spent all my nights in prayer and I had prayed and cried—yes, cried; I was a regular baby. But at any rate, while Mr. Moody was preaching about God being a Father and about his being ready to forgive us for our past if only our purpose is good—I can't explain it; it was a natural phenomenon that came over me. I had gone there a down-cast individual, not a young man but an old man. When I came out I felt as though the very sparrows in the trees were singing songs. Everything was changed and it seemed such a real experience. I can't account for it today, but I know this, I was happy for many years after that and I was more successful in my work.

The story of the years that followed—of his enthusiastic participation in church work, of his fall from grace, of his marriage to a faithful member of his church, a wife of whom he stood very much in awe, of his desperate attempts to maintain his self-respect, and of his final attempt to take his life—contains many points of interest, but it is not directly pertinent to our problem. We are concerned rather with his conversion experience and with the change it wrought in his life. The fact that there was backsliding which brought him to the hospital twenty-five years later does not make it any the less a constructive solution of the early crisis. Its typical character can be at once established by a reference to Edwin D. Starbuck's study of religious conversions.[2]

II

The first point to notice is that in the period preceding his visit to the doctor our sufferer had been a candidate for a mental hospital. He had worked himself into a state of mind typical of the onset of certain well-known forms of mental illness. It was likewise typical of that form of conversion which Starbuck has described as the eruptive breaking-up of evil habits and the turning of the vital energies into new and constructive channels following a sense of sin. It is to be noted that a medical writer, at the time Starbuck's findings were published, called attention to the fact that the condition he described was characteristic of certain forms of mental illness. Starbuck, however, like many other students of religion, did not see in this a lead to

---

2. *Psychology of Religion* (New York: Charles Scribner's Sons, 1899), chaps. xii and xiii.

be followed up but rather a charge to be refuted.[3] I am proposing in this paper to follow up that lead.

According to this man's account he suffered "unspeakable worry." This is a telling phrase; it would be hard to find a more accurate characterization of his difficulty. According to Dr. Franz Alexander,[4] it is the presence of disowned cravings which can be neither controlled nor acknowledged, for fear of condemnation, which is the cause of neurotic difficulty. This results from the fact that man is a social being. According to George H. Mead,[5] the personality is the subjective aspect of the culture to which one belongs. It grows much as the body grows through the constant assimilation of new experiences, and this process of assimilation involves socialization. It requires the discovery of relationships between the new experience and the organized experience, and the discovered relationship must be put into words and fitted into an organized framework taken over from the group. In fact, secrets seem normally to be forbidden. A happy experience wants to be shared. It tends to overflow. An unhappy experience tends to create a sort of vortex. When, therefore, in the course of development, experiences are encountered and tendencies appear of which we are ashamed, trouble is likely to result. If these tendencies are highly charged and if we are afraid to acknowledge them, they are likely to behave much like ill-digested food. They remain unassimilated because they are not fitted into the organization of the social self. The Freudians use the term "complex" to designate such highly charged unassimilated interests. They speak of them as being in the "unconscious." It should be recognized, however, that, far from being unconscious, they are simply clamoring for attention and give the sufferer no peace until they are in some way taken care of.

The sense of guilt, or sin, which psychopathologists today are recognizing more and more clearly as the primary evil in nonorganic types of mental illness,[6] is, then, due to something which we are afraid to tell and is therefore "unspeakable." Its essence is not to be found in any mere infraction of a code but in a rupture of the interpersonal relationships as inwardly conceived. The sense of sin is thus the social condemnation which we pronounce upon ourselves on the basis of standards which

---

3. *Ibid.*, chap. xiii.

4. *Psychoanalysis of the Total Personality* (Washington: Nervous and Mental Disease Pub. Co., 1930). See particularly chap. v.

5. *Mind, Self and Society* (Chicago: University of Chicago Press, 1935), particularly pp. 144-272.

6. Sigmund Freud's *The Ego and the Id* (London: Hogarth Press, 1927; *Das Ich und das Es* [Vienna, 1923]) was the first definite formulation of the problem of conscience on the part of the psychoanalysts. It has been of great importance in the subsequent development of their thinking and has had an important influence upon psychiatry in general.

we have accepted as our own.[7] It carries with it the sense of isolation and estrangement from that which is supreme in our system of loyalties, that which for the religious man is symbolized by his idea of God and which explicitly or implicitly is operative in the lives of all men.

It follows, therefore, that the word "maladjustment," which has been proposed as a substitute for the word "sin," does not convey the idea. It follows furthermore that the real difficulty is much better described by the singular than by the plural. What is involved in mental illness is not a number of petty or even serious infractions of law but a state of mind, a difficulty in the internalized social relationships and hence in the organization of the personality.

III

It seems clear that this particular boy was worried about the management of the sex drive. Since psychiatrists are often criticized for giving too much attention to this factor, it may be well to clarify certain issues. Such an attempt seems all the more in order in that there is today a swing in the opposite direction on the part of some psychiatrists. Dr. Karen Horney,[8] for example, holds that repressed sexuality as a factor in neurotic conditions has pretty much disappeared with the passing of the Victorian era. In its place she sees repressed hostility arising out of our competitive culture. Most psychoanalysts would regard that statement as entirely too sweeping. They would agree, however, in giving increasing attention to the hostility motive. In my judgment this tendency is due partly to an overreaction against some of the earlier Freudian formulations, partly also to an inadequate concept of conscience. Supporting the view that sex maladjustment is primary in most cases of mental illness and likewise in the sense of sin which precedes most dramatic conversion experiences are the following considerations.

1. The sex drive has to do with the perpetuation of the race—something for which the individual exists. There is in each individual a deep-seated but not always clear awareness of this fact and an extreme sensitivity regarding maladjustments in this field.[9] It is to be noted that full-blown mental illness seldom occurs before the adolescent period. It is apparently associated with the dangers incidental to sexual maturation.

2. The fact that the sex drive is surrounded with taboos and inhibitions and that, at least in our culture, it is something about which one does not talk freely,

---

7. W. A. White, *Foundations of Psychiatry* (Washington: Nervous and Mental Disease Pub. Co., 1921), p. 65.

8. *The Neurotic Personality of Our Time* (New York: Norton & Co., 1937), pp. 62ff.

9. Otto Rank, *Modern Education* (New York: Alfred A. Knopf, 1932). See particularly chap. ii for some very interesting observations.

means that maladjustments in this field are likely to be kept to one's self. This at once intensifies the emotional charge and increases the sense of shame and isolation. The sex drive is thus peculiarly liable to remain for the adolescent something at once fascinating and terrifying and unassimilated. It is, therefore, a potent source of that sense of guilt which is the cause of nonorganic forms of mental illness.

3. Sex love, as W. E. Hocking[10] points out, bears a close relationship to religion. It is not that religion is rooted in sex, as has sometimes been claimed, but that sex love at its best approaches religion. It wants somewhat the same thing that religion wants—union with the idealized other-than-self, and it can never be satisfied with the mere finite love-object. Because it is thus associated with the greatest of values, it is also a source of great danger and anxiety.

4. Repressed hostility may under certain conditions cause mental illness. A daughter sacrifices herself for her mother. She has for her mother a genuine love, but the mother has been demanding, sometimes unreasonable, and the daughter feels a resentment which is not in keeping with her idea of herself. She may even find herself wishing that the mother were out of the way. Finally the mother does die. She may then blame herself and become excessively depressed. Such cases do occur, but in the great majority of cases hostility is a reaction to the sense of personal failure and frustration. It is, then, a secondary factor. The boy who is uncomfortably aware of the fact that he is not making the grade toward manhood is likely to be surly and bitter toward anything that reminds him of his failings. He is likely to project his inner discomfort upon other persons. Hence the ideas of persecution which we see in patients of the paranoid type. Hostility also figures in many delinquent types. But to explain the severe self-judgment found in anxieties and depressions as due to inverted hostility seems a serious misinterpretation.

IV

It will probably be recognized that this boy had reason to worry, but that worry is in itself not an evil may not be so readily admitted. Medical men are inclined to direct their attention to the worry.[11] They may even try to deal with it by getting rid of the "antiquated good-evil antithesis." Such a tendency in its extreme form may be seen in a new treatment for serious agitations and depressions. Portions of the frontal lobes of the brain are excised, and worry is thereby eradicated. The neuropsychiatrist is thus seeking to remove the sense of anxiety and guilt just like a vermiform appendix.

---

10. *Human Nature and Its Re-making* (New Haven: Yale University Press, 1918), chap. xlii.

11. This viewpoint is brilliantly set forth in its more reasonable and persuasive form by Elton Mayo in his "Sin with a Capital S" (*Harper's*, April, 1927). This article is of especial interest in that it includes a consideration of Starbuck's study of the conversion experience.

It needs therefore to be pointed out that in this case the worry served a useful purpose. It drove this boy to make a visit to his doctor. Grave concern on the part of his friends might have been in order if he had not been worried. The true evil in such a case is the short-circuiting of the sex drive and the failure to attain to the next level of development. The worry in this case represented a desperate attempt at reconstruction, and it met with some measure of success. It was not an evil but a manifestation of nature's power to heal. As such it is analogous to fever or inflammation in the body. It is also typical of a fairly large group of religious converts whom Starbuck studied. Their experiences likewise were characterized by a marked sense of sin and by the eruptive breaking-up of evil habits. It seems to be nature's way, Starbuck concludes, to heal the breach between the ideal self and the actual self not by lessening the conflict but by heightening it.[12] My own studies indicate that, even though the worry and anxiety reach the point of acute mental disorder, it is nonetheless a manifestation of nature's power to heal.[13] The conclusion follows that the old theological doctrine that the consciousness of sin is the first step in the process of salvation is true in many cases.

From these considerations it will be seen that this young man went to Mr. Moody's meetings all set for something to happen. He had done his part. He had mustered up his courage and had gone to see the doctor. To him he had spoken of the "unspeakable worry." The cure was, therefore, already in process, because the real difficulty had been brought into the open and discussed with a wise physician. But this physician, after listening sympathetically, had referred him to religion. All that was now necessary was the right suggestion, and that Mr. Moody gave. He talked about God being a father and about his being ready to forgive our past if only our purpose is good. Perhaps some other suggestion might also have served, but we may recognize in these words the essence of all good psychotherapy and the essence also of the gospel of Jesus and of Paul.

In order to appreciate the significance of this suggestion we must bear in mind that in the task of internalizing the group attitudes and values, which is essential in all education, there are two chief instruments—fear and force, on the one hand, and love and admiration, on the other. In most cases there is a mixture of the two. In the case of this boy there was a love for his mother, but he describes her as "awfully soft." We wonder, therefore, how much he admired her, and we are sure that he did not fear her. We cannot be sure how much he loved his father. We can guess that he admired him, and we are sure that he feared him. In any case, it is clear that he accepted his father's authority and that his moral attitudes were governed chiefly by fear. His was a morality of the "Thou shalt nots." It was a static rather than a functional morality.

12. *Op. cit.*, p. 157.
13. *Op. cit.*, chaps. ii, iii, and v.

Now the essence of Mr. Moody's message, which was derived from the teaching of Jesus, was that the universe is governed not by force and fear but by a love that looks upon the heart and is ready to forgive even to the uttermost. In the eyes of love the important thing about any person is not what he is now, but what he is in process of becoming. Even the most faulty person is good and worthy of honor in so far as he is doing the best he can with what he has to work with, in so far as he is moving to become better.[14] The insight that God is a father and that he is ready to forgive the past if only our purpose is good went, therefore, to the heart of this boy's problem. It changed the basis of his moral self-judgment and set him free for the attainment of his true objectives in life.

Good psychotherapy depends precisely upon this principle. The psychotherapist must see the patient with the eyes of sympathetic understanding. This does not mean that he may not pass judgments. The "nonevaluating attitude," upon which some of my psychoanalytic friends insist, is neither possible nor desirable.[15] The physician's first task is that of diagnosis. This means that he must judge accurately. He may and often must condemn a patient; that is, he may be compelled to decide that a case is hopeless and does not warrant intensive treatment. But, if he is to help the patient, he must be quick to see the possibilities of usefulness amid the wreckage of apparent failure and the promise of beauty in what seems commonplace and unlovely. He must be equally quick to see through the shams and self-deceptions which are sheltering forbidden desires and are therefore blocking growth. His task is to reinforce or to kindle the patient's faith in himself and to help him to deal honestly with his frailties so that he may make a better job of his life. The good psychotherapist must then make accurate judgments, but he must do so as a trusted friend, seeing always through the eyes of the patient.

It follows, therefore, that psychotherapy is dependent upon the interpersonal relationship between the physician and the patient. Wherever the patient trusts the physician and the physician is able to think *with* the patient sympathetically and

---

14. Cf. John Dewey, *Reconstruction in Philosophy* (New York: Henry Holt & Co., 1920), p. 176.

15. Dr. James S. Plant in his *Personality and the Culture Pattern* (New York: Commonwealth Fund, 1937) draws a pertinent distinction between the attitude of the mother and that of the teacher or social worker. The latter assay Johnnie on the basis of his repeated delinquencies, his mediocre intelligence, his slovenly habits. Their attitude is determined by *what* he is. To his mother he is still her Johnnie. Her attitude is determined by *who* he is. She feels herself bound to him by ties which defy rational analysis. This type of relationship, Plant holds, is the deepest need of every child. It gives him a sense of belongingness, even though he may be a failure in the classroom and on the playground. This distinction seems important. It must, however, be supplemented by a distinction between the blind love which is based upon mere identification and the higher love which judges accurately and requires of the boy that he live up to his highest potentialities. The mother who believes that her boy is a white blackbird is likely to mother him. The attitude of the wise mother is not a nonevaluating one.

intelligently, there results are likely to follow. Technique is of secondary importance. One physician may stress dream interpretation, another free association, another may rely on moral re-education, another may even hand out advice or make use of hypnosis. What needs to be recognized is that the evil to be dealt with is the sense of inner disharmony owing to the presence of an "unspeakable worry" and that in some form or other there must be confession and forgiveness. The unsocialized and hence unassimilated interests must be resolved, and the sufferer must be able to feel himself restored to the fellowship of the best.

V

Experiences like that of our convert are commonly induced under fairly definite conditions. The Hindu mystic employs certain recognized techniques in order to induce the trance condition which he values. He concentrates his attention upon some bright object. He repeats over and over the magic syllable "Om." He thinks of certain ideas. In short, he narrows his attention.[16] The result is a deliberately induced autohypnosis. Narrowing of attention seems also to have been an important factor in the experiences of the great Hebrew prophets. They became absorbed in the problem of the fate of their people and of why Jahweh had forsaken them.[17] Narrowing of attention is likewise a factor in the onset of acute schizophrenia.[18] Clearly it was characteristic of our patient's condition at the time of his conversion experience. He had spent nights in prayer and weeping and had worked himself up into a state in which he could think of nothing but the one problem.

Such narrowing of attention is not conducive to balanced judgment. It means a loss of perspective which may go to the point of abnormality. But it may also mean a quickening of the mental processes. It may bring a new sense of reality and with it new ideas and new insights. This is particularly likely to be true where, as in the case of our convert and of the Hebrew prophets, the situation is genuine and highly charged emotionally. Our convert, as is characteristic of this type of experience, felt himself one with God. He had been downcast and despairing. Now the birds were singing, and the earth was full of joy. It was one of those experiences to which we give the name of "mystical."

This experience for the man who has it is something tremendous. Sometimes it is constructive, sometimes not. It may upset the foundations upon which the per-

---

16. George A. Coe, *Psychology of Religion* (Chicago: University of Chicago Press, 1916), chap. xvi.

17. Max Weber, *Gesammelte Aufsaetze zur Religionssociologie* (TÅbingen: Verlag von J. C. B. Mohr, 1923), III, 314, in a very illuminating study of the Hebrew prophets as compared with the founders or leaders of the other great religions.

18. Boisen, *op. cit.*, p. 79.

sonality organization is built. This is what happens in certain acute forms of mental illness. Such experiences commonly begin with a supposed manifestation of the superhuman.[19] The patient hears God talking to him or discovers that evil spirits are on his trail. If, with Mead, we look upon the personality as an internalization of the social order of which we are a part, we can perhaps understand the terrific impact of the experience of coming face to face with a different and superior social order. Destructive effects are particularly likely to occur when the experience is a solitary one and the dominant mood is fear. Under such conditions the individual may feel himself cut loose from his moorings. He will then not know what to believe. He will be sure of only one thing—that things are not what they seem. In everything he will see hidden meanings. In the case of our convert, however, there was social support. He had taken his problem to a doctor. The doctor had sent him to Mr. Moody's meetings. The experience thus came to him under group influence and conformed to a recognized pattern. The effect was thus not destructive but meant, rather, a new outlook on life and a new access of power. He was therefore happy for many years after that and more successful in his work.

It follows that we may look upon this experience as having creative value. This does not mean that he brought new ideas or insights into the stream of tradition. That is seldom clearly the case in experiences which take place within a social matrix. New insights are more likely to come to men who, like Jeremiah and Ezekiel and George Fox, wander away from the beaten paths. In the case of mental patients of the acute schizophrenic type, the experiences are solitary, and the new ideas are so different that there is a temporary or permanent break with the culture patterns of their time and race.[20] Our young convert did have new insights, but those insights had to do chiefly with the problem with which he was struggling— that of his own role in the drama of life. He saw himself now as one who had in him undreamed-of possibilities, and the beliefs and traditions in which he had been reared took on new meaning because they were associated with his role in life. They thus received emotional validation. He is, in this, representative of the great majority of those who under the influence of evangelistic meetings have a conversion experience. For this reason the radically mystical cults tend to be conservative in their theological beliefs.

One of the values of experiences of the dramatic type lies in the fact that they lift into the field of clear awareness problems which otherwise escape attention and throw new light upon them. The case we have considered has thus served to clarify the nature and significance of the sense of guilt. We have seen that it is essentially a rupture in the interpersonal relationships as inwardly conceived, owing to the pres-

---

19. *Ibid.*, p. 30.

20. John Dollard, "The Psychotic Person Seen Culturally," *American Journal of Sociology*, March, 1934.

ence of tendencies which can be neither controlled nor acknowledged for fear of condemnation—tendencies which are therefore "unspeakable." We have seen furthermore that all procedures of psychotherapy have to do with relief from the resulting sense of isolation. Psychotherapy thus resolves itself into a matter of confession and forgiveness. Man is, therefore, a social being, and the idea of God is the symbol of that fellowship of the best apart from which we cannot live and of which our standards of value are merely a function.

Salvation or cure is, then, not a matter of the correction of faulty habits or of the resolution of conflicts but of restoration to this fellowship. The significance of the conversion experience, as seen in this case, is to be found in the fact that, whatever the human instrumentality, there is a sense of being forgiven directly by God. It thus points beyond any finite therapist to that which is conceived as universal and abiding. More than that, it involves that sense of fellowship which is the essence of all religion and suggests the consideration that religion itself is a matter of those interpersonal relationships from which beliefs and values are derived. To be saved means, therefore, to be one with the best in our social experience and a contributing participant in the struggle for the attainment of the objectives thus determined.

COOPERATIVE INQUIRY IN RELIGION

Anton T. Boisen

[This article first appeared in the September-October, 1945 issue of *Religious Education*. In it, Boisen wishes to promote once again *his* particular perspective on the purpose of clinical training as an opportunity for cooperative (interdisciplinary) inquiry into religious experience. He provides a survey of journal literature as well as the work of contemporary theologians (including Reinhold Niebuhr) and other scholars and finds them deficient in their study of "living documents." He maintains that such a study can provide enlightenment in several major issues in the psychology of religion, that (admitting his bias) the best place to do this is still the mental hospital, and that this study will contribute to "the understanding of the normal personality and of normal religious experience." He also asserts that clinical settings are not the only place to study religious experience; it may be conducted in any setting of ministry. This was the basis for his book, *Problems in Religion and Life* (Abingdon-Cokesbury Press, 1946).]

Among those who have been chiefly instrumental in founding and promoting the plan for the clinical training of theological students there has been considerable difference of opinion on matters that are important. Dr. Cabot thus rejected the psychogenic interpretation of mental illness and considered the mental hospital, where the plan was first begun, as least important among the institutions which claimed the attention of the student of religion. Others saw in mental illness a problem which is fundamentally spiritual and considered the mental hospital to be of primary importance. On one point, however, there has been complete agreement: religious experience can and should be studied before it has gathered dust on library shelves, and the living documents are the primary sources for the understanding of human nature.

The task to which this paper addresses itself is a consideration of the present status of the point of view on which the Council for Clinical Training is agreed. It seeks to answer the question, "What is now being done in the matter of cooperative inquiry in the field of religious experience?"

What The Journals Show

Scientists are wont to say that the story of any science is to be found in its journals rather than in its books. The journal, they say, is the vehicle of the cooperative inquiry which is of its very essence. It reports the results of research while those results are still fresh and it invites criticism and interpretation. The book, on the other hand, usually seeks to cover some entire field from a particular point of view and it may or may not contain a new contribution. Most books, in fact, are not written for the scientific worker but for a more general circle of readers.

The first fact revealed by this study is the paucity of journals in the field of religion which can lay claim to scientific standing. Books are many but journals few. In spite of the size of the professional group concerned, there are certainly not more than nine such journals published in this country. The professional group of psychiatrists, on the other hand, numbering hardly 4,000 persons, has 13 scientific journals and these thirteen journals have in the aggregate more than twice the number of pages found in the religious journals.

The second fact is that in the journals which we do have, empirical[1] studies of human nature are conspicuous by their absence. Thus in the *Journal of Religion* for the 14 years from 1931 to 1944 there were 283 articles. These articles were distributed as follows: theology and philosophy of religion, 113; church history, 45; New Testament, 37; comparative religion, 29; Old Testament, 13; psychology of religion, 13; sociology of religion, 11; religious education, 8; biography, 7; current issues, 7. Of these 283 articles only 8 were empirical studies of religious experience, and only five other articles made use of empirical studies by other workers. A good many of the remaining articles represented careful documentary research, but the great majority represent merely unchecked observation and reflection.

In the *Review of Religion* for its first nine years the situation is much the same. The field which it covers is somewhat more limited. Its own division of its field is primitive religion, ancient religion, Oriental religion, Judaism, historical Christianity, contemporary Christianity, and general theory of religion. Nearly half of its articles would be classed under "general theory of religion" and about a third under "ancient religions" and "historical Christianity." Of its 102 articles none

---

1. For the purpose of this paper the term "empirical" is used to denote the point of view under consideration—controlled observation of actual experience before it gets on library shelves.

could be called empirical in its methodology and only two made use of empirical studies by others.

In *Religious Education* for the seven years from 1936 to 1943 there were some 200 articles. With scarcely an exception these articles dealt with contemporary Christianity. An examination of these articles showed that the overwhelming majority represented merely general observation and reflection. Many of them were indeed written by participant observers whose reflections were based upon accurate information, but there was seldom any attempt to marshal the evidence or to use quantitative methods. They were rather articles which might have been dashed off by a well-informed man on the basis of his general fund of knowledge. Not a few were symposia, involving the exchange of insight and information regarding some controversial subject, or some live current issue. Only fourteen were quantitative studies, attempts to check hypotheses by means of statistics, and only a few others were attempts to give an exact account of the present status and the historical development of some clearly defined and limited situation, group or institution.

The following is a list of the subjects and of the methodology used in those articles based on controlled observation and statistical verification.

An examination of these articles shows that most of the studies using the questionnaire method were of the type which calls for Yes-No answer or from a selection from a number of suggested answers. One is also struck with the peripheral, non-significant character of most of the questions asked and with the failure to relate the findings to universal principles.

Subject	*Method*
Reactions of Ex-Ministers to the Ministry	Questionnaire
College Experience and the Idea of God	Questionnaire
College Fraternities and Character	Questionnaire & Interview
New Light upon Adolescent Religion	Questionnaire
Why People Go to Church	Questionnaire
Student Thinking	Questionnaire
Why Do Students Lose Religion?	Case studies & Questionnaire
Student Attitudes towards Basic Values	Questionnaire
Honesty Attitudes in 300 College Students	Questionnaire
Student Interest in the Church	Questionnaire
High School Experience and Personality	Questionnaire
Religion in Education	Questionnaire
Comprehension Test on Lord's Prayer	Right-Wrong answers
Attitude of Rural Young People toward Church	Interviews, Questionnaire

Favorite Hymns of Young People.. Questionnaire

Religion in Hartwick College... Interviews & Questionnaire

Divided Protestantism in a Midwest County .... Case study, Interviews, Documents

Making Religious Education Religious... Case studies

Personality Traits of Religious Workers .... Bernreuter Inventory

Contributions of the Institute of Social and Religious Research

The Institute of Social and Religious Research, which was in operation from 1921 to 1934, has to its credit some impressive contributions. Among them are the following:

Studies of Town and Country Churches by Brunner and others,

Studies of City Churches by Douglass and others,

The Character Education Inquiry by Hartshorne and May,

The Education of American Ministers by Kelley and May,

The Laymen's Foreign Mission Inquiry,

Interchurch Relations by Douglass,

Middletown by the Linds.

There are other studies. The list is fairly long. The Institute's studies are characterized by thorough and painstaking work and exacting standards. From the standpoint of this study the question is whether in the effort to maintain scientific standards the Institute did not confine itself to more or less objective material and avoid those problems which relate more directly to the dynamic aspects of religious experience.

Living Documents and Printed Books

Theology

Theology may be regarded as the cooperative attempt to organize and test religious experience by scrutinizing religious beliefs and inquiring into the origin, the meaning and the consequences of these beliefs.

It is assumed in this definition that man is a social being and that religious experience is the sense of fellowship raised to the level of the universal and abiding, together with the resulting feelings, attitudes and actions. Religion is thus concerned with a biological fact which is operative in the lives of all men whether they recognize it or not.

Under this definition theology belongs among the social sciences. It has to do with the internalization and the modification of the socially accepted values and with the accepted hierarchy of loyalties. The question therefore arises, how far are its problems being approached through the methods of science. Our study of the journals may therefore be supplemented by an examination of some of the more important books.

From the standpoint of our problem, attention is at once drawn to a book which bears the title, *Theology as an Empirical Science.*[2] Examination of this book reveals, however, that the expectation evoked by the title is by no means justified. As an empirical science, according to this author, theology is concerned with the activities of God, and the scientific theologian must select from the manifold of religious experience those elements which give knowledge of God. These he finds in revelation. In his book he is therefore chiefly concerned with the problem of religious knowledge, and nowhere does he attempt to examine the religious experience of actual men. Neither does he draw upon the studies made by other men, even in his consideration of the conversion experience. In a later book on *The Problem of Religious Knowledge* the same author does give some attention to what psyhchologists and psychiatrists have to say, but he soon dismisses them and holds to the thesis that there is such a thing as cognitive religious experience which is able to stand the test of practical, intellectual criticism.

Another book whose title leads to high expectations is *The Psychological Approach to Theology.*[3] It is indeed an interesting and valuable attempt, but it suffers from the fact that its psychological data are not based on direct observation but are gleaned at second hand from the writings of Freud, Janet, Hadfield and others. Acquaintance with living human documents should have raised some questions in the mind of a competent student of religion regarding certain psychiatric short-sightednesses which this author accepts as authority.

Another prominent theological philosopher regards "radical empiricism" as the one valid method of getting knowledge. That term seems to mean to him something very different from the scientific principle of empiricism. His starting point is not the study of particular experiences or situations, made either by himself or by others, but rather certain common experiences and concepts. As a philosopher of religion he is concerned with that which is most worthy of devotion, that upon which man is dependent for love and for values of all sorts. His method of testing religious insights is the use of a precise and discriminating dialectic which defines clearly each term and then draws out the implications to see if the hypothesis stands up in the light of empirical reality.

---

2. Douglas C. Macintosh, Macmillan, 1927.
3. By Walter Marshall Horton, Harper, 1931.

Another influential theologian defines the task of modern theology as that of recapturing the human experiences out of which the classic doctrines of Christian thought arose.[4] He does not however place much reliance upon empirical studies of present-day religious experience. Even in his consideration of mysticism he merely reflects upon mysticism in general.[5] He does not attempt to examine the experiences of particular mystics; neither does he take account of the studies which others have made.

One of the most widely read of our modern books on theology is *The Nature and Destiny of Man*.[6] The author begins with certain Christian conceptions and "seeks to relate these to the observable behavior of men." His references to empirical studies of human nature are very limited. They are seemingly determined by the need of finding support for his own views. His discussion of the problem of sin leaves one with the impression that his standpoint is not that of one who is trying sympathetically to understand the frailties and misbehavior of men, but rather than of one who looks upon them from the standpoint of the Almighty and finds in pride the greatest of all sins.

One of the most important modern books is *God and the Common Life*.[7] This contains 34 pages of notes, whose value is, however, seriously impaired by their relegation to the back of the book according to the style so widespread in modern religious books. These notes cover a remarkably wide range. There are 40 references to philosophers, 50 to theologians, 28 to sociologists and social philosophers, 18 to psychologists, 9 to psychiatrists, 7 to physicists, 5 to biologists, 5 to astronomers, 8 to physiologists, 5 to mathematicians. In general, however, the data on which the conclusions are based have been gathered from books "twice or three times removed from the laboratories and the original papers of specialists." In dealing with the Christian doctrine of "vocation" this author starts with the historical positions of Christianity and ties into the findings of such men as Weber, Troeltsch, Tawney and others. He builds thus upon a more or less objective foundation.

These are just a few of the more important books on theology. They represent the best of modern liberal thinking relatively uninfluenced by the Neo-orthodox return to the authority of revelation. The value of these books is not in question. From the standpoint of this inquiry it is, however, a striking fact that these attempts to deal with the central problems of Christian faith makes so little effort to attack these problems empirically or to utilize empirical studies by other workers.

---

4. E.E. Aubrey, in *Journal of Religion* for 1932.
5. "Man's Search for Himself," Cokesbury Press, 1940, pages 63-70
6. Reinhold Niebuhr, Scribners, 1941.
7. Robert L. Calhoun, Scribners, 1935.

Church History

According to Henri de Pirenne,[8] all historical construction rests upon the postulate of the eternal identity of human nature. One cannot comprehend men's actions at all unless one assumes that their physical and moral beings have been at all periods what they are today. If we accept this view the question at once arises, where do our church historians get their knowledge of what is and what is not constant in human nature?

A glance through the journal articles and through several books on church history reveals very little effort to grapple with this problem.

A pertinent article is one by Professor Riddle in the *Journal of Religion* for 1932. He makes a plea for more attention to the psychological factors in the study of New Testament times. He proceeds, however, to minimize the constants in human nature and to magnify the role of tradition and of "ideology." Orientals, he holds, can hardly be understood at all by the Western mind. It is important to recognize that Jesus belonged in the Oriental, Jewish world, whose religion is one of achievement, whereas Paul belonged rather to the Graeco-Roman world in which individual salvation was the major interest.

A striking example of the failure to take account of verifiable assumptions regarding human nature is to be found in an article on "Demonic Confessions of Jesus"[9] in which the author says, "It is unnecessary here to attempt to answer the inevitable question as to the nature of demons, as to what we mean by the term, as to whether demons really exist at all." Later on he says, "But the mental content of insane or possessed persons varies from age to age and from one culture to another. Insane persons in any culture have the same ideas as normal persons in the same culture." For this statement no evidence is offered either in the shape of first-hand observation or of cited authorities. The author is clearly not aware of the fact that there is considerable evidence to the effect that psychotic ideation shows many important similarities regardless of race and regardless of culture.[10]

Comparative Religion

There is much emphasis today in anthropology upon the first hand study of primitive peoples. Students like Radcliffe-Brown, Malinowski, Rivers, and Margaret Mead have made expeditions to the East Indies, to Patagonia, to the South Sea Islands, and have spent years in getting acquainted with a particular people. In the

---

8. *Methods in Social Science*, Stuart A. Rice, Editor, University of Chicago Press, 1931, page 442.

9. *Journal of Religion*, 1944.

10. Cf. John Dollard, "The Psychotic Person Seen Culturally," *American Journal of Sociology.*, March, 1934; also, Alfred Storch, *Primitive Thought in Schizophrenia*, Nervous and Mental Disease Publishing Company, 1924.

field of religion there is a peculiar opportunity to make such studies due to the presence of foreign missionaries all over the world. So far as I am able to discover, however, empirical studies of religious experience in other cultures are deficient. There
are indeed some happy exceptions, such as Pratt's *India and Its Faith* and his
Pilgrimage of Buddhism,[11] Kulp's *Country Life in South China*,[12] and Embree's *Suye
Mura*,[13] but for the most part our studies of the great world religions are based upon
documentary studies with little attention to the *living* documents of today.

Psychology of Religion

At the turn of the century a movement for the study of the psychology of religion set forth with great enthusiasm under the leadership of William James, Stanley
Hall, Starbuck, Coe, Pratt and Leuba. This movement has to its credit some endur-
ing achievements, but it seems now to have spent itself or to have been diverted into
religious education or into the philosophy of religion. Most of the books which
appear today in this field lean heavily upon the writings of Freud, Jung, Adler,
Rank and Kuenkel, with only a slender basis in controlled, empirical observation.

In General

This survey of the present situation shows that there is indeed a strange lag in
the employment of the methods of cooperative inquiry in the study of present day
religious experience, and even in the use on the part of theologians of such studies
as have been made. It also reveals the difficulty of the task involved. It is no easy
matter to formulate the important problems of religion and theology in such a way
as to make possible quantitative verification. With few exceptions the quantitative
studies thus far made have dealt with peripheral factors rather than those of central
significance and the more penetrating studies have relied upon general observation
and reflection.

Issues in the Study of Human Nature

In the attempt to explore human nature there are, however, a number of crucially important problems which are demanding attention and must be answered if
they are answered at all by systematic, painstaking cooperative observation of actual
experience. Here are some which challenge the attention and the intelligence of the
student of religion.

1. *The Body-mind Problem.* Academic psychology has been proceeding on the
assumption that its task is to explain mental functioning in terms of physiological

---

11. Macmillan.
12. Bureau of Publications, Teachers' College, Columbia University, New York, 1926.
13. University of Chicago Press, 1939.

processes. In that task it has made little progress. The great contribution which Freud has made is a psychology built on the basis of desires and experiences of men rather than upon stimulus-response mechanisms. Meanwhile the interrelationship of body and mind is being attacked anew through the study of the interrelationship of emotion and organic disease. The body-mind problem is receiving increasing attention in the diagnosis and treatment of both mental and physical disease and it presents also a problem of great significance to the student of religion.

2. *Sin and Guilt.* Just at a time when many of our theologians were discarding the old idea of sin, the psychopathologists were discovering it. Among them it is a very live issue. Their findings call for careful reexamination of the old theological positions.

3. *The Nature and Function of Conscience.* Ever since Freud published his *Ego and Id* the doctrine of the "Super-ego" has been central in psychoanalytic theory. Few psychiatrists, however, have any acquaintance with Mead or Dewey or Hocking, and few students of religion have any understanding of the experiences on which Freud based his theory. Cross-fertilization is needed.

4. *The Foundations of Psychotherapy.* The procedures and the dynamic factors involved in psychotherapy are of profound interest to the theologian. What is involved is the problem of sin and salvation, and the principles relied upon are those of confession and forgiveness.

5. *The Social and Psychological Roots of the Idea of God.* Psychopathological experience indicates that the idea of God stands for something which is operative in all men whether they call themselves religious or not. It represents that which is supreme in the social relationships, that of which standards and values are merely functions. As such it crops out spontaneously under certain conditions, apparently without much regard to previous indoctrination. The forms which it assumes and the conditions under which it appears are challenging problems.

6. *The Nature and Significance of Mystical Experience.* Mystical experience tends to appear in association with crisis experiences and constitutes the fountainhead of religious movements. Some of these crises are turning points in the struggle for personal self-realization which in their more severe forms assume pathological features. Some crises such as war and economic depression, involved shared strain and are social in their nature. Such experiences need further investigation.

7. *The Interrelationship of Religion and Culture.* The types of religious and mystical experience and the symbols they employ in different cultures cannot be determined by the study of books. Only the study of living documents can give the answer. Such studies are much needed. So also are exact and specific studies of the influence of different religions upon the ways of living and working together.

8. *The Constants in Human Nature.* Henri de Pirenne's dictum that all historical construction rests upon the postulate of the eternal identity of human nature

calls for careful studies of the elements in human nature which do remain constant and those that vary as we pass from one culture to another and from one age to another.

9. *Major Religious Conditions.* Conditions under which they are made, mystical elements, emotional accompaniment, results, means of inducing them are important problems both from the practical and from the theoretical standpoint.

10. *The Concept of the Self and Its Significance.* Some students of the personality look upon an individual's idea of himself and of his role as the nucleus of the personality. What evidence is there for or against this view? What are its implications for the psychology of religion?

11. *Indulgence, Abstinence and Self-Control in relation to Religious Experience.* This is a problem of practical and theoretical importance on which we need additional evidence.

These are merely some of the problems, suggested for the most part by work in a mental hospital, which ought to be in some measure solved by means of controlled observation.

The Clinical Approach

The clinical approach is by no means the only one which provides an opportunity for the empirical study of religious experience. The rural parish, where everybody knows everybody else, the urban parish in its reflection of the pressures of city life, contact with service men seeking to adjust themselves to military discipline or to the horrors of battle, mingling with people of other cultures, these and many other areas of experience furnish their own unique advantages. But dealing with badly maladjusted or sick people (for which alone the term "clinical" should be reserved) seems especially important. Just as in medicine the study of disease has led the way to the knowledge of normal physiology, so also we may hope that the study of mental and physical breakdowns and social deviations may contribute to the understanding of the normal personality and of normal religious experience because it furnishes the nearest approach to experimental conditions with reference to the great drawing forces of human life. Clinical experience in any of the recognized training centers is not, therefore, to be regarded as an addition to the theological curriculum. It is rather a new approach to the problems with which theology has always been concerned and an attempt to modify the methods of teaching. A consideration of the different types of institutions in which clinical training is now being offered indicates that the problems with which each confronts the student fall within the following specialized fields:

The Mental Hospital:
    Psychology of religion
    Theology
    Social pathology
    Religious education
    Personal counseling
    Pastoral care
The reform school and the child guidance clinic:
    Religious education
    Social pathology
    Personal counseling
The general hospital:
    Pastoral care
    Personal counseling
The infirmary:
    Pastoral care.

This analysis is subject to some discount by reason of the writer's particular bias. His own work has been in a mental hospital. Perhaps if his lot had been cast in some other type of institution he would have discovered in them a wider range of problems. He is, however, very sure that in a mental hospital the student is confronted with problems whose implications for theology cut very deep.

THE SERVICE OF WORSHIP IN A MENTAL HOSPITAL: ITS THERAPEUTIC SIGNIFICANCE

Anton T. Boisen

[Perhaps a lesser-known but very pastoral aspect of Boisen's work among the mentally ill was his careful attention to chapel worship in the hospital. Concerned about the particular needs and reactions of patients regarding the words and symbols of worship, he compiled a worship resource entitled *Lift Up Your Hearts* in 1926. This article appeared in the *Journal of Clinical Pastoral Work* in 1948, prior to the publication of the fourth and final revised edition of this hymnal under the tile of *Hymns of Hope and Courage* in 1950.]

The occasion of this paper is a proposed revision of the hymnal[1] for use in hospitals which the writer first compiled twenty-four years ago. It has seemed worth while to formulate and re-examine the principles upon which that volume was constructed, and to consider changes which now seem desirable in the light of our accumulated experience in the ministry to the mentally ill.

The assumption which underlies the compilation of such a hymnal is that the service of worship, which has been distinctive of the Hebrew-Christian religion, is the outstanding exemplification of the group therapy of which we hear so much today and that its employment in a mental hospital calls for certain adaptations, if its potential effectiveness is to be realized.

---

1. *Hymns of Hope and Courage*, New York, Harper's, 1937.

The therapeutic significance of the service of worship can best be understood in the light of George H. Mead's theory that the personality is the internalization within the individual of the group organization by means of language.[2] It is, he holds, dependent upon the common response to symbols which arouse in us the same response as they do in others. The personality is thus a set of social responses which have become organized and habitualized. According to this view the social response which is the basis of the personality is not just to others in general but to those we love and admire and whose authority we accept, those who for the religious man are associated with his idea of God.

Now any crowd is likely to evoke an emotional response in so far as it is thinking and feeling together with reference to some common idea. If the feeling is at all strong, the previous organization, which is dependent upon verbal symbols, is likely to be swept away. The response to the organized best may thus give way before the response to the present living mass. The mob is thus likely to do what the individuals who compose it would not do in their sober moments. The mere mass of a crowd may thus carry it with a certain authority and the sense of identification with a crowd—as felt at a football game or called forth by the sight of the nation's armed forces on parade—is likely to carry with it a sense of exhilaration.

In the case of a religious assemblage attention is consciously focused upon what is conceived to be supreme in the hierarchy of loyalties. The Christian Church thus represents to the believer the fellowship of the best, and its meetings are designed to keep alive the loyalty to each other and the common loyalty to the God whom the worshipers regard as the source of their life, the controller of their destiny and the one to whom they owe unreserved allegiance.

At its best a church service calls forth in the participants a deep emotional response. It brings back tender memories of their loved ones and of those to whom they have most looked up, and it directs their attention back across the ages to a beautiful and luminous figure in whose life and teachings they see the norm by which to direct their lives. They see this figure glorified by a sacrificial death and exalted by the devotion of countless men and women who down through the centuries have responded to His appeal and have given all that they had to the cause He represents. These memories and associations can be used with telling effect by the able preacher, aided by religious symbolism and music, to stir the hearts and consciences of his hearers. Even those who are half-hearted in their devotion commonly turn to the church in the great crises of life when they find themselves standing on the threshold of the unknown. They turn to the church at the time of marriage, of the birth of children and of death, to seek its blessings and its support.

---

2. Mead, George H., *Mind, Self, and Society,* Chicago, University of Chicago Press, 1936.

Not only does the church service call forth an emotional response, but it provides also an opportunity for instruction and for re-thinking the fundamental beliefs in the light of changing conditions and for modifying the ethical standards in the light of growing knowledge. Most sermons are anything but stimulating, but the pulpit is there for the prophet, when he comes; and the class meeting is a medium for the exchange of experience and belief on the part of the people. Church and synagogue have then enormous social significance and the fact that the Hebrew-Christian religion is the only one of the great ethical religions which has religious assemblage for instruction and common worship may help to explain why that religion has been associated with dynamic and changing cultures.

In the mental hospital the religious gathering will have a somewhat different significance from what it has in the normal parish. Where the normal church is based to a large extent upon the family unit and the congregation is made up in large part of those who are bound together by ties of love and friendship, the religious gathering in the hospital is made up of individuals. The social and familial ties are lacking.

These individuals are likely to have one important common characteristic. They are persons who have taken life seriously. They may be sharply contrasted with the inmates of a reform school or penitentiary, who very commonly have rebelled or failed to take seriously the loyalty represented by their parents and by the church. The non-organic type of mental patient is one who has accepted that loyalty. Where the delinquent is judged by society, the mental patient has judged himself. There are of course many mental patients who in the face of moral self-condemnation have thrown up the sponge and have withdrawn into a private world of their own. There are many others who stubbornly refuse to admit defeat or error and resort to all sorts of concealment devices in order to escape self-blame. But there are others, not a few of them, who feel themselves face to face with the ultimate realities of life, persons in whom the better self is struggling desperately to gain control. For such persons the symbols of the church and of religion are likely to have profound meaning and it is among these that we find the largest proportion of recoveries.

It seems obvious that the ministry of religion in a mental hospital should concern itself chiefly with the latter group, those for whom there is still hope of rehabilitation. This does not mean that the leveled-off institutionalized patients and others of the less hopeful types are to be neglected. On the contrary their true needs will best be met as we focus on those whose problems are still acute.

The task of re-education must then be taken seriously. The aim must be not merely to re-awaken a faith which, in many cases, is based upon erroneous pre-suppositions, but also to modify and re-direct it, to substitute a wholesome religion for one which may have been associated with the patient's difficulties.

In the service of worship, therefore, the problem is how to make use of all available resources—music, pageantry, group participation, sermon—to re-inforce therapeutically valuable suggestions. Religious emotion is not to be looked upon as an end in itself, but as a means of re-making and stabilizing character. It is thus not to be regarded as sufficient that a particular hymn or tune should win immediate acclaim. What is important is the behavior sequences which result, especially in those who are in the process of re-making.

In the working out of the order of service as given in this hymnal, the aim has been to provide for much participation on the part of the entire group, not only in song, but in prayer and response. There is also provision for change of position, standing for the Gloria, for the Confession of Faith, for hymns of praise and action and commitment, kneeling or sitting with bowed heads during prayer or during the singing of prayer hymns. It is intended that these changes of position should succeed each other in such a manner as to be restful and stimulating. Care is thus taken not to keep the congregation standing to the point of fatigue or sitting until they become restless or sleepy.

The order of service as thus worked out provides for both repetition and variation. The following of a regular order, especially in a hospital congregation, is conducive to the orderliness and effectiveness of the service, and the repetition Sunday after Sunday of the Lord's Prayer, of the Confession of Faith and other selections of unquestioned value helps to impress them more deeply. Provision for variety may be made by the use of other prayers and passages of Scripture which deal constructively with the problems of the patients.

In the selection of hymns and tunes it should be assumed that the words really matter. Tunes are important but their function is to reinforce the words and serve as an aid to recall. To those who may object that we sing the tune and not the words, it may be pointed out that in pre-literate times it was the general practice to put into verse and music those things which it was important to remember. It seems safe to say that today religious ideas are implanted more readily through the medium of hymns than in any other way.

Careful consideration of the words will of course rule out a number of well-known hymns, and other widely used worship materials. The following are types of worship materials which should be excluded as likely to be disturbing.

1. References to enemies, as in the imprecatory psalms. Concern about enemies is a malignant reaction and needs no fostering.

2. Materials likely to reinforce the belief in the authority of "voices" and other subconscious promptings. For example: "O Christian dost thou see them?" evokes not only visual but also auditory and tactile hallucinations and calls for action besides. The writer of this ancient hymn has undoubtedly passed victoriously through an acute psychotic episode, but his hymn is strong medicine for a congre-

gation of mental patients. "O speak to me that I may speak," is a less striking example of a group of hymns which should be used sparingly in the mental hospital situation.

3. Materials likely to re-inforce belief in the magical. "There is a fountain filled with blood" and "Rock of ages cleft for me" are representatives of a large group which give expression to a magical concept of the atonement which is unsound therapeutically as well as theologically.

4. Materials likely to intensify the patient's sense of helplessness, fear and isolation. "Once to every man and nation" is thus a useful hymn in summoning men to social action in times of national danger, but it does not help discouraged patients to be told that "The choice goes by forever." "Before Jehovah's awful throne" and "O worship the King in the beauty of Holiness" are other examples of a considerable number which represent God as a stern judge and ruler and are therefore of questionable value.

5. Materials out of keeping with the situation and mood of those patients in whom we should be most interested. "Rejoice ye pure in heart," "Joyful, joyful we adore Thee," "For the beauty of the earth," and "My God I thank Thee who has made the earth so bright," are thus so out of place that they must seem like mockery to the thoughtful patient. Many hymns while not disturbing, simply do not apply to the hospital situation. Here belong most missionary hymns, social action hymns and children's hymns.

The excluding of materials which are clearly unsuitable is of course merely a first step. Then comes the task of selecting those materials which most effectively bring to bear the great resources of the Christian faith upon the actual problems and needs of mental patients. The following are the categories which may be recognized in the materials which have been included.

1. Materials giving expression to the consciousness of sin and need and to aspiration for the better life. It is here assumed, on the basis of controlled observation, that the consciousness of sin is a benign reaction[3], that it may indeed be a first step toward the realization of higher possibilities and that the confession of sin, or guilt, brings release from the sense of isolation and estrangement, in which, rather than in conflict and self-condemnation, the most potent factor in mental illness is to be found. The Fifty-first Psalm, the General Confession and such hymns as "Father to us thy children humbly kneeling," "Lord Jesus, think on me," and "Immortal Love, within whose righteous will" have therefore a place in this collection.

2. Materials portraying the love and forgiveness of God. Those who are already undergoing severe inner conflict do not need to be reminded of God's sovereignty and majesty. They do need to be reminded that their world is under the control of

---

3. *Exploration of the Inner World*, (Willett & Clark, 1936)—chapt.1.

friendly forces. Hence we say in our Confession of Faith, "We believe that the sufferings of this present time are not to be compared with the glory which shall be revealed to us hereafter," and use such hymns as "There's a wideness in God's mercy," "God is my strong Salvation," "Here in this maddening maze of things."

3. Materials giving expression to attitudes of resignation and faith. It is assumed that from the religious standpoint spiritual maturity involves the transfer of loyalty from the finite to the infinite and that dependence upon God becomes a source of strength as well as of comfort. Hence, such hymns as "Thy way, not mine, O Lord," "Father, whate'er of earthly bliss," "Still will we trust, though earth seem dark and dreary," give expression of these attitudes.

4. Expressions of courage and action. The need for these is obvious. "Believe not those who say," "Creation's Lord, we give thanks," "Father, hear the prayer we offer," "He who would valiant be" are among the hymns of this type.

5. Hymns of the Future Life. It must not be forgotten that there are not a few residents of the hospital community for whom the hope of a life beyond is about all that can make the present existence worthwhile. We see the expression of this hope in "Jerusalem the glorious," and "Hark, hark, my soul."

6. Materials dealing with special problems common among institutionalized patients:

Moods—"Twixt gleams of joy and clouds of doubt," "When we in darkness walk," "When shadows gather on our way."

Voices—"We pray no more, made lowly wise, For miracle and sign."

Locked Door—"Make me a captive Lord," "Not so in haste my heart."

Day-dreaming—"Abide not in the realm of dreams."

Frankness and Concealment—"Walk in the light."

7. Materials adapted to special purposes and occasions such as opening and closing of worship, morning, evening, Christmas, New Year's, Easter, Thanksgiving, Lord's Supper, etc.

The choice of hymns has to a large extent determined the choice of tunes. Given a fine hymn, the tune must be an appropriate one. Consideration must of course be given to established associations. The number of these associations is not, however, so great as might be supposed. Passing from one standard hymnal to another, one finds many variations. For a congregation made up of adherents of many different church bodies, as is the case in a large mental hospital, established associations are a factor in a relatively small number of cases.

In the 1932 revision of the hymnal we sought the help of two of the best advisers we could find, and we followed their advice, balking only in a few instances. The value of expert advice may be found in the fact that even though experts may differ one from the other, their differences will be far less than those of the rank and file and their judgments are far more likely to stand the test of our own best judgment later on.

One of the factors upon which our consultants laid great stress was that of pitch and range. In accordance with their advice about twenty of the plates in the original edition were discarded as being too wide of range or too high in pitch to meet the requirements of unison singing by the entire congregation.

In the book as it now stands there are 82 tunes. Of these 22 are in widest use, 38 are in general use and 22 are less familiar. A very few changes were made in established association. *O Quanta Qualia* was thus substituted for *Morecambe* in the case of "Spirit of God, descend upon my heart!" *Martyrdom* was substituted for *Serenity* in the case of "Immortal Love, forever full" and *Hursley* was used instead of *Maryton* in the case of "O Master, let me walk with thee." The musical editor regarded these tunes as so far superior as to justify the change. In the case of the less familiar hymns and of those without established associations our aim was to make use of the finest and most singable tunes available.

The printing of the entire hymn below the music was determined by the purpose of permitting the hymn to be read for its meaning. When the words are printed between the staves, this is difficult.

The purpose of a hymnal for use in mental hospitals and the needs which it should seek to meet may thus be summarized:

The perpetuation and re-creation of religious faith through the re-animation of the historic Christian symbols, beliefs and personages;

Re-orientation with reference to one's accepted loyalties with confession of sin and need as an indispensable condition of right relationship with God;

Reaffirmation of the love and forgiveness of God;

Surrender and commitment in accordance with the principle that spiritual maturity is dependent upon the transfer of loyalty from the finite to the infinite and the building of the life upon that basis;

Orientation in time, making one superior to the trials and vicissitudes of the present existence;

Courage and action leading toward the realization of one's accepted goals.

Modification of morbid religious beliefs is to be sought by means of the inclusion of therapeutically valuable materials and by the exclusion of that which is unwholesome and irrelevant.

It has now been eleven years since the latest revision. The book has not come into wide use. It has been criticized chiefly on the ground that too many of the hymns are unfamiliar.

The question which this paper is intended to raise is whether the principles observed in its compilation can be accepted as sound, and whether it may not be possible to meet the objection regarding paucity of familiar hymns by the printing of a supplement made up of old favorites, hymns which might not stand closest inspection but would be at least harmless.

Suggestions regarding the hymns and tunes which should be included in such a supplement will therefore be welcomed. We shall also welcome criticism of the book as it now stands. Such criticism, to be helpful, should be specific rather than general. We shall want to know what you disapprove of and why. Above all we are eager for suggestions regarding the principles upon which the book should be constructed in order to have maximum therapeutic value.

◙ ◙ ◙

THE MINISTER AS COUNSELOR

Anton T. Boisen

[This article appeared in the Spring, 1948 issue of *The Journal of Pastoral Care* and is reflective of the strong post-World War II interest in personal counseling, both in the church and in secular settings. Repeating a theme which appears in many of his other articles, Boisen criticizes the evangelical churches for "saving souls" without giving individual attention and follow-up to the particular needs of the person. However, he also criticizes the liberal churches for giving "neither treatment nor diagnosis" by referring persons to psychiatrists or psychoanalysts when its clergy should have been able to provide help themselves. Without naming it, Boisen endorses the "client-centered" approach of Carl Rogers in which the relationship, rather than a particular technique, becomes the source of healing. He also reflects the division within the pastoral care and counseling movement between those who became enamored with technique and skill and those, like himself, who sought an in-depth understanding of the individual through the case study approach.]

The rapid spread of the term "counseling" among the members of the profession to which I belong calls attention to a somewhat singular situation. The physician has his "patient" and refers to his activities in behalf of his patient as "therapy." The lawyer has his "client" and speaks of himself as "counselor." But what term has the liberal minister of religion for his ministrations or for the object thereof? In the absence of any generally accepted term the word "counseling" has come to him as a veritable godsend. It is used to denote his efforts to help the sick of soul by means of certain recognized techniques. Such, at least, is the definition upon which I shall proceed in this paper. I shall assume that the term "counseling" is the nonmedical equivalent of "psychotherapy," and since my own specialized work has been in the field of mental illness, I shall take as my theme the Church's obligation toward the mentally ill and the potential role of the minister of religion in their care and treatment.

The case of a college student who was brought to the hospital because of an acute disturbance will furnish a good starting point for this discussion and help to hold it down to reality.

> The patient in question was a tall, attractive fellow of some twenty years. His father was a successful business man, his mother a once-talented woman who for seven years had been an inmate of a hospital for the insane. The boy himself was a brilliant student, active in all departments of college life and intensely ambitious and idealistic. This boy, whom we shall call "Bernard C." had been active in church work and the summer before his commitment he had been a delegate to the Y. conference at Lake Geneva. He had there been profoundly stirred and had decided to devote himself to religious work. On his return home he went to his pastor and offered his services. The pastor, a wise and experienced man, saw at once that he was in no condition to do the evangelistic work he proposed to do. He therefore assigned him to some task in connection with his choir. By the end of the summer the excitement had subsided and he went back to college under instructions from his father not to engage in outside activities. These instructions he disregarded. He did do excellent work in his classes, but he also became involved in extra-curricular affairs. The break-down came about the middle of the year. It seems to have followed a "talk to men" by a speaker brought to the campus for that purpose by the college Y. The climax came when Bernard prepared a sermon and invited some of his friends to hear it. When no one showed up at the appointed time, he marched down to the college church, where the Sunday morning service was at that time under way, proceeded up to the pulpit and sought to deliver his message. He was of course hustled out and shortly thereafter he was sent to a sanatarium. There his condition became such that he had to be transferred to a state hospital. Here he was extremely disturbed, for the most part depressed and mutistic, some of the time violent and destructive. Throughout the period of disturbance he knew where he was, he kept track of the dates, and his answers, when he spoke at all, were relevant and coherent. He was, moreover, observant of all that was going on. But he had to be closely watched to be sure that he did not injure himself or someone else. After two months the acute disturbance subsided and he made an excellent recovery.

Here is an extreme example and yet a problem which concerns us all, a college student of considerable promise who under the influence of college religious agencies goes violently insane. To what extent were these religious agencies responsible for this disturbance? What might they have done to avert it? What obligation has the Church toward this boy during his disturbed condition? To what extent is he representative of others with whom religious workers in our colleges and communities have to deal?

The Factor of Inheritance

You will probably notice, first of all, that Bernard had a mother who was insane. This fact may be taken by some as the all-sufficient explanation of his misfortune. For such a view there has been much psychiatric support, especially in the days gone by. Heredity has often served as a mysterious Quantity X, supposed to explain certain equally mysterious disease entities which went under such names as "dementia praecox" and "manic-depressive psychosis." Today however we are beginning to see that such explanations are merely cloaks for ignorance which explain nothing at all and that disorders of this type are best understood as reactions to a difficult life situation. Heredity must then first register in experience before it manifests itself in the form of a psychosis.

In the case under consideration we have a boy of unusual ability, talented, high-strung, physically strong and attractive, who at the same time, in all probability, had more of his share of unmanageable sex cravings. Heredity in this case meant high potentiality. It meant also a certain handicap. His difficulties were undoubtedly accentuated by the influence of a mother who for some time before her commitment had been peculiar. Liability to disorder was increased by the fact that he knew his mother was insane and was acquainted with the prevailing views regarding the inheritance of mental disease.

Sense of Guilt

This boy, talented as he was, handicapped as he was, went to school. He did excellent work in his studies. He was active in the social life of the school, at times feverishly active. This activity may have been an attempt to escape from inner unrest and his hard work as a student an attempt at compensation for that of which he could not bring himself to speak. He was fairly well-liked by his mates and yet he felt himself separated from them because of uncontrollable cravings which he had been unable to socialize and thus assimilate. There is some evidence in this case, as in most functional mental disorders, that the primary causative factor was a sense of guilt and isolation, due to the presence of unassimilated matter which, like ill-digested food, was clamoring for attention and destroying his peace of mind. We may say, furthermore, that high ideals inculcated by the Church, were a factor in inducing this sense of guilt.

The "Soul Surgeons"

Then came the visit to Lake Geneva. Here he came under the influence of a religious group which lays great stress on "soul surgery." Just what happened here we do not know. We may assume that he found here those with whom he could talk over his problems. He was thus relieved of the overwhelming sense of isolation, which is the essence of the sense of guilt. As is characteristic of such experiences, he felt himself at one with a Greater-than-himself, and became profoundly stirred. He found within himself new possibilities and he proposed to go to New York to work among the fallen and the lost.

Minister and Psychiatrist

But now comes the question, What concern has the minister of religion with a definite case of psychosis? Is not such a case outside of his province? And why should I choose as a basis for this discussion an experience which was psychopathic in the extreme?

I therefore call attention to the fact that Bernard's experience at this time, even though it showed many morbid features, may be regarded as a dramatic conversion experience of the type which has been so prominent in the history of the Christian Church ever since the days of Saul of Tarsus and that the psychosis which later developed shows in exaggerated form many features of the religious conversion experience. The psychosis, like the conversion experience, was a desperate attempt to resolve a severe inner conflict. Acute psychoses of this type are to be sharply distinguished from malignant reactions such as withdrawal and concealment in their many forms. They are characterized by marked religious concern and by the sense of mystical identification, something which is generally absent in the malignant reactions. They may be looked upon as extreme manifestations of the consciousness of sin which theology has long regarded as the first step in the process of salvation. Like fever and inflammation in the body, such disorders seem to be manifestations of nature's power to heal.

It follows therefore that Bernard's experience, even in the frankly psychotic stage, belongs rightfully within the province of the specialist in religion. It is true that not many ministers are now equipped to deal with him. But what is involved are the most potent forces and the most delicate and profound laws of the spiritual life. His experience is an extreme exemplification of the honest and desperate struggle for salvation with which the minister of religion should be especially concerned. The student of religion should therefore have much to learn from him and from his kind which will not only enable him to contribute to the treatment of the full-blown disorders, but will equip him to deal with the more complex incipient disorders which abound in every normal parish.

Treatment without Diagnosis

It follows also that the Lake Geneva group which had a part in precipitating Bernard's disturbance was not necessarily at fault. They might have done him a real service by helping him to recognize and grapple with a serious accumulation of unassimilated experience, and by doing so before catastrophe had become an accomplished fact.

Where these "soul surgeons" were at fault was in the lack of adequate individual attention. When Bernard was aroused and eager to do something about his situation, he was left to shift for himself, and the minister whose guidance he sought seems to have had nothing better to offer than occupational therapy. He set him to work singing in his choir, when what he actually needed was intensive psychotherapy. This is a weakness which has characterized the Church's past efforts at evangelism. The old evangelists of the Dwight L. Moody type brought a message of salvation to the sick of soul and were of real help to many. But what they gave was all too often treatment without diagnosis. There was little attempt to sit down with those who "hit the saw-dust trail" and arrive at a real understanding of their particular problems. As for the modern liberal churches, it may be said with some justice that they have been giving neither treatment nor diagnosis, but have been referring to the psychiatrist and to the psychoanalyst many persons who needed the help they should have been able to give.

The Church's Task

On the basis of these considerations we are ready to attempt some generalizations regarding the minister's task as counselor. In the first place, the minister of religion is concerned always with the problems relating to mental health. This follows inevitably from his task as a servant of the Church. Thus in Bernard's case, he and also his parents had been brought up under the influence of the church, and its ministers had had much to do with shaping the standards by which he judged himself. His church happened to be one of the more liberal persuasion, but even so, those standards determined the inner conflict which resulted in the psychosis. The Church is often charged by psychiatrists with being responsible for much unnecessary suffering by reason of its perfectionistic requirements. As a servant of the Church, I admit the charge that it sometimes disturbs men's consciences. I only wish it did so more often and more effectively. That, as I see it, is inherent in its job. The task of organized religion is to perpetuate and re-create religious faith. This means not merely transmitting religious insights and moral achievements from one generation to another, but also awakening its people to new opportunities and coming dangers and leading them to new and higher levels of adjustment. The Church is concerned with that which is not yet but ought to be in personal character and in social order. For this reason it cannot be content with mediocrity and it cannot take the average as normative. It is and must be perfectionistic in its objectives. The fact that the sexual behavior of the human male, as revealed by Professor Kinsey's recent studies, gives us a picture of the average man which is by no means flattering, does not make that behavior any the less "ornery," or "vulgar," two terms which, significantly enough, are etymologically identical with "average"; nor does it release the servants of the Church from the duty of trying to awaken that man to his higher potentialities. The fact that man has always been war-like and that the world to-day is filled with wars and rumors of war does not release us from the obligation of summoning men to repent in sack-cloth and ashes for the nationalistic selfishness and blindness which threatens to destroy our entire civilization.

The Church's Social Significance

In the second place, the minister of religion is the leader of the world's outstanding exemplification of the group therapy of which we hear so much to-day. Even though he may disturb a man's conscience, he and his group have also the power to heal. In support of this proposition I may remind you that religious assemblage for the purpose of instruction and common worship, which seems to be peculiar to the Hebrew-Christian religion, has social significance of enormous importance.

We may thus recognize the part which religious assemblage has played in the re-thinking of fundamental religious beliefs in the light of changing conditions and in the modification of ethical standards in the light of growing knowledge. Herein we may find an explanation of the marvelous stability of Hebrew culture, of its capacity to survive and maintain its integrity over a period of some 2000 years, even though its people have had no homeland of their own but have been scattered over the face of the earth among people of other cultures. Herein also we may find an explanation of the flexibility of the Christian religion and its ability to adapt itself to such radically different cultures as Roman Imperialism, Medieval Feudalism and modern Industrial Democracy. Hinduism, Buddhism, and Confucianism have had no such institution. For this reason these religions have been the bulwark of the status quo and in very truth the opiate of downtrodden peoples; and their associated cultures have shown relatively little change.

But a vital church has another function which is of greatest significance from the standpoint of the problem before us. The church at its best is never a fellowship of saints—that is of persons who are already perfect in their own eyes—but rather an assemblage of those who are agreed regarding their loyalties and their objectives. It is a fellowship in which moral self-judgment is based, not upon some fixed code, but upon the will to do better. The emphasis upon the will to righteousness in imperfect men was central in the teaching of Jesus. It was Paul's great discovery in his concept of the Spirit as against the Law.

Thus in Bernard's case the disturbed condition began, as we have seen, with an experience which was near-akin to the religious conversion. It began under the influence of a group which took its religion in earnest and laid great emphasis upon confession of sin and sharing of experience. This group has sometimes gone under the name of the "First Century Christian Fellowship," a name which rightly calls attention to the fact that their earnestness in the pursuit of the better life, their profound conviction that they had tapped anew the source of spiritual power and their practice of confessing their faults and sharing their experiences with each other are traits which have been characteristic of the Christian Church in its more creative phases.

Down through the ages the Church has thus recognized and made use of the principles of confession and forgiveness which are today the foundations of psychotherapy. It has been offering to all who would accept it deliverance from the sense of guilt and from the tyranny of the standardized. It has been setting men free to strive for the objectives which it accepts as paramount. It has recognized that any one who shares in its purpose and who honestly seeks to face and correct his faults—no matter how serious those faults may be—is worthy of an honored place in its fellowship. It has thus shared what psychiatrists refer to, none too accurately, as the "nonjudgmental" attitude. It is concerned about *goals* rather than *standards*, about *growth* rather than *status*.

The mere fact that Bernard became a participating member of such a group must have had for him great therapeutic value. For many of those who undergo the conversion experience, that is in itself sufficient to maintain their stability and to hold them to the pursuit of the better life. In the group their consciences are enlightened, their purposes are reinforced, their faith re-kindled and their belief in themselves is supported.

But Bernard's stay at Lake Geneva was a short one. He had to return home. There he at once sought out his pastor and that pastor sought to meet his need by gearing him into his own organization. The pastor's plan was one which would normally have worked, even though his church was one which had become comfortably institutionalized. But Bernard's problems were unusually aggravated. For him this solution was not sufficient. He was in need of intensive therapy, or personal counseling—whichever term we prefer.

The Present Status of Personal Counseling

My third proposition is that the minister's role as leader of a group of socially-minded persons and as counselor to individuals in distress are two complementary tasks and that both are dependent upon a true understanding of the laws of the spiritual life. The two tasks have gone always hand in hand, and attention to the individual has always been central in the Church's program.

Thirty-five years ago, at a time when I was engaged in making studies of the social and religious conditions in several different regions of this country, I took occasion to inquire of many ministers and church leaders what they were trying to do. In the more liberalized East the answer would often be given in terms of "bringing in the Kingdom of God." Here in the Middle West, however, it was almost invariably, "We are trying to save souls." The latter answer may be regarded as substantially correct. The Church has generally operated by trying to change individual lives. It was also significant that the Middle Westerners, when asked what they meant by "saving souls" were somewhat hazy in their answers. The church's efforts to help the individual have been largely on a common sense or intuitive basis. There has been little attempt to exchange and criticize experience on the part of the professional group and thus to build up a body of organized and tested experience.

This weakness on the part of the Church has in recent years been spot-lighted by developments in the field of psychiatry. The medical profession, approaching the problems of the individual on the basis of their experience with the seriously disturbed, have made use of the methods of science to clarify many of the principles involved and have won increasing prestige.

It is none the less true that at the time of Bernard's breakdown twenty years ago, there was a dearth of persons who were equipped to give him the needed help. There were few psychiatrists and few analysts who had any understanding of the religious significance of his disturbance and few ministers of religion who were versed in psychopathology.

The situation today is somewhat changed. Under the guidance of the Council for the Clinical Training, of the Institute for Pastoral Care and several other agencies, opportunities to obtain experience under guidance in the service of the mentally and physically ill and of the delinquent are being offered, and during the past twenty years some 2500 ministers have availed themselves of these opportunities.

Lines of Advance

As one who had a part in the launching of this clinical training movement I feel much encouraged over this development. At the same time I am impressed with the crying need of certain important next steps.

One of these is suggested by the wording of the topic which has been assigned to me. I am thinking of the wide-spread tendency in our efforts at clinical training to emphasize the techniques of counseling rather than the basic understandings.

Without minimizing the importance of technique, or skill, I am more and more impressed by the fact that psychotherapy is not dependent upon any particular technique, but upon a relationship between therapist and patient which involves trust on the part of the one and understanding on the part of the other. Wherever such a relationship is established, results are likely to follow, even though the techniques may be clumsy and the theories all awry. This principle has been delightfully stated by Dr. Macfie Campbell in a lecture which, so far as I can discover, has never appeared in book form. It is worth quoting at some length.

> The psychotherapeutic treatment of Brown, a patient, by McConachie, a physician, consists in McConachie listening and talking to Brown. Is there any special technique in regard to this type of therapy? So long as McConachie is intelligent and listens long enough to the information which Brown can put before him, and so long as he is able to talk to Brown in a useful and constructive way, details of procedure, or technique, are of vanishing importance. They are to a large extent questions of taste and tradition and authority.
>
> One physician may wish to employ the dramatic technique of the hypnotic procedure in order that he may listen to Brown and talk to him. Brown may be docile and have no objections to this little drama, in fact, the mild mystery associated with it may somewhat exalt McConachie in his eyes. Primitive man has always been very sensitive to the magical forces associated with the medicine man, and the reactions of primitive man still continue beneath the more highly evolved functions of civilized man. Even when Brown is not especially influenced by these primitive mechanisms, he may have other reasons for accepting the hypnotic suggestion. It is less embarrassing to tell some things with head averted or with eyes closed; it is gratifying to have at the same time the possibility of unburdening and the official fiction that we are not really conscious of the facts we are disclosing. So in diplomacy, it is sometimes useful to communicate some information but at the same time to make a demonti officiel. This is in accord with the diplomatic tradition and the diplomatist retains his self-respect. So also in the hypnotic technique.
>
> Or another physician, an orthodox follower of Freud, may prefer to sit behind his patient, who lies stretched out on a couch and with eyes closed talks to the physician about whatever happens to come into his or her mind. Here too the patient has the opportunity to talk with averted face, and it may be more pleasant for the physician not to have the patient scrutinizing his face for an hour continuously. This setting too may give both to the patient and to the physician a diluted magical feeling which heightens the prestige of the physician.
>
> The essential fact about the situation is that Brown, an individual in trouble, whether in the hypnotic or psychoanalytic setting or sitting with eyes wide open on any convenient chair, is getting an honest chance to bring up important problems of his life before McConachie, the physician, who is seated upon some equally indifferent article of furniture, but who is honestly endeavoring to pool his special knowledge with Brown's lay experience to see whether poor Brown can, by means of his help, make a better job of his life and get along without his previous evasive reactions, whether the

latter consist of physical symptoms, special fears, domestic friction, economic inefficiency or social eccentricities.

According to this view the essence of psychotherapy is thinking with the
patient about his problems as a trusted and trustworthy friend. Skill is indeed
required. It is important to respect the personality of the man we are trying to help.
We must be able to listen to him and to refrain from imposing upon him our own
opinions and formulations. We must be able to interpret the symbols by means of
which he seeks to reveal his difficulties to those who have eyes to see and ears to
hear and to conceal them from those who have not. We must be able to sense
things which he leaves unsaid. But the primary requirement is to understand the
patient and to have a real knowledge of human nature in difficulty. This is essential
not only for effective work with individuals but also for the intelligent guidance of
the group. The present overemphasis upon technique at the expense of understanding involves the danger that even those who have had clinical training might not be
able to give Bernard the help he needed. We need therefore a thorough-going program of cooperative inquiry in the field of religious experience and mental illness.

In the acquisition of the needed understanding the progress is not as rapid as it
ought to be. Most of the progress achieved has been on an extra-curricular basis.
The empirical study of human nature either in health or in sickness, either individual or collective, is not yet part of the basic structure of theological education. The
other courses are historical, homiletical, and philosophical. In the great majority of
our theological schools it is still possible for a student to go through school and get
his degree without having studied the human personality either in health or in sickness or the social forces which determine it. And the humanistic sciences on their
part—psychology, sociology, anthropology and psychiatry—have not yet carried
their inquiries to the level of the religious.

Conclusion

My answer to the question which has been assigned to me may now be summarized. The churches and their professional servants have been performing a great
and important service in the realm of mental health. They have been helping men
to think and feel together regarding the things that matter most. They have been
helping them to determine and modify their beliefs and their standards of conduct
in accordance with changing conditions. They have been holding up high ideals as
objectives toward which to strive and have at the same time been setting men free
from the sense of guilt and isolation to strive for the achievement of their best
potentialities. But these things have been done on an intuitive and common sense
basis. There has been a strange lag among the professional servants of the Church in
the matter of applying the methods of science to the field which is distinctively their

own, that of religious experience. That field is still a terra incognita whose exploration promises untold possibilities for the understanding of human nature and the achievement of mental, or spiritual, health.

But I see neither the possibility nor the desirability of establishing a new profession of religious counselors. Specialists are indeed needed especially in the understanding and treatment of our much neglected mentally ill and the future minister of religion should be thoroughly grounded in the first hand knowledge of human nature both in health and in disease; but any new insights which may accrue from our growing knowledge of spiritual law can best be applied without any blowing of trumpets by the well-trained minister in the quiet discharge of his duties as pastor and preacher.

THE PRESENT STATUS OF WILLIAM JAMES'S PSYCHOLOGY OF RELIGION

Anton T. Boisen

[In this brief article published in the Fall, 1953 issue of *The Journal of Pastoral Care*, Boisen uses the 50th anniversary of the publication of William James' *Varieties of Religious Expreience* to issue a criticism of the clinical training movement as he saw it. One reason that Boisen entered Union Theological Seminary in 1908 was that it was a place where he could study the psychology of religion as interpreted by William James. He studied this with George Albert Coe, whose empirical approach became a major influence on Boisen. However, Boisen laments that, since World War I, the psychology of religion has become too Freudian and that clinical training programs have become too enamored with psychoanalytic theory and technique rather than the phenomenological study of the meaning of religious experience.]

At a conference on the present status of the psychology of religion held in 1938 there was general agreement among the distinguished psychologists present that the movement which had been launched so enthusiastically at the turn of the century and had reached so brilliant a climax in William James's *The Varieties of Religious Experience* had spent its force. Not only had there been a dearth of really significant new books in this field, but it was no longer academically respectable. If in any of our major universities a graduate student in psychology should submit a thesis in the psychology of religion, that thesis would not be accepted.

This paper will undertake to show that in so far as there has been a decline in the psychology of religion, it is only a recession which may be explained by the growing pains of psychology in general and that, actually, William James as a pioneer in this field is only now beginning to come into his own.

It is important to recognize that William James stood both at the beginning and at the end of an era. He was a pioneer and an explorer, but he was also a representative of the old order when philosophy and psychology dwelt together and the scientist was also a scholar who was at home in other departments of human knowledge. William James thus began as a specialist in physiology, but he became more and more absorbed in psychology, and he ended his life as a leader in the scientific study of religion and as a philosopher of the first magnitude. More than that he was a splendid incarnation of the old cosmopolitan culture, a man grounded in the study of Latin and Greek—without which he could not have graduated from college—and thoroughly at home in the language and literature of Germany and France. He was a man of broadest sympathies and widest horizon. He was a scholar of the old school at its best to whom the specialized new studies brought dazzling new vistas, which he had the power to describe in language unforgettable. Professor James's younger associates in the psychological study of religion shared in this broader outlook. They also were trained in philosophy as well as in psychology. But they fronted more the coming age, and this early group was succeeded by specialists, men trained in the time when philosophy and psychology had been divorced and psychology was bent on establishing itself as a respectable "brass-instrument science." From this group came very few who dared to carry their inquiries over to the level of the religious, while those whose interest lay primarily in the field of religion made little use of the scientific method.

A second consideration is to be found in Professor James's interest in the psychopathological. This interest permeates the *Varieties* and provides the basis for some of its most brilliant insights. He was convinced that the phenomena of mental disease threw much light upon the everyday problems of personality and offered much more that was important to psychology than did experimental psychology. His younger associates in this country did not share this interest. Some of these were crusading against the excesses of nineteenth-century revivalism and all were critical of his interest in the pathological and his tenderness for the mystical. Thus it came to pass that the original impetus was diverted into religious education on the one hand and into the philosophy of religion on the other, while still others offered explanations in terms of the social factors. Meanwhile the promising beginnings in France and Germany were destroyed by the horrors of war. In Europe the general trend was toward a return to orthodox theological beliefs which had received emotional validation through the religious experiences of men who in time of crisis and suffering had been forced to think and feel together intensely about the ultimate values of life. The empirical approach to the study of religious experience was thus in large measure by-passed.

Meanwhile a new interest has been developed in the problems of the personality, which promises to lead us back to William James's central insights. We are beginning to recognize more and more that the great driving forces of human life— love and hate and fear and anger and sense of failure and guilt—cannot be brought under laboratory conditions and that in the disorders of the personality we are dealing with the end-results of nature's experiments with just these forces. Hence a new interest in the psychopathological, due chiefly to the work of Sigmund Freud and his associates. They have found their chief source of understanding not in the laboratory but in listening to the patient in the interview situation. Instead of the old associationist psychology with its emphasis upon habit and the conditioned reflexes of the behaviorist school, they have given us a psychology based upon the stuff of experience, with wishes and dreams, love and hate, anxiety and belief as central factors. As yet the Freudians have shown little interest in religion and little understanding thereof. Freud himself regarded religion as a neurotic manifestation and most of his followers have been interested chiefly in reductive interpretations, particularly the mistakes made by parents in the early years of life. Nonetheless, students of religion have been quick to see the implications of psychoanalytic doctrine for the study of religion. Following World War I, books on the psychology of religion, especially in England, have been based largely upon Freudian teaching. But few, if any, of these books have been based upon first-hand study, and few, if any, have attempted to employ the methods of science. Most of them have been semi-popular treatises built upon foundations which are not likely to endure.

Along with the new interest in the psychopathological has come the movement for the clinical training of clergy and theological students. As originally formulated, this movement saw in mental illness a problem which concerned the student and minister of religion quite as much as it did the medical man. Mental illness, it held, was the price we had to pay for being men and having the power of choice and the capacity for growth. It was due to the operations of conscience, and certain of its forms are manifestations of healing power analogous to fever or inflammation in the body. As such they are closely akin to the dramatic forms of religious experience so prominent in the history of the Christian Church since the days of Saul of Tarsus. These forms, which are to be sharply distinguished from those in which adaptations to defeat and failure are made and accepted, are frequently characterized by the sense of mystical identification which figured so prominently in James's philosophy of religion. In many ways this movement represented a return to William James and an attempt to take up where he left off. With him it believed that sickness of soul might have religious significance. With him it saw in mystical experience the creative source of institutionalized religion and it proposed to employ the methods of science in attacking the problems involved.

As a cooperative attack upon the problem of religious experience the clinical training movement has, for this writer, been disappointing. It has shown considerable vigor, but its main interests have diverged widely from those of William James in his *Varieties*. It has often been content to accept psychoanalysis as authoritarian doctrine, and it has often placed its main emphasis upon early conditionings and upon the techniques of counseling and of group work. The questions of central importance to the student of religion and of theology are not being asked and valid methods of cooperative inquiry are not being developed.

The anniversary of the publication of the *Varieties* therefore brings with it a special challenge to those engaged in clinical pastoral training, that of undertaking the exploration of the important territory in which William James has blazed the way in the effort to build up a body of organized and tested experience relating to the religious life and the laws that govern it.

INSPIRATION IN THE LIGHT OF PSYCHOPATHOLOGY

Anton T. Boisen

[The following article from the October, 1960 issue of *Pastoral Psychology* is a commentary on the case of one of Boisen's favorite patients at Worcester State Hospital, an African-American named Ben Mickle. Mickle was named and quoted in many of Boisen's published and unpublished works, probably because his religious ideation provided the type of case in which Boisen was most interested. It is obvious, especially in the "Personality" section, that Boisen had great respect and appreciation for this man and his potential. The statements at the conclusion of the article are illustrative of Boisen's advocacy for the mentally ill prior to the similar efforts of R. D. Laing and Thomas Szasz. Affirming that auditory hallucinations "may represent the operations of the creative mind" (his own experience), Boisen sought to have Mickle released from the hospital but was blocked by Mickle's occasionally violent nature.]

Among the problems which confront the student of religion in a mental hospital there is none more challenging than that of the would-be prophet and the phenomena of inspiration which he presents. The beginnings of all vital religions are to be found in experiences interpreted as communications from a superhuman source, either in the person of the believer himself or of some significant person whose authority he accepts. Such experiences arises spontaneously under the stress of crises situations when men are brought face to face with the ultimate issues of life and are forced to do fresh and creative thinking. For this reason new prophets are constantly appearing, some true, some false, some giving expression to beliefs which are forward-looking and superior, others to beliefs and practices which are inferior and regressive; some worthy of devotion and admiration, others who are rightly consigned to institutions for the insane.

In every mental hospital, therefore, we find patients who believe that God has spoken to them, that he has given them some important mission to perform and that they have some important role to act out. Among these there may be some potential George Fox or John Bunyan or some Saul of Tarsus who has it in him to change the course of history. It is therefore a matter of first importance to be able to recognize and give a helping hand to the moulting genius and to have our eyes opened to the significance of such experiences.

A Twentieth Century Jonah

In the belief that the mental hospital has something to tell us about the phenomena of inspiration, I am offering a brief study of one of our borderline prophets, a quaint Negro who went by the name of "Mickle," who thought of himself as the prophet Jonah, and who believed that he had been called to preach to the wicked city of Nineveh, entirely unaware, as he later found out, that Nineveh "done been destroyed twenty-four hundred years ago."

This patient had been picked up for vagrancy more than a thousand miles from his native Savannah and had given utterance to such strange religious ideas that the police took him to the hospital.

In appearance he was a dark-skinned Negro of about thirty-eight years, some-what below average in height and weighing about 135 pounds. What hair he had was kept closely clipped. He had snapping, bright eyes and a pleasant, happy expression. In walking, he took long strides with a peculiar swing of arms and hips, getting over the ground with remarkable speed.

The hospital staff classified him as "dementia praecox, paranoid type; based on delusions of grandeur in an individual who is following explicitly the hallucinated voice of God, and whose entire life is under the direction of that voice."

In the psychometric examination he was eagerly co-operative and was naively delighted with each success, but his score was only at the eight year level. Some of his answers were of interest.

In the *Ball and Field* test, which resulted in a failure, he made a simple straight line to the center of the circle, remarking, "Something tell me to come in and stop in front of that mark (a water-mark in the paper). I works by the Spirit, you know."

Induction test, also a failure. Here he got one right. He was greatly delighted at this and said, "There's a man inside telling me."

Fables: His response to the fable of the *Fox and the Crow* was, "A fox is a kind of dog that loves to play around a chicken anyhow. He thinks he can come through with his sweet talk."

Vocabulary: 21 out of 50 words defined correctly. Here are some of the definitions:

Ramble: It's just like as if you goes into the woods to hunt a coon or a rabbit or a possum and you has to travel around this way and that to find that beast.

Hysterics: It's when a person's mind comes and goes and he talks by spells.

Nerve: Now that's another nationality. It's what makes you do things you don't want to do.

Curse: The devil, he deal with all such jobs as that.

Lecture: It's just like you setting down here asking me all sorts of questions to see if I'se crazy.

Patient's Own Story

It's not difficult to get Mickle to tell his story. He has evidently told it many times in the past and he delights in telling it. Here is the way he gave it to me in the first interview:

> I was born in Charleston, South Carolina, lived twenty years in Savannah. I used to be a wicked man. I was called first in 1912 to go and preach to the heathen race. I had been very wild and rough, very fond of frolic. I went home one Sunday morning from the frolic and lay down on my bed. I see a white man, a big man all dressed in white clothes. It was God's spirit talking to this man, yes, me. He took me by the hands. He say, 'Mickle, you are arrested. There is a wicked city over in that direction. It was on sale 60 or 70 years ago to be destroyed. But before I destroy it, I will send a man to notify the people. This people never has repented of their sin, and there's four and a half million head of people in that city. I tell him I can't read or write and I'se a wicked man. He say, 'I just want you to go down there and stand up and I will talk through you to the people myself. And after you get through talking, I will sweep that whole place out. That nationality is very onruly.'
>
> But I went out and I went back to the gaming table. I worked as a brakeman on the Seaboard Air-Line four years. After that I went back to Savannah and worked four years toting furniture for the Benton Transfer Company.
>
> In 1922 the Spirit came by where I was working and said, 'Come and go with me.' I went home to my house. He say, 'You remember, Mickle, what you promised God? You promised God you would go to that wicked city. I want you to go there now. There's a man named Ananias. He will tell you what to do.'
>
> After I am baptized in Savannah, I am a number one speaker. You see I am just a young preacher, a Missionary Baptist preacher, but I'se the biggest missionary in the United States. (Here follows a detailed itinerary of his journey through Georgia into Alabama, then back into Georgia and from there up through the Carolinas, Virginia, Maryland, Pennsylvania, New Jersey, New York, Connecticut, Massachusetts. Vermont to the Canada line and then back to Massachusetts, all the way on foot.) He then concludes:

When I got back to Worcester, I had walked 3400 miles. I was on my fifth pair of shoes and I had been arrested seven times. I was a give-out vessel and I'se very happy when I end my journey walking into Worcester Hospital. I felt a great rejoicing when I landed in the wicked city of Worcester.

Supplementary Details

Because of the distance to Savannah it was not possible to check his story and we were forced to rely upon the patient himself. The information derived from many interviews may be summarized as follows.

Concerning his early years he reports, "I couldn't go to school. I had to work. My father was a bright-skinned man. He go all around. He leave my mamma. My mamma, she marry another man. He fight me. My father was converted afterward and became a preacher. He came back and want to take me, but my mamma, she wouldn't let me go."

He claims to have been a good worker, earning $30 to $35 a month and holding his jobs for considerable periods. His regular earnings seem to have been supplemented by what he took in as a "banjo-picker" and dancer. In the hospital he did little or no work. This was not due to laziness, but to his idea of what was becoming to a man of his high calling. It was also a reaction to the institution of slavery. To work under orders is slavery, and this he would not do.

He says of himself that in his younger days he was a "bad man after the wimmens." He was "a man crazy after big fat wimmens." He also claims to have been "a very lucky man with female folk." With one woman he lived for four years and ten months. "She weigh 220 pounds. She love me pretty well. But I give her up. The Spirit tol'me, it's a wrong thing for a single man to live with a woman."

During his sojourns in the hospital, especially in the earlier period, he seems to have been little occupied with sexual matters. He would rarely bring up the subject spontaneously and when questioned on the subject he would answer without evasion or embarrassment. He stated that he had no use for female folk and explained, "If you eats a lot of corn and that corn make you sick, you doesn't have anything to do with that corn any more."

Concerning his religious life he reports that before his second call he had been attending meetings in the Reverend Danright's church in Savannah. It seems that Mr. Danright said some things that "sturbed" him. "He talk about shooting craps and running around after other men's wives and getting drunk. All that hit me pretty. Rev. Danright was a live fellow and a good preacher and he had been converted just like me. But when I went and ask him to baptize me, he wouldn't do it. He say, 'That the way God call you? I don't deal with no such man as you.' I feel pretty bad at that. I go then to Rev. J. H. Wiley. He baptize me. Did Rev. Danright think there was something wrong with me? Yes, he did. He though I was a crazy colored man. But he's badly fooled. It's an awful queer thing that a preacher doesn't know a religious man when they see him."

Personality

Mickle's chief delight was in his conversations with the Man Above. This Man Above would appear to him, especially at night, and bring him comfort and counsel and warning. Sometimes he would bring a choir of angels to sing to him. The common term for these communications was "signals." When he got good signals he was happy. When for any reason the signals were not functioning, or when they were disquieting, he would be irritable and cross. I asked him once if these signals sounded like my own voice in talking to him. His answer was, "No, he tell me things to tell you. He speak much like a natural man, but he don't speak like a natural man. When God speak to me, it ain't no idea that comes into my mind. There's a man down in here (pointing to his chest). But the Spirit don't talk like you talk. He don't say no dozens of words. I don't hear him with my ears. I hears him here." (He points to his chest.)

Frequently in talking with Mickle, a far-away look would come into his eyes and he might explain, "He's talking to me now." This was likely to happen when for any reason he was deeply moved.

Time and again I have found that in my efforts to change some attitude the one effective way was to get the Man Above to give him orders. Such orders he would not "jump." Within the limits imposed by his system of beliefs, the advice thus received was generally sound. The Man Above would reprove him for losing his temper. The Man Above would tell him to go into the packs. The Man Above would tell him to look upon his hospital experience as a school and assure him that all was in accordance with his will and in many other ways he would help him to cope with some really difficult situation.

Mickle was not without some share of mystical identification, but he was somewhat canny regarding it. He rarely went further than to say, "You doesn't know who I is." On one occasion he went on to explain that he couldn't tell because he didn't want people to run from him. On another occasion he announced, "I am behind Norah and Jonas and Paul." Asked whether this meant that he was one with God, he replied, "No, I didn't say that." Usually he identified himself with Jonah. This identification seems to have come from the circumstances surrounding his second call. "I tell God," he explained once, "that I feels like Jonas." It seems that in reply God said to him that he was Jonas and gave him the commission to preach in Nineveh. This commission he took quite literally, believing in his ignorance that Nineveh was a "sure enough city." He did not discover his error until he got clean to New York. However, this discovery did not faze him. Worcester became Nineveh and his great ambition was to preach the message of doom to that wicked city.

His system of beliefs was thoroughly fixed and organized. His whole life was unified around the idea which had carried him on his three thousand mile journey. He said of himself once, "I wants to be different from everybody else. I want to walk different, talk different, act different." But in his peculiarities there was no confusion and no uncertainty. He always knew his own mind. And there was no self pity, no seeking of alibis, no tendency to transfer blame.

No picture of Mickle would be complete which did not take account of his courage. "I never moans or cries," he remarked once after a series of reverses which included the loss of a cherished parole, "I jes' keeps right on." I can testify to the accuracy of that statement. He had the true fighting spirit. After a fight with another man in which he got the worst of it, his only comment was, "That sure some man."

For me, Mickle always seemed a work of art or, better perhaps, an artist himself. I have found no little enjoyment in some of his shrewd observations and quaint phrases. Here are some examples.

The Conversion of Paul

You see, I was called just like he call Paul. Paul was a very wicked man. He went through the world 'stroying people. One day God come along while Paul was going out to kill people. God knocked Paul a double somersault off the hosses. Paul rise up and say, "Lord what will you have me to do?" The Lord say, "Go down there, Paul. There's a man names Ananias. He will tell you what to do." Paul became the finest preacher there ever has been in the United States.

Jonah and the Whale

God told the whale, "You take Jonas back to Nineveh and put him in drydock." The whale started back. He went three hundred miles an hour.

Advice to Preachers

A preacher, preaching, must branch off on three roads, first, second, third. On the first you makes them open up their eyes. Then you comes back and you throws another switch and you digs in after the way people live. You tells them they's getting worser and worser. On the third you knocks them sprawling all over one another.

What Makes a Man Go Crazy

What tears a man's mind worse than most anything else is to have something covered up in your mind. It's just like as if you shuts up milk or meat. They 'gins to stink. That's what keeps a million thousand people here in this 'sylum. They's minds is all muddied up. My mind used to be that way. But God cleaned it out. God just p'litely took a scrub brush and scrub it out. But I ain't never been crazy. That comes from worriation, and I never worries. I just gets mad and that lets the stink out that quick. But God is curing me of that now.

When a man worries, the worriation go into his heart and the heart get sick. The heart telegraph it to the brains, and the brains, they gets addled up, just like addled eggs.

Comments

Many questions may be raised by the story of this quaint prophet. Why was he adjudged insane and kept in the hospital while Father Divine goes free? Why was it that with all his picturesque and attractive qualities he failed to win any followers? On these and other questions much time might be spent. This paper, however, is particularly concerned with the "signals" and with the mystical identification so closely associated therewith as a problem of special interest in any consideration of the interrelationship of religious experience and mental disorder.

We may begin by recognizing that Mickle's "signals" were identical with the "voices," or auditory hallucinations so frequently encountered in a mental hospital. The medical record, compiled by an able psychiatrist, thus describes Mickle as "an individual who is following explicitly the hallucinated voice of God and whose entire life is under the direction of that voice." Most psychiatrists would probably agree. In the mental hospital vernacular he might be described as one of those who "hallucinate all over the ward." Such phenomena are common in a mental hospital. It is assumed that these voices are the product of repressed and dissociated wishes and that their presence is evidence that the personality is in process of disintegration. There is therefore seldom a psychiatric interview in which the patient is not questioned directly or indirectly as to whether he has "heard voices," and if his answer is Yes, he is likely to be labeled "schizophrenic" and to be give a gloomy prognosis.

What are these "voices," and what is their significance? This is a question in which I have long been interested and for many years I have made it my business to talk with patients who are said to "hear voices." I have found that most of them, if left to themselves, will describe this experience in different ways. The commonest term is "voice," but most such patients make a sharp distinction between such voices and those they hear with their ears. Here are a few examples.[1]

> Patient 1 heard a voice which seemed to be God's voice and words from the Bible came into his head. He had an idea so big that it just carried him away and he ran out into the street in his underwear. When questioned, he explained that he didn't exactly hear anything. "It's just like when you sit and think. Something comes to you."
> Patient 2 began to get directions. Ideas came to him. The greatness and the allness of it drove him goofy.
> Patient 3 got such funny thoughts and felt himself under some sort of control.

---

1. Cf. Boisen, A.T., "Onset in Acute Schizophrenia," *Psychiatry* (1947) 10:159-166.

Patient 4 got inner pushes.

Patient 5 heard voices repeating his thoughts.

Patient 6 heard God speaking to him, saying that judgment was coming upon the human race. He got messages. He discovered things through transference.

Patient 7 got such funny thoughts. Things popped into his head.

Patient 8 heard God and the devil talking. The voices said he was to be cut up.

Patient 9 heard voices saying "crucify him."

Patient 10—God put thoughts into his head. God hypnotized him. God did the talking.

Patient 11—"I can't explain it. It was just the way I felt. I got the idea. It came to me as a revelation in a dream."

Patient 12—"I began to have a flood of mental pictures as though an album within were unfolding itself. Communications came to me from out of the ether. I felt as though I were directed by someone higher than myself."

Patient 13—"I had to give up my work and sit around and brood. Then ideas came to me. I didn't have to search for words. It was just like I was commanded to say certain words I had never heard of before."

Patient 14—"I got the inspiration to write poetry. It just seemed to flow without my trying. There weren't any voices. Ideas just came to me. I got up one morning at 5 a.m. and wrote my first poem."

I could give many other instances, but these may be sufficient to indicate that the psychological process involved is found outside the mental hospital and that it is not uncommon. It is that of the "inspiration," or "verbal automatism," that of the idea or thought formation which after a period of incubation darts suddenly into consciousness so vividly, sometimes, that it is ascribed to a superhuman source. It is a mechanism which is common to poets, to inventors, to creative scientists and, according to Professor Coe, it is the primitive root of all mystical experience from spiritism to religious ecstasy at its best.[2]

Professor Eliot Dole Hutchinson has described this dynamism as among the phenomena of "insight." His words are worth quoting.

The scientist, the artist, the thinker of whatever variety has before him a problem involving some production or decision. For months, or it may be for years, this problem remains unsolved, the creative intention unfulfilled. Attempts at solution have ended only in bafflement. But suddenly, usually in a moment when work has been abandoned temporarily, or attention had been absorbed in irrelevant matters, there comes an unpredicted *insight* into the solutions. As if "inspired," or "given," ideas arise which constitute real integration of previously accumulated experience. An answer, a brilliant hypothesis, a useful "hunch" paves the way to artistic or scientific advance. Exhilaration marks such moments of insight, a glow of elation goes with them, a feeling of finality, adequacy, accomplishment.[3]

2. Coe, G. A. *Psychology of Religion*, chapt. 16; also 11 & 12.

3. Hutchinson, Eliot Dole. "The Nature of Insight" *Psychiatry* (1941) 4:31-43.

Professor Hutchinson goes on to point out that the distinction between religious and scientific or artistic insight is to be found in the nature of the problem which is at the focus of attention. In the case of the artist, and especially of the scientist, the new insight will pertain to something which can be more or less readily verified by others and fitted into the structure of organized and tested experience. In the case of the mystic the new insight is likely to be intimately personal and have to do with his own role in life. It is therefore not so readily subject to verification and it involves tremendous affective reactions.

Herein we may find a clue to what has happened in the case of our Negro prophet. We do not have all the facts, but we do know that about the thirty-fifth year of his life, there came a sudden and dramatic change in his concept of himself. He had been a "wicked man, very wild and rough, very fond of frolic." For some time apparently he had been deeply discontented with his way of life. In any case, the solution to his life problem came in his sudden call to preach to Nineveh, and around this new role his life is completely re-built. This change seems to have taken place without any serious disorganization of the personality, but it must have been attended by profound emotion and narrowed attention, and the initial "call" was followed by other "signals," or messages. As he gives up everything in obedience to this call and starts forth on his great adventure, his conversation with the Man Above, the "signals," as he calls them, take on increasing importance. Interpreting them as communications from God, he pays attention to them and cultivates them, and because his personality is truly unified around a great controlling interest which is associated with that which is supreme in his system of loyalties, the signals become more and more insightful. They even approach the level of genius, as in his explanation of what makes a man go crazy.

These considerations may help us to understand why it is that mental hospital workers have come to regard the presence of "voices" as an ominous symptom. They have had abundant opportunity to observe that it is the seriously disturbed and also the more fragmented types who are most likely to hear voices and they lump these all together without recognizing the constructive aspects of the acute schizophrenic disturbance and the significance of the voices which characterize it.

It is important to recognize that the acute disturbance usually begins with a period of preoccupation and sleeplessness during which the patient is intensely concerned about his own role. There is a narrowing of attention which is conducive to creative mental activity but unfavorable to balanced judgment. In any case it will be fertile in new ideas growing out of what is on the patients mind. Pathological features are most in evidence when there are serious maladjustments and the patient is overwhelmed with the sense of personal failure and defeat. His eyes may then be opened to his unsuspected importance. New insights in the form of voices come to him regarding the magnitude of the disaster and his own responsibility therein and the entire personality will be stirred to its bottommost depths and its forces marshalled in an attempt at healing which may either make or break. Frequently the forces of destruction get the upper hand. When that happens the voices are likely to persist, giving expression to the fears and to the disowned tendencies. Not infrequently the patient who hears God talking to him makes a good recovery and we seem justified in looking upon such disturbances as problem-solving experiences which are closely related to the dramatic forms of religious experience.

In those cases in which the outcome is constructive, either of two things may happen. The patient may return to normal, and the strong emotion and with it the voices may disappear, or else he may rebuild his life on the basis of the role envisioned in the mystical experience. In the latter case the voices may continue to function more or less as a creative factor. This is what happened in the case of George Fox, of John Bunyan, of Saul of Tarsus. This is likewise what happened in the case of our Negro prophet. Whether we classify such persons as paranoiac or recognize them as religious geniuses, depends entirely upon the value of their message and of their achievement. The important question, therefore, is not the presence or absence of voices, but what the voices say and how the patient reacts to them.

There were, of course, many difficulties with Mickle's religion. One of these was his reliance upon force. When he "got a mad on," he would fight like a tiger, hurling flower pots and swinging swabs with reckless abandon. He could not be persuaded that the Man Above would have given him two good fists if he were not to use them in fighting. It was this fighting proclivity which kept him in the hospital and blocked my efforts to set him free. Another great difficulty was his lace of reverence. His was a tiny universe, limited to himself and the Man Above. Nevertheless he had found something which enabled him to bear up and keep going in the face of devastating frustrations and disappointments. The source of his courage we may see in his sense of fellowship with the Man Above, in his conviction that the Man Above had a plan for him and that this Man Above was in full control. As to the signals, the medieval mystics had to learn the lesson that some of the ideas which came surging into their minds could hardly come from God. They assumed that they must come from the devil. Perhaps we of today need to learn the converse lesson, that all auditory hallucinations do not necessarily come from the devil but may represent the operations of the creative mind.

IDEAS OF PROPHETIC MISSION

Anton T. Boisen

[This article, which appeared in the Spring, 1961 issue of *The Journal of Pastoral Care*, was a paper read before a meeting of the New England Section of the Association of Mental Hospital Chaplains at Westboro State Hospital, Westboro, Massachusetts on May 4, 1959. One of Boisen's last publications before his death in 1965, it reflects his awareness of the contemporary practice of giving psychological tests to candidates for the ministry. Because of his own experience, Boisen cautions seminaries against being too quick to reject persons with a special sense of mission, because such "craziness" has been seen in many religious leaders since the time of Paul. Reaffirming his thesis that "the divine is nearest when the struggle is keenest," Boisen offers ways in which a special call can be tested in an academic and community context.]

In a recent account of his experience as a psychiatric consultant to the Garrett Biblical Institute,[1] Dr. Carl Christensen states that candidates for the ministry who lay claim to special calls are suspect in his eyes. Such calls he explains in terms of a "weak ego." He regards them as indicative of mental illness so serious that such persons should seldom be encouraged to proceed with the training course. In this opinion Dr. Christensen reflects a common medical view, but it is of special interest as coming from the psychiatric consultant of a Methodist seminary. Some of us can remember the time when dramatic conversion experiences and special calls to the ministry were highly esteemed among our Methodist brethren. This view is of special interest to me as one who must plead guilty to just such a call. Not only

---

1. Carl W. Christensen, "The Role of the Psychiatric Consultant to a Seminary," *Journal of Pastoral Care*, IX (1955), No. 1, 1-7.

that, but my own call was attended later on by a severe psychosis. I have often wondered what would have happened to me if Union Seminary, fifty years ago, had been psychiatrically sophisticated. Fortunately for me it was not. I was not screened out, and the years I spent within its walls I count among the happiest and most profitable of my career. Hence the question which I am raising in this paper: In the light of thirty-five years of service as a mental hospital chaplain, what would I say if I had been called upon fifty years ago to pass judgment upon myself as a candidate for admission to a school for the ministry?

I may begin by agreeing with Dr. Christensen, at least in part. I recognize that many, perhaps most of those who lay claim to a divine call, are or have been mentally sick, and that those of them who have rebuilt their lives upon that claim are likely to be hard to live with.

Where I differ from the prevailing view is in my interpretation of their sickness. I see them in their acute phases as representing a type of disorder which is closely related to religious experience and should be sharply contrasted with the rank and file of mental hospital cases. The latter are commonly persons who make and accept some malignant adaptation to defeat and failure. They escape into alcohol. They indulge in erotic phantasy. They become bitter and suspicious. They maintain self-respect by blaming others or by developing an organic scape-goat. Their's is a chronic character difficulty. Such persons seldom show religious concern and their chances for recovery are poor. Those, on the other hand, in whom calls to the ministry are most likely to be found are persons in whom the better self has been struggling so desperately for possession that they become temporarily disordered. In that struggle they are likely to feel themselves face to face with ultimate Reality. Their eyes may be suddenly opened to their undreamed-of importance, and great responsibility seems laid upon them. In such periods religious concern is much in evidence and the creative forces are exceptionally active. So also are the forces of destruction. They are periods of seething emotion which tend either to make or to break. As such they are analogous to fever or inflammation in the body. They may thus be regarded as manifestations of the power to heal and closely akin to the conversion experience so well known in the history of the Christian Church since the days of Saul of Tarsus. With such experiences they form a continuum in which the degree of freedom from malignant tendencies and the value of the results achieved become the significant variables.

I therefore agree with Dr. Christensen that those who undergo such experiences are sick, sometimes very sick. They may even be sick enough to receive the label, "schizophrenia, catatonic type," and the outlook for recovery may indeed be very grave. But that does not alter my conviction that such experiences have religious significance. May it not be that the divine is nearest when the struggle is keenest and that the call to preach which comes so frequently under such conditions has a significance and a validity which needs to be reckoned with?

Most students of religion will probably agree that vital religious movements begin with experiences which are interpreted as communication from a superhuman, divine source. They arise generally under the stress of crisis situations when the individual feels himself faced with the ultimate issues of life and is forced to do fresh and creative thinking. The religionist speaks of such experiences as "inspirations," or "revelations" and ascribes to them a greater or less degree of authority. But the suggestion that there was anything in common between these "inspirations" and the phenomena of pathology would be likely to fill him with horror.

The psychiatrist has probably the greatest opportunity to become acquainted with such phenomena, but he has seldom seen them in their true significance. He calls them "voices," or "auditory hallucinations." According to his observation they are most in evidence among his acutely disturbed and disorganized patients. He explains them in terms of repressed and dissociated wishes, or impulses, and he assumes that their presence is evidence that the personality is in process of disintegration. There is seldom a psychiatric interview in which the patient is not questioned directly or indirectly as to whether or not he "hears voices," and if he says, "Yes," he is likely to be labeled "schizophrenic" and given a gloomy prognosis.

It has long been my conviction that the phenomena of "voices" furnish the best key to the understanding of those complex disorders which are grouped together under the name of "schizophrenia." I have therefore made it my business to talk with many patients who were said to "hear voices." I have found that, if left to themselves, they will describe the experience in different ways. The commonest term is *voices*, but most patients make a sharp distinction between such *voices* and those they hear with their ears. Here are a few examples:

Patient 1:
"I heard a voice which seemed to be God's voice, and words from the Bible came into my head. I had an idea so big that it just carried me away and I ran out into the street in my underwear. No, I didn't exactly hear anything. It was just like when you sit and think. Something comes to you."

Patient 2:
"I began to get directions. Ideas came to me. The greatness and the allness of it drove me goofy."

Patient 3:
"I began to have a flood of mental pictures as though an album within were unfolding itself. Communications came to me from out of the ether. I felt as though I were being directed by someone higher than myself."

Patient 4:
"I had to give up work and sit around and brood. Then ideas came to me. I didn't have to search for words. It was just like I was commanded to say certain words I had never heard of before."

Patient 5:
"I got the inspiration to write poetry. It just seemed to flow without my trying. There weren't any voices. Ideas just came to me. I got up one morning at five and wrote my first poem."

Patient 6:
"I got inner pushes."

Patient 7:
"I got such funny thoughts. Things just popped into my head."

Patient 8:
"It was shown to me that I should take the name of Jesus."

Patient 9:
"I can't explain it. It was just the way I felt. It came to me as a revelation in a dream."

Patient 10:
"It seemed as though something were controlling me. Words formed themselves within my mind and I found myself talking about the coming Day of Judgment and about the necessity of fleeing from the wrath to come."

I could give other instances, but these will be sufficient to indicate that the psychological process involved in the schizophrenic's *voices* is not confined to mental hospitals and that it is, in fact, identical with the *inspiration,* or *verbal automatism,* so frequently encountered in religious experience and in the creative operations of the human mind. As such it may be explained as an idea, or thought formation, which after a period of incubation in the region of dim awareness leaps suddenly into consciousness, so vividly, sometimes, that it is ascribed to a superhuman source. It is a mechanism which is common to poets, to inventors, to creative scientists and, according to Professor Coe, it is the primitive root of all mystical experience from spiritism to religious ecstasy at its best.[2]

Professor Eliot Dole Hutchinson has described this "dynamism" as among the phenomena of "insight." His words are worth quoting:[3]

The scientist, the artist, the practical thinker—the profession makes little difference—has before him a problem involving some explicit production or decision in life situations. For months, or it may be for years, this problem remains unsolved, this creative intention unfulfilled. Attempts at solution have ended only in bafflement. But sud-

2. George A. Coe: *Psychology of Religion;* University of Chicago Press, 1916, Chap. 16.
3. Eliot Dole Hutchinson, "The Phenomena of Insight in Relation to Religion," *Psychiatry,* V (1942), 499.

denly, usually in a period when the work has been abandoned temporarily, or when attention has been absorbed by irrelevant matters, there comes an unpredicted *insight* into the solution. As if "inspired," or "given," ideas arise which constitute a real integration of previously accumulated experience—an answer, a brilliant hypothesis, a useful 'hunch,' forming, it seems, a short-cut to artistic or scientific advance. Exhilaration marks such moments of insight, a glow or elation goes with them, a feeling of adequacy, finality, accomplishment.

Professor Hutchinson goes on to point out that the distinction between religious and scientific or artistic insight is to be found in the nature of the problem which is at the focus of attention. In the case of the artist, and especially of the scientist, the new insight will pertain to something which can be more or less readily verified by others and fitted into the structure of organized and tested experience. In the case of the mystic, on the other hand, the new insight is likely to be intimately personal and have to do with his own role in life. It is therefore not readily subject to verification and it arouses tremendous affective reactions.

The profounder struggles of the human soul, in which mystical experiences so often appear, begin usually with a period of preoccupation and sleeplessness, during which the sufferer is intensely concerned about his own role. There is a narrowing of attention which is conducive to creative mental activity, but unfavorable to cool and balanced judgment. Perspective is therefore lost and wide limits are set to the validity of inner promptings. It is therefore not to be wondered at that such states of mind are fertile in new ideas growing out of what may be on the patient's mind.

The ideas which present themselves in such disturbances are a bewildering array. They are seemingly meaningless and most of them may actually best be explained as due to the play of imagination when the brakes are off and the mind is stirred at its deeper levels. But some of these ideas are recurrent, common to many cases and probably to all cultures. Such is this idea of prophetic mission, the "call to preach." It appears in case after case along with ideas of death, of world disaster, of rebirth, reincarnation and cosmic identification.[4] Where we find one of these ideas we are likely to find the others also. Nearly all such patients show profound religious concern and a relatively large proportion make good recoveries.

Is there any special meaning in these recurrent ideas? I think there is. Their basis may be found in the structure of human nature and in the significance of the acute schizophrenic disturbance. The idea of world disaster thus represents death or failure of the individual in its more far-reaching ramifications. The idea of rebirth stands for the hope of a new beginning which so often accompanies death or tragic loss. The sense of cosmic identification reminds us that we are social beings, each one important beyond his wildest dreams. These ideas, coming as they usually do in

---

4. A. T. Boisen: *Exploration of the Inner World*, Harper and Brothers, New York, 1952, Chap. 1.

the form of voices or revelations, offer a solution of the problem on the patient's mind, that of his own role, and the predominance of such ideas, when free from malignant trends, such as hostility and fault-finding and transfer of blame and crude eroticism, means usually that the healing forces are at work, that hidden difficulties are being brought to light and that the sufferer is striving earnestly to face what for him is ultimate Reality.

Among these recurring ideas that of the call to the ministry seems especially significant. It may be recognized as a true insight which comes to the disturbed person who is honestly trying to answer the question, "Who am I? What am I in the world for?" That answer is that we exist, each one, not for himself alone but for the sake of humanity and of humanity's God. In the sense of prophetic mission and the willingness to give one's life for the great Cause, lies the basis of all vital religion. In such prophets and their followers we may see religion in its creative stages. They are persons who have taken their religion in earnest. With all their crudities we may see in them provision for the re-creation and perpetuation of religious faith and we may trust the social process and their own critical judgment to sift out the superior from the inferior beliefs.

Any candidate for the ministry who laid claim to a special call would command my serious and sympathetic consideration. If I should see in him features which seemed to me pathological, that mere fact would not rule him out. I should not, however, be easy on him. Here are some suggestions which might guide me in my decision. I offer them for what they may be worth.

1. I would neither accept or reject a candidate on the basis of some purported "call," but upon his ability to measure up to the school's standards.

2. I would condition his admission upon his readiness to accept the guidance of a competent counselor and to abide by the social judgment of some recognized group.

3. My Protestant up-bringing inclines me to believe in a sanctification of the secular which would turn religious zeal into the service of this suffering world and lead to a broader interpretation of the "call to preach."

4. I would want to be sure that the candidate's motives were not contaminated with self-regarding ingredients and that the readiness to be called was balanced by an equal readiness to be denied the call.

5. I would consider his potentialities rather than his past record, his tomorrows rather than his yesterdays, what he is striving to become rather than what he now is.

6. I would take careful account of his reaction to frustration, not hesitating to change a negative decision if he accepted it in really fine spirit.

Part II

A CRITIQUE OF
BOISEN'S LIFE
AND WORK

FATHER OF THE
CLINICAL PASTORAL MOVEMENT

Fred Eastman

[Boisen began corresponding by letter with Fred Eastman (a Union Theological Seminary classmate who also did survey work with him after graduation) very shortly after his first psychotic disturbance in the fall of 1920. This correspondence continued throughout his fifteen months' stay at Westboro State Hospital; the letters were significant reflections upon the meaning of his experience and explorations of his thesis regarding mental illness in light of his reading. Thus, as one of a small number of trusted friends who saw Boisen through this crisis and then helped him to realize his vision, Eastman was well-qualified to assess Boisen's pioneering role in the establishment of clinical pastoral education (even though it appears that, at this writing, Eastman did not have the whole story of what precipitated Boisen's breakdown). This article appeared in the Silver Anniversary issue of *The Journal of Pastoral Care* (Spring, 1951) when Eastman was Professor of Biography and Drama at Chicago Theological Seminary, where Boisen served on the faculty from 1924 to 1942.]

Russell Dicks has asked me to tell briefly the story of the origin of one of the most heartening ventures on the frontiers of religion and something about the man— Anton T. Boisen—who started it. The frontier is the one where pastors are trying to minister to the sick and troubled, not only in private homes but also in hospitals, prisons, infirmaries, and reform schools. I knew the pioneers in this venture when they blazed their first trails.

Forty years ago a pastor received little or no training for such a ministry. If he was a consecrated Christian with a good schooling in Bible theology, church history, and the rudiments of pastoral care for normal persons, it was thought he needed nothing more than what he would learn on his visits in the homes of his parishioners. But with the increasing complexities of modern life—the stress on nerves and hearts due to wars and depressions and the general depersonalizing of individual life—human beings in great numbers have broken under the strain. They have need of ministers specially trained in understanding the psychological factors that wreck mind and nerves and character.

One of the first to realize this need was Richard C. Cabot, a noted physician and author who also taught in Harvard Divinity School. He had introduced the case method into medical education and had a large share in the inauguration of hospital social work. In 1925 Dr. Cabot published an article in the *Survey Graphic* in which he proposed that something radical be done about this need for better prepared pastors. He suggested that every student for the ministry be given a kind of clinical training for his pastoral work similar to the clinical training a medical student receives during his internship.

Behind Dr. Cabot's proposal lay not only his medical experience but his acquaintance with the work already begun by Anton T. Boisen, a middle-aged minister who had come through a serious nervous breakdown that had confined him for several months in a mental hospital. Boisen had a unique cultural background. His ancestral family tree was heavy with college teachers and presidents. He had graduated from Indiana University, Yale Forestry School, and Union Theological Seminary. He had received a Master's Degree from Harvard University. He had been a sociological investigator for the Presbyterian Department of County Church Work, had spent five years in the rural pastorate, and had made extensive surveys for the Interchurch World Movement. The collapse of that movement brought to a sudden end this sociological work and precipitated a nervous breakdown.

Being a genuine scholar, he studied his own case and those of his fellow patients; and upon his release from the hospital he enrolled in Harvard University to study further the problem that had confronted him. There he found a group of men admirably suited to guide his thinking—Richard Cabot, Macfie Campbell, William McDougall and Elwood Worcester—all deeply interested in the vagaries of the mind. With their help he prepared himself for a ministry to the mentally ill and, at the same time, for further researches which would be foundational for the more effective training of future ministers.

To have a great goal is one thing; to realize it is quite another. The difficulties he faced were staggering, chief among them the lack of financial resources. On the other hand, he had no family responsibilities.

The first step came when William A. Bryan, superintendent of Worcester State Hospital with its 2200 mental patients, offered the Protestant chaplaincy of that hospital. Boisen accepted and soon demonstrated that a chaplain giving full time to an intelligent, day-in-and-day-out ministry to mental patients individually and in groups was far more effective than the plan in most hospitals: simply having pastors of local churches come in on Sundays to conduct a worship service.

Next, in June 1925, came the introduction of theological students. There were four that summer, one each from Harvard, Boston, Union, and Chicago. There were four also in 1926. In 1927 there were seven, in 1928 eleven, in 1929 fifteen. These students worked on the wards, at first ten hours a day, then part time only. They wrote letters for patients. They also conducted recreational programs—baseball, play festivals, group singing, checker tournaments. They took walks with patients around the grounds. They made records of their observations. They read up on psychiatry, psychology, and religion. They attended psychiatric staff meetings and had special conferences with Boisen and the medical staff. Through it all they made friends with the patients and with each other.

The financing of this work constituted one of Boisen's major problems. The hospital could pay his modest salary and a limited amount for attendants' wages. It also provided room and board for the students. Other expenses had to be met from outside sources.

Obviously Boisen needed the support of an organization that would help on this financing and enlist the cooperation of theological seminaries, doctors, and ministers. One of his early students, Philip Guiles, who had become so convinced of the value of the training that he had stayed on with it, volunteered to help secure funds. Fortunately, his own father-in-law, having previously manifested his interest, agreed to make a substantial contribution provided those who had been foremost among Boisen's helpers and advisers would form a corporate body to finance and otherwise promote the work. They agreed.

On January 21, 1930, Richard Cabot, Henry Wise Hobson (now Episcopal Bishop of Southern Ohio), Samuel Eliot of the Arlington Street Unitarian Church of Boston, William A. Healy of the Judge Baker Foundation, and Ashely Day Leavitt of the Harvard Congregational Church of Brookline met in the study of Dr. Eliot, adopted a constitution and by-laws, and signed the incorporation papers for The Council for Clinical Training of Theological Students. Philip Guiles was made the executive secretary and Helen Flanders Dunbar, of the 1925 group, the medical director.

An important fact needs stressing at this point. The founders made it clear to every student that he must not think of himself as under training to become a psychoanalyst or a psychiatrist. That would take years of specialized graduate work in the proper institutions. The Council aimed only at bringing the minister-to-be face to face with human misery in various institutions and there, under competent supervision, to accomplish three things:

"1. To open his eyes to the real problems of men and women and to develop in him methods of observation which will make him competent as an instigator of the forces with which religion has to do and of the laws which govern these forces;

"2. To train him in the art of helping people out of trouble and enabling them to find spiritual health;

"3. To bring about a greater degree of mutual understanding among the professional groups which are concerned with the personal problems of men."

Underlying these aims and the whole undertaking were three assumptions which Anton Boisen stated:

"1. That the living human documents are the primary sources for any intelligent attempt to understand human nature;

"2. That the study of human ills in their terminal stages is a most important means of enabling us to grapple with them in their more complex incipient stages.

"3. That service and understanding go hand in hand. Without true understanding it is impossible to render effective service in that which concerns the spiritual life, and only to those who come with the motive of service will the doors open into the sanctuaries of life."

While the founders agreed upon these major objectives, they differed on others. Cabot thought that the main emphasis upon the training of the students should be placed upon developing ability and skill in dealing with persons afflicted with bodily troubles—the ill or dying, the blind or deaf, the otherwise disabled. He, therefore, preferred to see most students trained in general hospitals.

Boisen, on the other hand, was chiefly concerned with mental hospitals where the students would come in contact with types of mental illness in which patients were breaking or had broken under the strain of moral or spiritual crises. In such cases, he held, they could see the problem of sin and salvation in flesh and blood. He had—and still has—the conviction that a minister in his parish is dealing all the time with the problem of mental health and that he meets a large number of persons in the incipient stages of mental trouble; he should therefore be trained to recognize them and help the troubled person in his struggle for mental health.

Both points of view—Dr. Cabot's and Mr. Boisen's—had validity, and the students were given their choice as to which kind of training they preferred. Some of them chose both and put in the extra time required.

The State Hospital at Elgin, Illinois, caring for 3600 mental patients, called Boisen to become its chaplain. He had been offering courses on religion and mental health at the Chicago Theological Seminary for some years. He could continue these and make the Elgin Hospital not only a training center for the Council but a basis for fundamental research, a laboratory where theological students could discover fresh insights which would bear upon their work as students and as ministers. So he accepted the call and served both institutions until his retirement. And in his retirement he continues his researches. Out of them have come his great book, *The Exploration of the Inner World* (1937), his manual for pastors, *Problems in Religion and Life* (Abingdon-Cokesbury Press, 1946), his service book for hospitals, *Hymns of Hope and Courage* (1930). Just now he is completing another book.

Meanwhile the movement for the clinical training of theological students has grown steadily. There are now some thirty training centers where 140 theological students from twenty-five seminaries work for periods ranging from five weeks to twelve months preparing themselves for more adequate service as pastors of churches and as specialized workers in hospitals and reformatories. More than 2,500 students have availed themselves of the opportunities to study in these centers.

Boisen has thus spearheaded the way to a field of far-reaching importance. His constant emphasis upon the firsthand study of persons in difficulty has brought forth published works of real significance by those who have been associated with him. These include such contributions as Flanders Dunbar's *Emotions and Bodily Changes* (Columbia University Press, 1935), *Psychosomatic Diagnosis* (Harper & Bros., 1943), and *Mind and Body* (Random House, 1947); Russell Dicks' *Art of Ministering to the Sick* (Macmillan Co., 1936), which he wrote in collaboration with Dr. Cabot, his *Pastoral Work and Personal Counseling* (Macmillan Co., 1949), and *My Faith Looks Up* (Westminster Press, 1950) and his monthly department in *The Pastor;* Carroll Wise's *Religion in Illness and Health* (Harper & Bros., 1942) and Seward Hiltner's *Religion and Health* (Macmillan Co., 1943) and his newest book, *Pastoral Counseling* (Abington-Cokesbury Press, 1949).

Many of his former students now hold positions of strategic importance. For example, Donald Beatty is in charge of the training of chaplains for the Veterans' Administration; Wayne Hunter is associate director of the Chaplains' Training School at Carlisle Barracks, Pa.; Harold Hildreth is chief psychologist for the Veterans' Administration; Fred Kuether is executive secretary of the Council for Clinical Training; Seward Hiltner for the past twelve years has been Secretary of the Federal Council of Churches' commission on Religion and Mental Health and is now leaving that position to join the Federated Theological Faculty of the University of Chicago.

But the vast majority of the students have remained in the pastorate, as Boisen and the Council intended from the beginning. The grateful testimonies of these pastors cheer the Council leaders when the going gets tough. And they warm the heart of their spiritual godfather who started this great adventure. Here is but one sample:

> "I have found my clinical training increasingly helpful in understanding the reactions of the people to whom I seek to minister. Instead of becoming discouraged, I realize that there is something troubling them, of which they may not be fully aware, but

which forces them to act as they do. Sometimes, because of my training I can help them to discover what it is, and to help correct it. I minister to their needs with a sympathy and understanding that I would not have had without my training."

THE HERITAGE OF ANTON T. BOISEN

Seward Hiltner

[This editorial appeared in *Pastoral Psychology* in November, 1965, following Boisen's death in October of that year. It gives evidence of the profound influence which Boisen had on Seward Hiltner, who was then Professor of Theology and Personality at Princeton Theological Seminary. Hiltner's pioneering work in defining the field of pastoral theology and making it "academically respectable" grew out of his long association with, and appreciation for, Boisen's work. Hiltner was one of Boisen's first students at Elgin State Hospital in the summer of 1932 and then worked closely with Boisen in the development of the Council for Clinical Training.]

These words are being written—a little hastily in view of deadlines—immediately after receipt of the news that Anton T. Boisen died on October first at the Elgin, Illinois, State Hospital. This hospital had been his home since he became its chaplain in 1932. Following his retirement as chaplain more than twenty years ago, he continued to make it his residence. His unusual vigor enabled him to continue most of his activities until two or three years ago. Since then his activities have declined; and, since last spring, he has been bed-ridden with his general health on the decline. He came within a few days of being eighty-nine years old at his death.

A memorial service for Anton Boisen will be conducted during the autumn on a date that has not been set at this moment of writing. Information may be secured from the Chicago Theological Seminary, 5757 University Avenue, Chicago 37, Illinois, on the faculty of which Boisen served for many years until his retirement.

I had the great good fortune to be, first, a student of Boisen, and then a colleague in clinical training and other enterprises. During the years 1950 to 1961, when I was on the Chicago faculty, Boisen was still able to be about and to drive his car; and over those years I saw him rather regularly once every week or two. In those later years he was a preoccupied and absent-minded motor vehicle operator, and we often wondered how he managed to avoid automobile accidents.

Others of his former students and subsequent colleagues were personally closer to Boisen than I was, especially Donald C. Beatty, recently retired as Assistant Director of the Chaplain Service of the Veterans Administration, who was a colleague of Boisen first at the Worcester, Massachusetts, State Hospital, and then at the Elgin (Illinois) State Hospital and at the Chicago Theological Seminary. I think also of the late Wayne L. Hunter, at his untimely death a few years ago serving as director of the U.S. Army Chaplain School; and of the late Francis W. McPeek, at the time of his death directing the City of Chicago's efforts for better interracial relations. Of the many others who were close to Boisen at various stages of his life and work, many are dead except his recent associates at the Elgin State Hospital. He was especially appreciative in these later years of the work and friendship of Chaplain Charles Sullivan, of Philip Bower, the Hospital's chief psychologist, and of Marjorie Peters Bower, a literary agent and teacher by profession, who gave Boisen much help on his own later writings.

In view of the magnitude of his contribution, and of the steadily growing recognition in many circles of Boisen's originality and depth, no brief article, even by a grateful student and colleague, could possibly do justice to his memory nor appropriately evaluate our collective heritage from him and his work. These remarks are, therefore, tentative, preliminary, and even halting. For, as I know from having tried on several occasions when Boisen examined something I had written about him, he was never wholly pleased with what anyone said about him and his contribution although always appreciative of every honest effort.

His heritage to us seems to fall into six categories. Although these are interrelated, it seems not possible to subsume any of them under the others without risking the loss of something unique and original. I shall deal briefly with each area in turn.

Theology through Living Human Documents

Boisen's own religious and theological views were an amalgam of four kinds of elements and influences. First, there was his early religious heritage in the late nineteenth century, a critically-oriented and intellectually alert view of Christian faith, but with strong elements of moralism and pietism included. Second, there was the influence of the theological liberalism of the early twentieth century, with Albert Schweitzer and George A. Coe having an especially strong impact upon Boisen (Coe was his teacher). Third, there was Boisen's own serious mental illness, erupting in his mid-forties, the significance of which he came to interpret religiously and theologically, and which clarified for him the critical mysticism that was also part of his view. And finally, there was the conviction, growing out of his personal experience and his studies of psychiatry and the social sciences, that theology was method as well as content, and that the study of "living human documents" was an indispensable aspect of that method.

This unusual diversity of theological views and interests has thrown many otherwise able theologians off the track in trying to place him theologically. The old-fashioned liberals were baffled by the pietistic element; the neo-liberals were puzzled by both the pietism and the mysticism; mystics could not understand the devotion to empirical and scientific inquiry; scientists could not quite reconcile themselves to the mysticism and the mental illness; and so on. Boisen did not always make it easy for the theological critic. He was not concerned to bring forth a "constructive theology" except at the one point of including methodologically the study of "living human documents." It is precisely this last, I believe, that will constitute his theological heritage.

Mental Illness as Attempted Re-Adaptation

From the time of his own severe mental illness in 1920, Boisen contended that some forms of mental illness are to be understood as akin to some forms of religious experience. As he wrote on the first page of his classic work, *The Exploration of the Inner World*:

> . . . both may arise out of a common situation—that of inner conflict and disharmony, accompanied by a keen awareness of ultimate loyalties and unattained possibilities. Religious experience as well as mental disorder may involve severe emotional upheaval, and mental disorder as well as religious experience may represent the operation of the healing forces of nature.

Boisen then added the more general conclusion, which was strange and generally unacceptable at the time he wrote it, but has subsequently been widely accepted in psychiatric circles: "The conclusion follows that certain types of mental disorder and certain types of religious experience are alike attempts at reorganization." The outcome was not necessarily guaranteed by the process. Boisen felt that, when the outcome was constructive, the notion of religious experience was appropriate. Whether or not one associates religion always with the "good guys," the basic thesis remains: that, to use language other than Boisen's, at least much mental illness is an attempt, whether successful or not, at readaptation, and is not, therefore, to be understood merely as weakness, as giving in, or as regression. In recent years, this very thesis has been most ably documented and asserted by Karl Menninger and associates in *The Vital Balance*. For the long-run understanding, treatment, and prevention of mental illness, and despite its apparent simplicity, it may well prove to be the twentieth century's most significant insight on this subject.

Clinical Pastoral Education

Although Boisen always gave great credit to William S. Keller, M.D., the Cincinnati physician who in 1923 took the first group of theological students into health and welfare institutions and agencies as a part of their theological education, preceding Boisen's own experiment at the Worcester, Massachusetts, State Hospital by two years, history will undoubtedly continue to credit Boisen as the founder of clinical pastoral education. With no denigration of Keller's vision and energy, we must nonetheless note that his original "theory" of the training was simply to get sheltered students in contact with life including its sufferings. From the start, Boisen had a theory about clinical experience as an aspect of the study of theology. Not the study of theology on one side and of human beings on the other, but the study of theology by way of the study of "living human documents." It is this fundamental theory, and not alone the actual contact with people in need, that lies at the center of the clinical education movement.

Boisen had four students at Worcester in 1925, during their summer vacation period. He followed this with a larger group in 1926, and before long had some students and graduates who remained for longer periods, including, in the nineteen twenties, such persons as Donald C. Beatty, A. Philip Guiles, Carroll A. Wise, and Alexander Dodd. Before 1930 two or three "missionary outpost" centers had been established; and in 1930 the Council for the Clinical Training of Theological Students was organized. Thus clinical pastoral education (as it later came to be called) became a movement including constitution and by-laws, officers, minutes, and some very strong and not entirely compatible personalities. In the movement's development, although Boisen was pleased to see the basic idea spread, there were aspects that Boisen feared might subvert his basic intent, i.e., the study of theology via living human documents. He also preferred decentralized organization. In various degrees he gradually disassociated himself from the formal bodies. For a time a group of younger leaders of the movement, while properly deferential to Boisen as the founder and grandfather, nevertheless paid little attention to his ideas and convictions. That adolescent period is, I think, past. The wisdom of Boisen's basic original conception is now clearer within the movement than it has ever been since the earliest days. On this front too, Boisen's influence is likely to be more permanent than, during a few dark and lonely days of the past, he believed.

The Psychology of Religion

The psychological study of religious phenomena was a largely-American discipline that received its greatest impetus from G. Stanley Hall and the group of psychologists he brought to Clark University in the late nineteenth century. Inspired both by Darwin and the more flamboyant Herbert Spencer, they proposed to try to understand religious life as developmental and evolutionary phenomena. Some of them made and reported on remarkable first-hand observations, especially Starbuck. Others shrewdly analyzed, even dissected, various forms of religious life, sometimes to the point of debunking, as by Leuba. But the towering figure was William James and, above all, *The Varieties of Religious Experience*. The cases James used were collected mostly by others; but he showed, for the first time, what a case method could accomplish in examining religion psychologically. Unorthodox as James was theologically, and even philosophically, he was so compelling and so winsome, and indeed had such deep respect for religion in actual people, that even those who were repelled by his theoretical views were charmed and lured by his explorations.

George A. Coe, Boisen's teacher, was very much in this tradition, and in addition believed that the resources of education and of sociology should be combined with those of psychology in the empirical investigation of religious phenomena. Gradually even some theologians began to study "the psychology of religion," none of the original investigators having been a theologian. By the 1920's this field of study had settled down to a definition according to its "classic" period of Hall, Starbuck, James, and others. The study was being "tamed" for positive theological use, but its roots and perspectives were not being radically re-examined.

Boisen was, in my judgment, the first person to make such a radical re-examination. Like James, he studied extreme instances (mentally ill persons). Like Starbuck, he studied first-hand. But unlike any one before him, he studied his cases in depth, and by that time with the aid of Freud's insights, and he refused to make a radical distinction from the beginning between "health" and "illness," or between "religious experience" and "psychopathology." To what extent Boisen actually followed, in his specific studies, all the canons of scientific investigation, is a matter for historical determination. But the fact is that he is the first investigator who made any serious pretensions of this kind at all, whose major investigation included detailed study of nearly two hundred cases, who combined some kind of "counting" with individual examination in depth, and who had a clear operational hypothesis that was being tested.

Boisen was pleased that, during these last few years, as shown for instance in the work of the Society for the Scientific Study of Religion, there had been a great revival of interest in the psychological investigation of religious matters. For some of the most constructive aspects of this, he is undoubtedly the progenitor.

Pastoral Psychology

If "pastoral psychology" is, as we suggested in the first (February 1950) issue of this journal, a discipline that brings together insights from psychological studies and perspectives, examines them for their relevance and applicability to the work of the clergyman, and sets them within the proper theological point of view, then it must be said that Boisen's contribution is more evident to some aspects of this discipline than to others. Specifically, his contribution lies in the first and third items of the definition, and rather little in the second.

That there are insights from psychological studies and perspectives, indeed, that ministers and theologians have an opportunity and obligation to increase those insights from their own studies, is the major Boisen contribution. But it is also a Boisen emphasis that the insights ought, finally, to be seen in their theological significance. Boisen respected, and believed in, the second term of the definition: practical application of the insights in the work of the minister, his counseling and pastoral care, his preaching, his administration, his evangelism, and his social outreach into the community. His own work, however, contained only "thought-starters" about such applications. Indeed, he had some fear that a "pastoral psychology" movement might become so practically and pragmatically oriented that it might forget to do studies in depth or to link those studies with theological perspectives and insights.

As a discipline, it seems to me now as always that we should take seriously both Boisen's contributions and his warning. Wherever psychological insights might come from, he believed we should attend to them. If Freud had truth, let us not insist that Freud be baptized before we appropriate the truth and acknowledge it as such. Let there be no misguided insistence on some kind of "tribal" road to truth. But at the same time, there is the Boisen insistence on a theological perspective. As he often said, the theological student in the mental hospital may indeed learn from what psychiatry and its allies have found out; but he is there primarily to study "the problem of sin and salvation" through "living human documents."

It is possible, as Boisen feared, that "pastoral psychology" could become so practical, even flat, in its interests and inquiries that all depth, whether seen psychologically or theologically, could be "practiced" out of it. Generally speaking, I believe Boisen approved our own *Pastoral Psychology*. He recognized it as a proper obligation on our part to be as relevantly and practically helpful as we could to busy ministers who face all kinds of practical problems. I believe he felt that we had avoided becoming merely "practicalistic." At any rate, his warning is as important as his contributions.

Personal

There is, finally, a personal heritage from Boisen. As with all complex persons, this is most difficult of all to write about. Case-fashion, a couple of incidents might demonstrate the dilemma better than could abstract discourse.

I recall, on the one side, the large great superintendent of the Worcester State Hospital, William A. Bryan, M.D., who had had the courage to hire Boisen, an ex-mental patient, as chaplain, and who became a strong promoter of the clinical pastoral education movement. On one occasion Bryan, who was given to expansive moods and half-humorous hyperbole, was expressing his conviction that the clinical education movement for the clergy had great strength and potentiality. "It certainly must have real strength," he said, "to get where it has with all the unattractive personalities who started it." He meant Boisen. As administrator, he had to say no on many occasions to Boisen's single-minded devotion to getting the budget he needed for his work. He meant that, where conviction was concerned, Boisen could set friendship aside.

On the other side, I recall the first occasion when Boisen was in our home after my marriage. My wife had been hearing, ever since we met, of this great teacher of mine, with all the stories and folklore that had grown up about him. She would have been prepared, I think, if he had been gruff, or had sat all evening in a corner, or had given a lecture over the dessert. When he left she said spontaneously, "He is charming." And he was! He listened to her better than I have been able to do before or since!

When *The Exploration of the Inner World* was first published in 1936, most of us noticed the deeply moving dedication of the work to "A.L.B." A very few of Boisen's closest friends knew that A.L.B. was Alice Batchelder, a remarkable woman whom Boisen wanted to marry, to whom he was devoted for nearly all his adult life, but who, while being his friend for many years, refused any closer association. In 1936 most of us thought that A.L.B. must be some Boisen somewhere, perhaps a mother or so. Only with the preparation of his autobiography, *Out of the Depths*, published in 1960, did most of us learn about Alice Batchelder and what he had meant in Boisen's life. If Alice had ever said yes, it was Boisen's judgment, expressed in the final chapter of his autobiography, that he might have become "a passably successful minister" and would thereby have failed to found the "clinical-training movement." He may have been right. Perhaps, on this point, Boisen and Kierkegaard were brothers under unrequited love. At least in this regard, clinical pastoral education and existentialism may have something in common.

No reader of *Out of the Depths* can avoid admiration for the fidelity and single-mindedness of Boisen's romantic attachment. In his final chapter he wrote:

In all that I have done she has been an indispensable factor, and hers the harder and more difficult role. She had to suffer for my mistakes and slowness of mind. She was a rarely gifted woman who, on my account, never found her highest usefulness. . . . Her compassion on me, her wisdom, her courage, and her unswerving fidelity have made possible the measure of success achieved.

But the "Epilogue" in which these words appear is not entitled, as one might expect, "Alice." It is called "The Guiding Hand." The last word is of God's providence, "I would surely be a man of little faith if I did not recognize in this story the guiding hand of an Intelligence beyond our own."

Today it is not the theological fashion to see God as "Intelligence." He is love, grace, patience, acceptance, and much else, but hardly ever, these days, intelligent. Perhaps it is a nineteenth century voice that, in this regard, speaks through Boisen. Perhaps there is more here of Locksley Hall or the flower in the crannied wall than there is of Heidegger, or Barth, or Tillich. But it may indeed be, as it seems to have been in Sigmund Freud, that in Boisen the deep streak of romance, while publicly invisible, affected all that his hand and mind were turned to. Perhaps its very simplicity and single-mindedness can help to counteract some of the sophisticated but uncritical and double-minded romantic trends that threaten our own culture.

ANTON T. BOISEN AND
THE PSYCHOLOGY OF RELIGION

Paul W. Pruyser

[In this article from the December, 1967 issue of *The Journal of Pastoral Care*, psychologist Paul Pruyser, then Director of the Department of Education at the Menninger Foundation, provided a balanced assessment of Boisen's contribution to the psychology of religion. He affirmed Boisen's unique approach as one who not only communicated with others via his own experience but also viewed mental illness from a pastoral perspective. However, he also found it curious that Boisen, as a follower of James' phenomenological method, would be so dogmatic about "valid" types of religious experience and would also rigidly reject the experience of patients with organic disorders.]

In 1953 a senior citizen of seventy-seven years reflected as follows on the psychology of religion. "In so far as there has been a decline in the psychology of religion," he said, "it is only a recession which may be explained by the growing pains of psychology in general." He added that "Actually, William James as a pioneer in this field is only now beginning to come into his own."[1] Little did he know that today some of us would like to say the same thing about the man who wrote these lines, Anton Theophilus Boisen, who was born ninety years ago, whose major book was published thirty years ago, and who died one year ago, in Elgin State Hospital.

If he was at all like other children, he must have given thought to the meanings of his given names. *Anton* means priceless or praiseworthy; *Theophilus* means lover

---

1. A. T. Boisen, "The Present Status of William James' Psychology of Religion," *Journal of Pastoral Care*, 7 (1953), 155-158.

or friend of God. We do not know whether these names have consciously influenced his ego-ideal, but in retrospect there can hardly be any doubt that he richly deserved both names. And lest I be accused of gnostic propensities in attributing deep personal values to names of people whose importance is felt to lie in their public works rather than in their inner world, I hasten to add that in Boisen's case such a distinction is highly artificial. Except for his first few scientific articles on forestry and the sociology of rural churches, almost all his writings are intensely autobiographical,[2] and his vocational choice was profoundly personal. "Boisen's case" was indeed his case, with all the paraphernalia of case history, case record and case study. From his first psychological paper on "Religious Experience and Mental Disorder" in 1923 to his last book, *Out of the Depths*, in 1960 he worked on his own case, and the cases of many others with whom he shared personal tragedy. In the Foreword to this last book, he stated with great frankness that he had written it "because now for forty years I have been making it my business to inquire into the problems here involved, and my own case is the one I know best." And I remember vividly his deep chagrin in telling me, seven years ago when he was working on this book, that the superintendents of the mental hospitals where he had been a patient had persistently rebuffed him when he had earnestly asked that his own case record be released to him for study.

While such an enduring preoccupation with his own psychiatric syndrome, its causes and implications, was not without obsessional features, it had also another side. I find it most pointedly and movingly stated in his Foreword to another book, *Hymns of Hope and Courage*, which he designed "to deepen the aspiration for a better life, to strengthen faith in the love and healing power of God and to foster attitudes of hope and courage." He was an inveterate meliorist, an ardent perfectionist and a studied optimist whose own hope and courage were not only to guide him, but which he felt should be exemplary and inspiring to others as well. We should not lightly gloss over the existence and the title of that remarkable hymnbook. Amidst the dreariness of such designations as *The Methodist Hymnal, The Lutheran Hymnal* or *The Hymnal, Published by Authority of the General Assembly of the Presbyterian Church in the United States of America*, and the effervescence of *Triumphant Serving Songs*, it stands as a compassionate, sober and tender work, in content and title. Its title is a statement of a life's goal, an ethos.

These introductory statements about Boisen may already have confirmed suspicions in some self-respecting scholars that the man cannot be counted as an important figure in the psychology of religion. With so much personal involvement and so much self-confessed psychopathology, with such ministerial aspirations and such an urge to share his frustrated love-life publicly, indeed with such a *religious*

2. A complete bibliographic list of his writings can be found in A. T. Boisen: *Out of the Depths*, Harper and Brothers, New York, 1960.

orientation, can a man be trusted as a scientist? Can he be seen as a psychologist at all?

Were his observations objective? Are they repeatable? Did he have hypotheses, or were his leading thoughts only pet peeves or exalted hunches? Did he use respectable methods of sampling, data gathering and statistical analysis? Was he not, after all, a somewhat odd or sick clergyman? Would it not be safer to describe him as a crusader, an enthusiastic organizer or a dedicated and intelligent missionary? Or, for dignity's sake, as a religionist?

History will answer these questions and give its verdict. But it is incumbent upon us, in the present decade, to make our own assessment, in full awareness of the fact that psychology has its own short periods or cycles in which it perpetually defines and redefines the canons of science.

One can sometimes place a man in the meandering stream of a discipline by asking what intellectual company he kept. A simple count of the frequency of references in his books and papers shows that Boisen referred most often to Delacroix, Coe, Dewey and Freud. The next order of freqtency comprises Hocking, Mead and Starbuck; after them we find Hoch, Jung, Rank and Sullivan. Then comes James, Leuba, Pratt and Schweitzer. Most of these men were his contemporaries, some of them were his teachers. The majority were psychiatrists and psychologists, in about equal numbers. An influential philosopher and educator, a noted social theorist and several philosophers of religion and culture complete the ranks of his intellectual friends. It is thus clear that Boisen, well before 1936, took a vigorous interest in psychiatry, particularly in the thoughts of the leading dynamic psychiatrists whose interests were theoretical as well as therapeutic and who comprised the so-called second psychiatric revolution. His loyalty to the new psychiatry is all the more remarkable because, in his practical life and work, he also kept the company of Cabot, an internist and pathologist who was vigorously opposed to the psychogenic viewpoint, and the biochemical research men at Worcester, whose painstaking work he found simply unremunerative. Yet these were some of the friends who aided him in his professional career as a mental hospital chaplain pioneering in clinical pastoral training.

In other words, he was discriminating in his intellectual and professional loyalties. He was also discriminating in what he would accept or reject from each man who stimulated him. There is not a little deceptiveness in a mere counting of Boisen's references, because some of them were used monotonously for only one or two phrases which he repeated over and over, while others were cited polemically, with protests. He used from Freud mainly the general tenor of the libido theory, and the notion of intrapsychic conflict, and had only a vague appreciation for the dynamic unconscious, while always protesting against the structural viewpoint and the idea of energy economics. He never quite understood the psychoanalytic concepts of the superego and ego-ideal, despite his references to both Freud and Alexander. He had a lifelong apprehension of psychoanalytic treatment goals and techniques, always fearing that somehow the stringency of superego demands would simply be "reduced," which he saw as a dangerous tinkering with ethics. He sided with Jung against an alleged sexual reductionism in classical psychoanalytic thought, and admired Jung for advocating a teleologic interpretation of mental life.

What really might have attracted him to psychoanalytic thought most of all, despite his misgivings, are three ideological premises. The first one is Freud's determination to bring sexual behavior under scientific-psychological scrutiny, and his successful attempt in relating sexual dynamics to the symptomatology of mental disorders. Boisen obviously admired the candor of it and felt identified with it to the point of frequently alluding to sexual tensions and practices as a prelude to his own psychic breakdown. The second psychoanalytic premise which Boisen affirmed is the developmental and dynamic continuity between child and adult, healthy and sick, normal and deranged, which implied for him also an interdependence of psychology and psychiatry, and a fusion between normal and abnormal psychology. However, he labored under a strange inconsistency regarding the continuity principle in his concepts of psychopathology, which I shall describe later.

But what comes most alive in his writings is the third premise of psychoanalytic thought and the thrust of all dynamic psychiatry. It is that the mentally ill are not hopelessly fixed in their miserable condition. They can be helped when one realizes that in their symptoms they are already trying to help themselves. Mental illness is somehow beyond good or evil; it is "the price we pay for being human," as Boisen often said. Life has its crises, and mental illness is an accentuated crisis experience. It is purposive, adaptive, understandable and thus potentially curable rather than an odd and unchangeable freak of nature. It can be approached with "hope and courage" and one can rise up "out of the depths."

Boisen, however, had had the unique opportunity of keeping the company of a third group of people: the patients and staff members inside the old custodial mental hospital. This world, in which he was in every sense a participant observer, had made a tremendous impression upon him. Ill as he was, he made good observations, not only about the dreariness of the patients' lives and the rigors of discipline, but about the patients' symptoms, their regressions and progressions. He also noted the conceptual framework of the staff and their attitudes and jargon. He soon found himself steeped in psychiatric nomenclature, nosology and taxonomy, and he discovered more quickly than some psychiatrists of his time the bankruptcy of the Kraepelinian system, particularly in regard to the problem of schizophrenia. He lived in an era in which the older term *dementia praecox* was abolished in favor of *schizophrenia*, as defined by Bleuler, which in turn became redefined as *schizophrenic reaction* through the holistic and adaptive viewpoints of Meyer. And then came

Sullivan, who put even greater emphasis than Meyer on the factors of social role and social learning in producing these profoundly disordered conditions, and who recognized the quality of panic in the incipient stages of the patients' adversity.

This rang a bell with Boisen. He had experienced panic himself, he had seen it in other patients, and he had noticed how most of the hospital staff persistently tended to ignore it. Now all the pieces fell into place; if he, Boisen, had indeed suffered from the condition called catatonic schizophrenia in which Sullivan had noted the dynamic importance of panic, and if he, Boisen, had rather quickly recovered from the early attacks thus confirming the relatively good prognosis in those conditions, then there must be some striking differences between catatonic and other schizophrenic reactions. Perhaps it was primarily a condition of unbearable bewilderment, an intense crisis in which a person becomes either remade or broken. For Boisen and for a few other patients he saw, this terrible thing *dementia praecox* had plainly been an acute attempt at reorganization; he would later observe that for others it could be described as a way of life.

And here Boisen got into an odd difficulty, mostly because he did not go far enough in pursuing his keen insight. In the appendix to *The Exploration of the Inner World*,[3] which defines technical terms and concepts, he discusses the concept of "psychosis" with the following wry remark: "The descriptive groupings are not without significance but we would probably be better off if our psychiatric staffs would stop giving so much attention to a meaningless classification and more attention to the attempt to understand the real meaning of the experiences with which they are dealing." Despite that very appropriate judgment, and his efforts at introducing plain English into clinical work, he yet became himself at times a captive of the traditional jargon and its awkward conceptual baggage. What he did with both amounts to a description of his methodology.

From the outset he divided the mentally ill into two rigorously distinct groups: the organic and the functional disorders. The first group has "some disease of the brain which has so affected their social adjustments that they are said to have a 'psychosis.'"[4] He simply did not deal further with these patients in his writings, as if to imply that their minds are entirely epiphenomenal to their bodies. I think this is a strangely dogmatic position for a man who knew and admired Helen Flanders Dunbar, and who had read Alexander. In this respect he denied a continuity which he had earlier affirmed. An alternative reason for his silence on the organic disorders may have been political: he did not want to tread on the domain of physicians.

His next step was to define the functional disorders as attempts to solve conflicts. Two distinctions were then brought in, of different order, but both

---

3. A. T. Boisen: *The Exploration of the Inner World*; Willett, Clark and Company, 1936, reprinted by Harper and Brothers, 1952. Torchbook No. 87, p. 314.

4. *Ibid.*, p. 313.

involving sharp dichotomies. One regards outcome, and holds that positive conflict solution entails religious insight or a quickening of religious sentiments; whereas a negative solution entails a worse or more chronic mental disorder. The other distinction regards differential diagnosis and holds that catatonic conditions tend to be more productive of fruitful resolutions than the other types of schizophrenia: the simple, paranoid or hebephrenic varieties.

In his research hypothesis and documentary work the two dichotomies became both fused and overplayed. The catatonic state, if resolved, became equated with a mystical experience and also with a relatively good prognosis. It could thus be religious as well as productive from a social or hygienic standpoint. If it was not resolved it would tend to give way to the other clinical forms of schizophrenia, which Boisen had meanwhile come to see as three styles of life: (1) drifting off into a world of fantasy and easy pleasure-taking; (2) face-saving attempts through delusion formation, either by blaming others or by fictitiously enlarged self-importance; (3) gross demoralization with almost complete disintegration of feelings and social propriety.

And now we are ready to see what I regard as two dominant features of Boisen's thoughts. One is his lasting preoccupation, if not obsession, with the typology of schizophrenia and his lifelong unhappy search for outside validation of his own diagnosis, which should have been, in that same awkward terminology which he decried so much, neither more nor less than "schizophrenic reaction, catatonic type, acute, with trend toward improvement." The other one is that he took, willy-nilly and rather haphazardly, mystical experience and conversion to be paradigmatic of religion, despite his having noted elsewhere that religious conversion experiences appear to be time-bound and culture-bound and were significantly in decline among church populations during his own life span.[5]

In regard to the second feature, Boisen's work ties in with a venerable tradition within the psychology of religion. Many students of that discipline before him and several of his contemporaries had taken the acute mystical episode of a conversion experience as their model for the study of religion. It is still a preferred ideal-type among students of religion, and several investigators of today have turned, knowingly or unwittingly, Boisen's acute illness process into experimental procedure by ingesting or administering various psychotomimetic or psychedelic drugs. Starbuck, Coe, de Sanctis and others had made the study of conversions the focal topic for the psychology of religion. James, always more broad-minded and rich than others, had also given it much attention. And even Erikson, in his study of Luther, gives considerable prominence to what Boisen once called "acute upheavals or mutation periods."[6]

---

5. *Ibid.*, p. 234
6. *Ibid.*, p. 209

Boisen's uniqueness in this tradition lies, of course, first of all in his great ability to communicate his own experience of such a "mutation" to others, and to capitalize in his studies on introspection and retrospection. But, because he had chosen to become a clergyman, he was not content with merely describing what he saw in the members of his odd flock. He added the pastoral perspective, which means that he tried to understand the process of his patients' cataclysmic episodes with a view to helping them come to a good ending. Recording and reporting is not the same thing as aiding and guiding. And albeit that much of his pastoral work was organizational and administrative, since he shunned face to face pastoral conversations, he relied on the pastoral zeal of his students to make up for his aloofness.

Another aspect of his uniqueness is that he used first-hand observations instead of the second-hand reports which most his his predecessors relied on. Not that he scorned such reports; as a matter of fact, he collected dozens of them and rewrote them for teaching purposes. But he had started with direct observations, precisely because he was a patient, a co-patient and a chaplain, and he could thus look at literary resources with the trained eye of an insider and of a clinician. His uniqueness as a student of conversions and mystical episodes comes through with great force to anyone who has had the opportunity to read the unpublished case studies he collected about his hospital patients.[7] These show that he was not easily fooled by one-shot impressions. He studied his cases longitudinally and was fully aware of the ups and downs, the contradictions and inconsistencies, the morbid fantasies or the healthy reality testing which one patient would manifest over a stretch of time. In other words, he did study the process and the outcome of his patient's "dark night of the soul" and usually acted as a representative of physical and social reality in confronting the patients during pastoral contacts and in worship.

These case studies also show that Boisen had an eye for the pedestrian aspects of religion. He made frequent notes about such things as church attendance, prayer, depth of belief, Bible knowledge or unfaithfulness to religious habits in his patients. But the curious trend in his published writings is that he seemed to have succumbed to the need to single out a "valid" type of religious experience[8] from a presumably invalid or less valid type, although he avoided using the latter terms. I note and state this with some vigor, because it seems to me that some such distinction has plagued the psychology of religion for a long time and I find it a serious defect. It imposes a normative or valuational view of religion which, however useful this may be from an ethical, pastoral or theological viewpoint, unnecessarily shrinks

---

7. Mimeographed case studies, collected at Worcester State Hospital and Elgin State Hospital; unpublished, deposited in the A. T. Boisen Archives at Chicago Theological Seminary and at The Menninger Foundation, Topeka, Kansas.

8. See the chart "Personality Changes and Upheavals Arising out of the Sense of Personal Failure" in *The Exploration of the Inner World*, p. 148.

the scope of the field. For the psychology of religion, *all* religious phenomena are bona fide. Whether they be primitive or highly developed, vague or articulate, feelingful or conceptualized, childish or mature, healthy or sick, ritualistic or mystical, constructive or destructive, divine or satanic, highly individualistic or broadly corporate and collective, deistic, theistic or non-theistic, they are all worth describing and studying from a psychological point of view.

The attempt to select and focus on a so-called "valid" religious experience is like organizing a zoology for nice or beautiful animals only, an economy that only knows profit and abundance, or a physiology which only knows health and life everlasting. Indeed, it is as embarrassing and artificial as systematizing a theology that has no room for the problem of evil. Boisen, like other students of the psychology of religion, had practically nothing to say about the ordinary, nonspectacular psychological processes of religion in everyday life. Except that he tended to see any religious concern as *ipso facto* positive, he seems to have recognized nothing religious in those other disturbed people whose subsequent course of illness he described as drifting and the concealment reactions. But why exclude these? Are religious aspects of these behaviors simply irrelevant? Cannot they be placed in religious perspective also? Whether one uses the old terminology of the seven deadly sins, the moral descriptions of vices, or the modern existential categories, such behaviors as sloth, alienation, callousness, pride or bitterness are authentic data for a religious perspective and therefore also data for the psychology of religion.[9]

The situation from which these questions arise merits a closer look, which Boisen's work in particular enables us to take. This work straddles two disciplines: psychology and sociology. It uses two methods: the clinical case study and the sociological survey. The latter is particularly illustrated in his two books *Problems in Religion and Life* (1946) and *Religion in Crisis and Custom* (1945). Before he became a mental hospital chaplain he was a rural minister who conducted many surveys on his own and for his church boards, thereby undoubtedly relying on the statistical training he had received in his previous work in forestry. And Boisen had a penchant for a simultaneous vision of the trees as well as the forest. As a clinical worker and while focusing on the individual, he placed great emphasis on social roles and social learning, in which he felt buttressed by the works of George H. Mead and Sullivan. His aim for the "better life" of the individual always meant a socially more responsible life, and ethics was for him a corporate phenomenon.

---

9. See *The Exploration of the Inner World*, p. 212, where religion is said to be "not characteristic of the concealment and drifting reactions." Apparently Boisen found it difficult to admit that religion can be an escape from reality. He had to hold fast to the value-laden conviction that it "is to be regarded as an attempt to fall and grapple with the realities of life, not to escape from them" (pp. 212-213).

What attracted him to the study of George Fox was precisely this double vision of the lonely, sick, weird and unique George who was also the socially responsible Fox, symbol of a group and founder of the Society of Friends. It is not difficult to find passages in Boisen's work in which he appears to champion the individual,[10] whose heroic attempts at problem-solving he portrays in intimate detail. But he also regarded these personal problems as social in origin and consequences, as he demonstrated so keenly in his analysis of Jesus, Paul and other leaders. All things that really matter in life, the things which produce the tragic crises of existence, are in the last analysis the problems of the relation between the individual and his groups. Throughout his writings, I find his key words to be: *isolation, loyalty, conscience,* and *acute mental illness.*

There are many reasons why Boisen would have thought that way. His own psychopathology had convinced him of some basic wrongness in his social adaptation. As a patient he had seen the power of social interaction in the hospital, which induced utterly estranged individuals to assume definite roles toward the staff and each other. Yet he felt that patients who blamed their tragedy on their social conditions (in the paranoid reaction) were somehow escaping from the obligation toward selfhood which demands that one assume personal responsibilities for the subsequent course of one's life. I think that this double-aspect vision was also engendered by his pastoral vocation: in organized religion everything has an individual and a group aspect. In a sense all religion is organized religion and Boisen's own pastoral services were predominantly organizational.[11] The founders of new sects who break away from old traditions are as much corporately influenced as bishops of the establishment, yet both can have unique private experiences which Kierkegaard would have admitted as "individual" to the highest degree.

What happened in Boisen's actual writings, however, has occurred frequently in the psychology of religion: The more private aspects of religious behavior, accentuated in the ultra-private mystical experience, became paradigmatic for psychology, while the more public aspects of a person's religious behavior, whether truly group behavior or not, were relegated to sociology. The totality of religious behavior became thus polarized between two disciplines, each with its own conceptual framework, methodology, and "primary aspects." The result was, with Boisen and others, that a large amount of religious behavior fell between the benches and was neglected by both disciplines. The "valid" personal experience was seen in mystical states and conversions; the "valid" corporate experience was seen in group conformity, church attendance or social mobility within the stratification of churches.

---

10. For instance, pp. 186-187 of *The Exploration of the Inner World.*

11. See "Journal of the Wabaunsee County Improvement Association, A. T. Boisen, Secretary" in The Menninger Foundation Museum Collections, and the Chicago Theological Seminary Collections on patient activities groups at Worcester and Elgin State Hospitals.

I am not mentioning this polarization as an example of professional strife between two disciples, which I do not think it is at all. Rather, I see it as an instance of loss of relevant data and observations. I also note in this connection the striking absence in Boisen's writings of references to the work of Otto, Heiler, Mueller-Freienfels and Jones, all of whom have had much to say about the ordinary, not-so-intense, day-by-day phenomena of religion manifest in ritual, prayer habits, observances, prevailing ideation, language peculiarities, etc. While emphasis on peak experiences may put the ordinary religious phenomena in bold relief, it can also falsify our understanding of religious realities when we forget the rarity of such experiences or overlook how contrived they may be, and then walk the slippery path of assuming that religion and intensity of experience are synonymous. For the psychology of religion, all religious phenomena are "valid"; it is sheer mysticism to consider only the mystical experience as a particularly valid or significant religious experience.

Much of Boisen's work is polarized in the manner just indicated; on the one hand the "crisis experience," on the other hand "religion of custom." He wrote that "religious experience is rooted in the social nature of man and arises spontaneously under the pressure of crisis situations."[12] He also observed that "the end of all religion is not states of feeling but the transformation of the personality."[13] This definition seems to me to imply an undue polarization, and a faulty dichotomy, which would deprive the psychology of religion of fascinating observations. On the other hand, he contributed much to the psychology of religion by his minute clinical studies of just those "transformations of the personality" which he found in himself, in mental patients and in the biographies of great religious leaders. But even on this point one must note an oddity: in assembling a list for a minister's library (in *Problems of Religion and Life*) he put his own *Exploration of the Inner World* under the rubric of Psychopathology, together with psychiatric textbooks, while he placed under the rubric of Pyschology of Religion only the works of his teacher Coe, with those of James and Starbuck. All this, after having emphasized elsewhere that the study of the mentally ill is indispensable to the understanding of the laws of the spiritual life.[14]

It behooves us at this point to return to Boisen's reflections about William James. After having noted James' interest in the psychopathological, he added that many of his younger associates did not share this interest and were critical of it and his tenderness for the mystical. "Thus it came to pass that the original impetus was diverted into religious education on the one hand and into the philosophy of religion on the other, while still others offered explanations in terms of the social

---

12. *Religion in Crisis and Custom*, p. 3.
13. *The Exploration of the Inner World*, p. 212.
14. *Ibid.*, p. 132.

factors."[15] Boisen's own work did much to integrate these various strands. He turned James' brilliant vignettes into full-fledged case studies, with a longitudinal perspective. He focused the preoccupation of the workers in religious education on the question of outcome: How does education promote that desired transformation of personality? He gave the philosophy of religion an ethical turn by insisting that religion lead to the "better life." He dealt with the social factors in many ways: by inducing individuals to assume social responsibility and by asking the group to consider the lot of the mentally ill.

I have indicated elsewhere that Boisen created also a drastic change in the psychology of religion by his organizational work.[16] Largely due to his pioneering efforts and his work as a teacher and supervisor we can see the laboratory of our discipline shift from the university campus, with students as the typical subjects, to the hospital, with patients as the sources of observation. He helped also bring about a change from detached observation, with pencil-and-paper tests inserted between examiner and subject, to participant observation in therapeutic face-to-face encounters. Despite his criticism of the clinical pastoral training movement, which was his own brain-child,[17] his work as an organizer enriched the cadre of psychologists of religion with men of different professional qualifications: hospital chaplains, pastoral counselors and other clinically trained clergymen who have added important works to the body of the psychology of religion. He furthered the integration of psychiatry and psychology by his observations and concepts.

Lastly, he has given us all some homework to do. Just a few years before he said farewell to the world he gave us a book that solved the riddle of his strangely frustrated love life, and that seemed at first blush little more than a sentimental or nostalgic review of his checkered and colorful career. More perspicacious readers may have seen it as an *oratio pro domo* or *apologia pro vita sua*. I myself have entertained all these thoughts, but in immersing myself for the sake of this study once more in the writings of Anton Boisen I have come to a different conclusion. He has bequeathed us finally, with his own case study, a truly longitudinal study of his crises and quiet periods, of the stages in his development from childhood to senescence, of all the significant people in his life, of his learning, his studies, his work and his faith. Of all the case studies he assembled, this is the richest and the most purposive: to show the dynamics of faith at work in the nooks and crannies of one lonely man's productive existence. I am sure he would want us to see his *Out of the Depths* as one of the varieties of religious experience, and as an exploration of the

---

15. *V. supra*, p. 156.

16. P. W. Pruyser, "Some Trends in the Psychology of Religion," *Journal of Religion*, 40 (1960), 113-129.

17. In his paper on James.

inner world, and to study it until we can understand the roots of his hope and courage.

Anton T. Boisen and Theology Through Living Human Documents*

Henri J. M. Nouwen

[This article from the September, 1968 issue of *Pastoral Psychology* is written partly from the perspective of a personal interview which Nouwen had with Boisen in August, 1964. Nouwen's quotation of his letter from Paul Pruyser provides a rare picture of Boisen the man; this is also seen in Nouwen's recounting of Boisen's supervisory style. Nouwen's discussion of the various influences on Boisen's life and work provides insightful commentary on Boisen's relationship with Alice Batchelder and the symbolic importance of Boisen's favorite flower, the trailing arbutus.]

Introduction

The discussion of the case method in theological education as developed by Anton Boisen is intimately related to the discussion of Boisen's own case. Therefore the life history of Boisen himself offers the best framework to explore and evaluate the nature and implications of his case method. In this essay, "theology through living human documents" is the core phrase and Boisen himself the core document for understanding and illustration.

*Grateful acknowledgement is due to Dwight Norwood for his invaluable help in the preparation of this article.

The Man

Many people who knew Boisen socially or worked with him professionally voice ambivalent feelings when they talk about him. He can hardly be called an attractive personality. His preoccupied mind and distant personality made it difficult to feel close to him. His own students, who had strong positive feelings toward him, were often strongly irritated by his rigidity of thought and sometimes even experienced him as a hindrance in their own professional development. They avoided certain topics in his presence and did not always pay attention to his many monologues, which tended to be repetitious and dull.

Paul Pruyser, reflecting on his meeting with Boisen, expresses these mixed feelings in a very articulate way when he writes:

> The most outstanding feature of the man at the time I knew him was his flat affect. There is an awful psychiatric expression referring to chronic schizophrenic patients, who have made a good hospital adjustment, or sometimes have been discharged and live on the outside. That expression is 'burned out case.' This phrase came into my mind time and time again when I talked with him and saw him act. He was not without humor and delicacy, but something had happened to his feelings and their expression.
>
> He was very courteous to me, interested in some of my thoughts, and whether he himself talked about pleasant or unpleasant things in his life, it was all stated in the same monotonous, deliberately affect-free language. He also had a faraway look. Yet I must say that there was something very likeable about the man, perhaps in part because of the tragic stamp on his life. I have always felt that his *Out of the Depths*, which came out a year or so later, conveys in its tone and selection of topics exactly the impression I gained in my personal confrontation with him. The language is beautiful, the topics are moving, but there is something utterly pathetic about it all. There is something of homesickness in it, ennobled by a sense of suffering. In his presence I felt respect towards him for there was an odd distance between himself and the rest of the world. I also felt at that time that he knew he was dying, slowly and with several ups and downs physically, so that one felt somehow in the presence of a man preparing himself for death. This certainly augmented my sense of reverence towards him, but again, made it difficult for me to invest myself in him.[1]

This ambivalent feeling about Boisen reveals the most dramatic reality of his life, the fact that he was not only the chaplain of a mental hospital, but also a patient. The mental hospital was home. In 1920 he entered it following an acute psychotic breakdown. In 1924 he returned to the mental hospital as chaplain and after his retirement in 1942 he continued to make it his residence until his death in 1965. Chaplain and patient, two identities which seem so different to be together in one man, formed exactly the basis of Boisen's peculiar personality. He never would

---

1. Paul W. Pruyser: Letter to H. J. M. Nouwen.

have become the productive chaplain if he had not been so familiar with the world of the patient through his own experience. Even after the recovery from his major breakdown, he remained a patient and suffered from the basic conflicts involved all through his life. But his own suffering offered him the core insights of the clinical training movement and became the source of inspiration for new views in the psychology of religion.

Until his mid-forties, Boisen had not found his vocation in life. He tried languages, forestry, entered the ministry, wrote field surveys, but never would have become the father of the clinical training movement if he had not had to go through "the wilderness of the lost." Boisen's psychotic breakdown when he was 44 years old was the culmination of a long struggle and frustration, but also the beginning of a new life. In a way, we can say that Boisen's own psychosis became the center of his identity. He became the "man who went through the wilderness of the lost" and he made his own illness the focus of his life. There he found his true vocation: the ministry to the mentally ill. There he found the main concepts of his most important publication, *The Exploration of the Inner World*, and there he found the basis of his idea for the clinical training of theological students.

Boisen's work is intensely autobiographic. Not only his last book, *Out of the Depths*, but all his publication in the field of the psychology of religion as well as his activities in pastoral training have a strong autobiographical imprint. His own case forms the core inspiration. Just as the mental hygiene movement is intimately connected with the personal psychotic experience of Clifford Beers, described in his autobiography, *A Mind That Found Itself* (1908), so many new trends in the education for the Christian ministry are unthinkable without the story of the man who walked through "a little known country," A. T. Boisen.

This fact gives a prophetic quality to Boisen's life and work. His deep personal involvement in practically everything he wrote and the intense personal commitment to the things he did, made it possible to accomplish a remarkable task and to give this task an original flavor. But the same fact also explains many of the problems which mark Boisen's life. It was the reason for the repetitiousness of many of his writings, of the stubbornness of his ideas about clinical training and of the conflicts which arose when his students want to branch out in directions different from his own. And finally it caused the estrangement of Boisen from his own movement, with the development of which he could not keep pace, and led him into a very isolated position, often forgotten or misunderstood by his own students.

The Central Experience

"To be plunged as a patient into a hospital for the insane may be a tragedy or it may be an opportunity. For me it has been an opportunity."[2] No better words can express the importance of Boisen's illness, as these opening lines of his main work. Boisen's hospitalization not only was an opportunity for him, but even the focal experience of his life. So far as he was concerned, without it "there would have been no new light upon the interrelatedness of mental disorder and religious experience. Neither would there have been any clinical training movement."[3] We cannot stress enough the centrality of this experience to Boisen's life and the great ideas and events which came out of it. Everything he did and said since that moment was "in the light of my own experience."

In the chapter of his autobiography, "A Little Known Country," Boisen gives an extensive description of his experience. In October 1920, when Boisen was 44 years old, he found himself still uncertain as to his task and vocation in life. Although, after many other attempts to find his true profession, he had received the call to the ministry and finished his studies at Union Theological Seminary in 1911, the years following had been "years of wandering." Between 1911 and 1920 he worked for the Board of Home Missions of the Presbyterian Church, was involved in two surveys about the church and school conditions in rural Missouri and Tennessee, and was a rather unsuccessful pastor in Wabaunsee, Kansas, and North Anson, Maine. Moreover he spent two years in Europe with the American Army during the first world war and was director of the North Dakota rural survey.

But he was aware of the fact that he still had not found his real vocation: "I still felt that my chief contribution ought to lie somehow or other in the religious experience through which I had passed, rather than in the gathering of facts on social and religious conditions."[4] He looked for a pastorate but was forced to wait. During this time of instability and uncertainty, he felt the need to "reformulate his message" and to "reexamine his religious experience." This rambling life in the ministry had not yet given him the sense of meaningfulness he was looking for and at this point of temporary standstill he started to work on a statement of religious experience and belief.

This task, in which he became deeply involved, led him to the mental hospital, first as a seriously disturbed patient, later as a prophetic chaplain who had found his true vocation in life. On October 9, Boisen was brought to the Boston Psychopathic Hospital and seven days later transferred to Westboro State Hospital,

---

2. *The Exploration of the Inner World.* (Will be quoted as E. I. W.) 1936, Willett Clark and Company; 1952, Harper & Brothers; 1962, Harper Torchbooks, p. I.

3. *Out of the Depths.* (Will be quoted as O. D.) 1960, Harper & Brothers. p. 209.

4. O. D., p. 75.

where he stayed as a patient for fifteen months. Most remarkable about the fifteen months in the hospital is Boisen's constant attempt to understand as fully as possible his own condition and to draw conclusions which are applicable far beyond his own case. As soon as he "snapped out" of his acute disturbance two weeks after his transfer to Westboro, "as one awakes from a bad dream,"[5] he became interested in finding out just what had happened to him. His active, well-trained mind went to work as soon as possible and all through his hospitalization, notwithstanding serious relapses, he kept asking the question: What does this mean and especially what does this mean for me, a minister who is trained in the psychology of religion? With an amazing sharpness Boisen studied and analyzed his own case and was able to find, time and again, enough distance to formulate the main insights which would guide his future life. Although Boisen himself never denied that he suffered from a mental illness (he denied an organic cause), his whole life became a witness to the idea that his experience was part of a plan which made him find his vocation.

From the very beginning Boisen's future plans show two sides: ministry to the mentally ill, and the study of the interrelationship between religion and certain forms of insanity. These two aspects of his future task have been closely related to each other and have remained connected all through his life. Many of Boisen's disappointments were related to the growing separation between the research and the ministerial aspects of theological education, which for Boisen cannot be isolated from each other without serious harm. They are the essential ingredients of his new approach to theology: the study of "living human documents."

Boisen himself is the first human document that asks for careful study. When Boisen formulates his main hypothesis: "That certain types of mental disorder and certain types of religious experience are alike attempts at reorganization,"[6] he asks: Why is the outcome for some people a happy solution and for others an unhappy one? Boisen's answer is: the difference depends partly on what went on before the onset of the illness. What was the input? What was brought to the disturbed period? This gives us the key for the discussion of Boisen's own case. The outcome of Boisen's experience: a new vocation, a new hypothesis, and a new approach to theology, can never be fully understood without a careful analysis of the input. After all, Boisen was 44 years old when he entered the hospital and he brought to the disturbed period a great wealth of experiences, thoughts, and feelings which were grounded in his illness and molded into a life project.

---

5. E. I. W., p. 4.
6. E. I. W., p. Viii.

The Input

The input was 44 years of intensive living. Many things happened during those years and many small and great events gave shape to the personality who entered Westboro Mental Hospital in October 1920, but it seems that we will stay most in line with Boisen's own view of his life if we describe these years in terms of the many personal relationships that played a role in his formation.

In his autobiography Boisen mentions 176 different names, only a few of which are those of authors. Most of them were people whom he had known personally and whom he felt had some influence on his development. This is even more meaningful when we consider the fact that Boisen considered the primary evil in mental illness to be in the realm of social relationships. "We have found," he writes, "one characteristic common to the group as a whole: they are isolated from their fellows through a social judgment which either consciously or subconsciously they accept and pronounce upon themselves."[7] Overlooking his own life, Boisen was deeply convinced that his successes and failures were dependent on the sense of fellowship he could obtain. But the word "dependent" seems to indicate not only how much Boisen was influenced by his surrounding family, friends, teachers and students, but also how much he needed them.

Family background

Anton T. Boisen was born in 1876 in Bloomington, Indiana. The milieu in which he grew up was that of the University of Indiana. There his father, Hermann B. Boisen, who emigrated from Germany to the U.S. in 1869, was a teacher of modern languages. There his mother was one of the first women to enroll. There his grandfather, Theophilus Wylie, was professor in "pure mathematics," and there his grandfather's cousin, Andrew Wylie, was the first president.

Besides being academic, Boisen's milieu was clerical to some extent. In the ancestry of both his parents we find clergymen. His mother's paternal grandfather was a pastor in Philadelphia. The second generation counted three pastors in the family and Boisen's grandfather nearly yielded to the family idea that he should be a minister. Boisen's academic and religious interests were both to remain very strong during his life and their fruitful interaction was to provide the particular creativity of his later years.

Parents

Although Boisen dedicates some of the most beautiful passages of his autobiography to his mother, he allows us only a rather distant look at her. In contrast with

---

7. E. I. W., p. 28.

the articulate and critical picture that he gives of his father, it seems that he does not want to blur any of the sweet memories of his mother.

Boisen's father, or better, the memory of his father, had the greatest influence on his life. His figure never completely left him and at all the turning points of Boisen's life the image of his father is there to guide him and co-determine the road he will take. Anton was only seven years old when his father died but:

> . . . his memory, reinforced by my mother's picture of him and that of others who knew him, has remained a potent force in my life, one which for me has been associated with my idea of God.[8]

It seems at times that Boisen's life is the long story of his admiration for his father and all those whom he related to him in his romantic fantasies, but a fearful admiration of a weak and fragile boy who always looked up to an unreachable ideal. This ideal image of the perfect and severe father entered into many of his relationships with his teachers, his muse, and finally with God. It played a role in his decisions to study languages, to go into forestry and to enter the ministry. This relationship with his father is a major thread through his life; it is the source of a great strength, but also of great suffering.

Anton carried with him the heritage of these two parents, a gentle, retiring mother, who relied more on persuasion than compulsion, and an energetic, domineering father, whose sense of order and discipline was stronger than his patience and tolerance. The sensitivity of his mother and sense of systematic inquiry of his father both became a part of him. And in many ways we can see his life as a struggle to reconcile and integrate these often polar characteristics.

Significant Others

To three men Boisen feels himself very much indebted during his years of formation. Dr. William Lowe Bryan, his "second" father during the college years, Dr. Raphael Zon, his supervisor as a forester, and Dr. George Coe, his professor at Union Theological Seminary. Their intellectual influence on Boisen was intimately related to their confidential relationship with him. They were all at one point confessors to whom he felt free to talk about his most disturbing feelings.

William Lowe Bryan: *the road to psychology.* Although the name of Dr. Bryan only occurs in Boisen's story about his early life, this man had a definitive influence on his thinking and even laid the foundation for Boisen's major thesis on the relationship between mental illness and religious experience. Dr. Bryan was a professor of philosophy and psychology at Indiana University in Bloomington and later the president of this university. After the death of Boisen's father, Dr. Bryan became the great male-figure of Boisen's youth, his second father, his ethical model. It was

---

8. O. D., p. 27.

against the background of a personal friendship loaded with memories of Boisen's father that Bryan's intellectual influence becomes more obvious. Dr. Bryan set Boisen on the road to psychology. After his graduation Boisen stayed at Indiana University and started to study the *Principles of Psychology* by W. James, under Bryan's guidance. Bryan seems to be greatly responsible for Boisen's growing interest in psychology, which remained his central interest during his life. And although the man who taught him most in this field was George Coe, Bryan laid the foundations.

After an experience of personal disorder and confusion on Easter morning 1899, closely related to his sexual tension, Boisen found in Dr. Bryan a man to discuss his problems. But Dr. Bryan did more than counseling. He also offered Boisen a theory which later helped him understand the crisis of his early years. Through application of Bryan's "law of the plateaus in learning," Boisen saw the Easter event as an upward turn which brought him to a higher level of functioning. Through sharing the experience with others, the obstacles were removed, the difficulty was socialized and the plateau of what for him was "abiding and universal," was reached. Bryan's law, which was a law of learning in telegraphy, seems to be the core of Boisen's later ideas about the relationship between mental disorder and religious experience. So it is not so strange that Boisen dedicated his last and most personal book to Dr. William Bryan, "my teacher and friend."

Raphael Zon: *the road to clinical observation.* In a discussion in August 1964, fourteen months before his death, Boisen said that the man who influenced most of his scientific thinking was Raphael Zon, a Forest Service scientist. This might be surprising, since in his autobiography Boisen only mentions him incidentally, in three places, and from this one would hardly suspect the importance of this man for Boisen's life. But on closer scrutiny, this is less unlikely than it seems.

As Bryan was the main figure during the time in which Boisen studied languages, so Zon was the significant man during his second career: forestry. In Raphael Zon he found a scientist who not only strengthened Boisen's "clinical sensitivity" but trained him in the systematic survey. Scientific investigation was one of Boisen's primary concerns: first in the forest, later in the parish, and finally in "living human documents." The educational background of Boisen in which the emphasis was always on the empirical approach, using surveys, questionnaires and statistical analysis, has determined a great deal of his own contribution to the field of the psychology of religion. His own hospitalization certainly was the deciding factor in the choice of his subject for investigation, but the empirical approach to this subject had its roots long before the climax of his illness. In this approach he was trained during his forestry career under the inspiring leadership of Raphael Zon.

George Albert Coe: *the road to the psychology of religion.* George Albert Coe is undoubtedly the main figure during Boisen's years at Union Theological Seminary. It was Boisen's call to the ministry in 1905 which brought him there three years later. After his training in Yale Forestry School and three years of practice in the Forest Service, he started his study at Union in 1908. Boisen was then thirty years old.

One would expect a growing interest in theology during these years, but Boisen's interest was already set in another direction: psychology in general and the psychology of religion in particular. Boisen's lack of interest in theology requires more explanation. Different factors play a role here. First, the preoccupation with his own case, which narrowed his interest considerably. "My own problems were not theological, they had to do with my inner adjustments."[9] His own problems were and remained central, and his main criterion in the selection of his subjects was their relevance for the clarification of his own problems. Certainly, a second factor was that he entered the seminary with a mind already set in the direction of the psychology of religion under the influence of Bryan and his own readings. A third more distant but not less important factor was the liberal theological milieu in which Boisen grew up. The attitude of Boisen's parents as well as his education at the University of Indiana had kept him free from the fundamentalist religion of his days.

Although during the first year at Union Boisen was disappointed with the lack of interest in the psychology of religion, in the second year things looked better for him, when George A. Coe joined the faculty as professor of religious education and psychology. Boisen developed a relationship with Coe which gave him great support. While in Westboro Hospital in 1921, he received many supporting letters from his former teacher and even considered going back to Union to study his problem with the help of Coe.

While Boisen's work is considered by many to be the most important contribution to the field of the psychology of religion since James' *Varieties*, this never could have been true without the inspiring guidance of George A. Coe. He made Boisen familiar with the research in the field, he was an example of the systematic researcher of the problem of conversion, he encouraged Boisen in his later research notwithstanding the differences in opinion and, finally, he was one of those "significant others" on whose friendship Boisen could depend even in times of crisis and despair.

---

9. O. D., p. 39.

The Great Motive

The great motivating factor in Boisen's life was Alice Batchelder. She was also the hidden motive, about whom only very few people knew. Whereas all during the years after his hospitalization he felt free to claim and proclaim his own life experiences as the source of his ideas, it is only very late in his life that he revealed the great motive which formed the undercurrent of his whole life: the love relationship with Alice Batchelder.

Out of the Depths is primarily a book about Boisen's great love. Alice is the center of this book and all the events and persons are grouped around her. She was for him what Beatrice was for Dante and Regina Olsen for Kierkegaard—the woman he never married but who remained the source of his inspiration all through his life. Boisen himself is aware of the fact that the unreachable love was not only the main cause of his suffering but also the main motive for his creative work. It is not so easy to evaluate the nature of the relationship of Boisen with Alice. Are we dealing with an adolescent love affair, a therapeutic relationship, or a guiding hand to God?

Whereas *Out of the Depths* gives us a very good picture of Anton Boisen himself, which is often painfully critical and direct, it is very difficult to get a concrete idea of Alice Batchelder. From the first to the last page she remains a mysterious, vague figure who never becomes a real person with strengths and weaknesses, with a history and a future. She seems without parents, brothers and sisters; only good, full of wisdom, courage and unswerving fidelity—more a guardian angel than a woman of this world, more an unreachable star than an attractive girl friend. For a "distant" reader, the relationship between Anton and Alice is very unhealthy, immature, and unrealistic. Alice never really loved Anton and told him this. So it was in the beginning and so it would ever be. And if it were not for the many other reasons which make it worthwhile to pay attention to the person of Boisen, *Out of the Depths* would be the sad story of a boy who fell in love with a girl when he was 26 years old, in an adolescent fashion, and remained fixated on this level for the rest of his life.

If we study more closely the way in which Boisen describes Alice, it reminds us often of the way in which a patient would describe his psychotherapist. She is for him like the curing authority, to which the patient becomes more and more attached, but who is also able to make him slowly aware of his attachment so that he is able to develop a more independent, mature relationship. She keeps warning him when he "goes too far" and violates the contract, which is phrased in sentences such as: "She gave her consent (to me to write) only insofar as it might be of help to me."[10] But why did Alice allow him this begging and humiliating behavior, know-

---

10. O. D., p. 153.

ing that a marriage never would be possible for her? It seems as if she sensed that Boisen needed her, if not as a wife, then certainly as a point around which to center his life. And if we see how most of Boisen's creativity is related to this distant, Tantalus-like relationship with Alice, perhaps she realized that Boisen could do more with her distance than with her closeness. She wrote him on official stationery,[11] and was very cool to him when he visited her unannounced.

In many ways we are tempted to think that Boisen transferred his deep feelings toward his father to Alice. It is remarkable how his memory of his father, as well as his love for Alice were associated with his idea of God. His call to the ministry is not only described by him as related to the memory of his father.[12] He also says:

> Through her I was led into the Christian ministry, and with the passing of the years my love for her has become more and more interwoven with my religious faith.[13]

But Boisen also speaks about Alice as a guiding hand to God. How was Boisen's love for Alice interwoven with his religious faith? In Boisen's view, psychotherapy has a religious connotation because it aims at the removal of the "the sense of alienation by restoring the sufferer to the internalized fellowship of the best."[14] Alice's role in Boisen's life was exactly to remove this sense of alienation and to bring about the internalization of the highest values of his social relationship. After a long relationship of painful dependency Boisen seems able to stop using Alice for his own needs. Notwithstanding different setbacks, their relationship develops into a friendship which shows more strength and maturity on Boisen's side; and finally, when Alice dies in December, 1935, Boisen seems to be able to stand on his own feet and give more than take. Boisen's adventure in theological education, his many publications, and his inspiring relationship with many people are expressions of the new strength which came forth out of his purifying relationship with Alice. Where on the one hand, Boisen considers his life a failure because he was not able to prove his manhood and the devotion he professed to her whom he wanted as a wife, he also considers her the sensitive guide on his way to a fuller and more productive life.

Boisen's health, vocation, and God—all three became intimately related to the development of what at first glance looks like only an immature adolescent love affair. During his life Boisen came to a growing awareness of the religious dimensions of his "love affair." Already, shortly after his breakdown in 1920, he writes to Dr. Elwood Worcester: "The love affair was not rooted in friendly association but rather in inner struggle and in what might be called quite accurately the need of

---

11. O. D., p. 206.
12. O. D., p. 56.
13. O. D., p. 209.
14. O. D., p. 197.

salvation."[15] It seems as if Boisen is saying that he used Alice for his savior, but that his real salvation only came about by the internalization of the values which were deeply hidden in this relationship and which had to be distilled and purified by a long and painful process.

The Symbolic Flower

Boisen entered the mental hospital in 1920, certainly not "cum tabula rasa," with a blank mind. The input was rich and complex. His milieu and parents, his teachers and friends, and especially Alice Batchelder, all played a part in the information of this sensitive man. But we would miss the full meaning of all these influences if we did not pay special attention to the particular symbol which binds all these together and expresses them in a very powerful way: the arbutus. Many of the beautiful passages which he dedicates to the arbutus suggest that more is involved than just an idiosyncratic hobby. This rare flower is a rich symbol which evokes associations with his mother, who told him about it, with the memory of his father, who discovered it, with the University of Indiana, which adopted it as the college flower, with Dr. William Bryan, who shared Boisen's love for it. The arbutus is in the background of his decision to study forestry, of his call to the ministry, and of his failure with Alice.

Boisen pictures himself as always looking for the mysterious arbutus. This quest for the arbutus is like the quest for the Grail, which disappeared because its keepers were morally impure. It meant for him the search for his deceased father, for the great love, for the liberation from his sense of isolation, for the state of purity, and finally, for God. This flower becomes the symbol of all Boisen's great ideals. The ideals have different names: forestry, ministry, Alice, recovery, the guiding hand of God, the fellowship of the best, the ultimate loyalty. But Boisen is aware of the fact that only after much experimentation in life will he find the conditions under which his flower will come to its fullest bloom and show its hidden splendor.

Discovering the conditions under which arbutus grew is perhaps one of the best ways of symbolizing Boisen's life work: discovering the ways in which man can overcome the sense of alienation. This was the motive for the exploration of his inner world, this brought him through the wilderness of the lost, which he calls "a little known country" and this led him to the final discovery that "love between man and woman can be truly happy only when each is a free and autonomous being, dependent not upon the other, but upon God."[16] In this struggle for purification and detachment, Boisen compares himself with Dante. Boisen saw in Alice his Beatrice. Like Beatrice she became a spirit of heaven who guided him through the turmoil of his inner world and liberated him from the terrible isolation. His

---

15. O. D., p. 139.
16. O. D., p. 208.

whole life was a long struggle to overcome this alienation, and of this struggle the continuous search for the trailing arbutus became the binding symbol.

The Outcome

Cabot and the Case-Method

In January 1922, Boisen left Westboro, entered Andover Theological Seminary and started to take courses at Harvard. Here he met Richard C. Cabot, M.D. The meeting of Cabot and Boisen not only made the start of the clinical training movement possible, but also offered him the model for theology through living documents. Boisen always gave full credit to Cabot as the one who first proposed the idea of a clinical year for theological students.

By Boisen and others, Cabot is considered the "inventor" of the case-method in medical education. The use of cases in teaching was not new. The case approach is as old as medicine, and cases were presented and discussed in general and mental hospitals long before Cabot. But Cabot's case-method was of a very special nature as becomes clear from his famous clinicopathological conferences in the Massachusetts General Hospital, where he exposed to students the painful diagnostic struggles of the medical doctor. When Anton Boisen was asked which of Cabot's publications had been the most important for him, he did not mention any of Cabot's writings on social ethics, but Cabot's most known medical work: *Differential Diagnosis*, the two volumes which resulted from the clinicopathological conferences.

This study gave Boisen the clue for much of his late work: the case-method. The theological student may have read about and discussed the problems of his fellowmen during many years in the seminary, but when confronted with a concrete situation he still feels helpless and confused. Cabot found this to be true with physicians and writes, "experience shows that a man may possess a considerable acquaintance with physical diagnosis and with the course of disease, and yet be quite helpless in the presence of a suffering person, simply because he cannot apply his knowledge to this case. He can observe, he can remember, but he cannot constructively think and experiment."[17] The emphasis of Cabot, and accordingly of Boisen, is diagnosis. The main question was: "How can I go beyond the apparent symptoms and find the actual cause?"

It is exactly this emphasis which we find in all of Boisen's later writing. After two years of study under Cabot, Boisen wrote this article "The Challenge to our Seminaries," in which he defends the case-approach in theology. The focus is clear: *a case-approach*. Boisen calls this "investigation of living human documents." His

---

17. Richard C. Cabot. *Differential Diagnosis*. Philadelphia. London 1911, p. 19.

vocabulary explains this: Careful scrutiny, seeking patiently and systematically and reverently, discovery, laying foundations, and building. It is primarily a scientific task. Cabot says to the physicians: ". . . we must reason and inquire our way back into the deeper process and more obscure causes. . ."[18] Like an echo Boisen says to the theologian: "(We must) discover the motive forces and the machinery which are involved and . . . formulate the laws which govern them."[19] In both formulations the focus is on Differential Diagnosis.

It is this aspect of the clinical case-method that became one of the most important ingredients in the clinical training of theological students as Boisen saw it. The case-method for Boisen was primarily a way to help the student to think in alternatives, alternatives in terms of possible causes and possible explanations, and to help him to make the leap from the possible cause to the probable, and from the probable to the real. Later when the clinical training movement developed, this diagnostic principle remained central, yet broadened in its application. Other alternatives in terms of possible ways of relating to the supervisor, students and patients, and even possible ways of self-understanding were considered.

Boisen's main concern was with the empirical approach to the study of religious experience and he was deeply convinced that "a program of instruction should be based upon a program of research."[20] And although Boisen differed basically from Cabot in his view of the nature of mental illness, the methods he used to study it came from the years he worked as a student of Cabot.

Boisen and the Case-Method

On July 1, 1924, Boisen was appointed as chaplain in Worcester State Hospital. It was there that he established the invaluable precedent of the minister as fully recognized member of the therapeutic team and claimed a due place for the minister in the circle of the helping professions. If today in all the hospitals and institutions where clinical training programs are established the chaplain-supervisor and his students form an integral part of the hospital staff, can participate in the staff discussions, and are free to consult all the files, they are indebted in large part to the strong conviction of Boisen that the chaplain is also a scientist, specialized in the religious aspect of the case under consideration.

The presentation and discussion of cases was for Boisen the essential aspect of his training of theological students. Boisen himself was not a great group leader. He was often too preoccupied by his own view on the matter to freely acknowledge and utilize the ideas which came up in the discussion. He often left the group members

---

18. Richard C. Cabot. *Ibid.*, p. 18.

19. A. T. Boisen. "The Challenge to Our Seminaries." *Christian Work*, Jan. 23, 1926. New York.

20. A. Boisen. *Types of Mental Illness, a Beginning Course* (Mimeographed Edition), p. 1.

free for twenty or thirty minutes without interruption. If he felt that the discussion had moved too far away from his own ideas, he delivered a short monologue and let it go on from there. And when the discussion was over, Boisen gave a straight lecture, with a few questions. He hardly paid attention to what the students had said. It is clear that Boisen was much more a teacher than a supervisor and that, although he had discovered the power of the case-study from Cabot, he was not able to make it the sort of interchange between students and teacher which Cabot had in mind.

Boisen's case-method in the training of theological students was not only based on his general conviction that living human documents are a source for an empirical theology, but also on the specific typology by which he related certain types of mental illness with certain types of religious experience. This explains Boisen's selectivity. In fact, Boisen's primary concern all through his life remained with cases like his own, and it became more and more clear that his students wanted to extend their interest far beyond the particular preoccupation of Boisen himself.

But what they learned was a new approach in which the point of departure was no longer an idea, concept or theory, but a living person, with a unique history and a unique problem. The Case of Benjamin Mickle, for instance, raised questions for theological students, which up till then had looked rather academic and abstract, such as the meaning of vocation, problems of sin and salvation, the role of voices and signals. Through the case-study these questions were made highly "practical" and concrete. Boisen says: "I wanted them (the students) to learn to read human documents as well as books, particularly those revealing documents which are opened up at the inner day of judgment."[21] For him the problems of sin and salvation, of hell and heaven, of atonement and judgment, could not only be understood by the careful study of the many theological treatises written during history, but also through firsthand observation of those who were struggling with the basic realities of their lives. It is therefore that Boisen feels that we must not begin with tradition or systems formulated in books, "but with open-minded exploration of living human experience in order from that to build up a body of generalizations."[22]

For Boisen, no better place for this theological endeavor could be found than the mental hospital, because there the pain was most visible, the issues most bare, the struggle most obvious and man most approachable for understanding and help. In daily life the student of religion probably would have many more difficulties in discovering the real ultimate problems of human existence. But if he had seen these struggles in their dramatic vehemence, in their nakedness of panic and despair, he might be more sensitive to the little hints and small signs by which a man indicates his need for help and salvation. It is precisely for this reason that Boisen considers

21. E. I. W., p. 10.
22. E. I. W., p. 251.

the mental hospital the ideal laboratory for the theologian. And although he recognized the value of clinical training in general hospitals as this developed later, he always stressed the unique opportunity which the mental hospital offers.

Growth Through Conflicts

In the summer of 1925 Boisen welcomed his first four students to Worcester Mental Hospital. In 1928 there were sixteen summer students, and a second training center was established. The pioneer spirit of the first students was so contagious and the movement had such a rapid growth, that in 1931 three new centers were opened. In 1945 the movement counted fourteen training centers, and when Boisen died in 1965 the Clinical Training Movement had become a known and powerful factor in theological education with numerous centers all over the country related to mental hospitals, general hospitals, prisons, boys' industrial schools, centers for the retarded, and other institutions. As far as the stormy development goes, Boisen gives all the honor to his students, and even feels that he often was more an obstacle than a stimulus to its growth.

Boisen was not altogether wrong in his modesty. He indeed became a background figure. The Council for Clinical Training, which in many ways was his own creation, did not support his research proposal and even at one point felt that he was incompetent as a supervisor. At Elgin State Hospital, where he was chaplain from 1931 and where he began, as he says a "vigorous" training program, he was succeeded by a man who worked along lines quite contradictory to his own ideas. Many "rebels" came to Boisen often deeply frustrated with their own theological school education. Using the opportunity to try new ways, they often moved in a direction quite different than Boisen had envisioned. Although in his later years he spoke with pride about the accomplishments of many of his students, he had to forgive and forget many moments of disappointment and often bitter conflict. Boisen himself entitles the last part of his life history "growing pains."[23] Just as his moments of happiness and satisfaction were directly related to personal relationships with his teachers and friends, so also were his pains and disappointments a part of personal conflicts. But these conflicts were not just disturbing; they helped to clarify many key issues in training and also developed new possibilities of the case-method.

The first new development was the growing attention to the pastoral conversation, which asked for a careful analysis of verbatim reports. Dicks "discovered" this method. But Boisen was critical of its lack of psychodynamics.

---

23. O. D., p. 172.

The second development was a growing interest in the relationship between supervisor and trainee. The psychotherapeutic milieu had helped to focus on this aspect of the pastoral training. However, Boisen was afraid not only of the unchristian inspiration of certain psychotherapeutic theories but also of a shift in emphasis from the patient to the student.

The third development had to do with the relationship of the clinical training movement to the theological schools. Boisen regretted lack of contact with the theological schools and their courses. It was mainly through the work of Carroll Wise, Wayne Oates and, in particular, Seward Hiltner, that this contact developed. In many ways Hiltner gave Boisen's ideas the status they deserved and integrated many aspects which had been rather disconnected. In the case-method he not only accepted the value of the verbatims without losing sight of the psychodynamics of the case under consideration, but he opened a new perspective—the theological dynamics of living human documents.

It was only through many conflicts and pains that Boisen's great idea was fully understood in all its consequences and possibilities. And twenty-five years after its beginning the Clinical Training Movement was not any longer a movement of some revolutionaries in theological education, but an idea accepted and appreciated in most Protestant seminaries.

The Last Years

In 1938, when Boisen was sixty-two years old, he left Elgin State Hospital where Donald Beatty became his successor, and devoted himself full-time to teaching and writing at Chicago Theological Seminary.

Although after his retirement from the seminary in 1942, and after a year of lectureship at the Pacific School of Religion, he returned to Elgin and functioned for different periods of time as acting chaplain, his main activity was his research. Many important articles were written between 1938 and 1960. In 1946 his book, *Problems in Religion and Life*, appeared; in 1955 his work, *Religion in Crisis and Custom*, found a publisher and, finally, in 1960 his autobiography, *Out of the Depths* was completed. There is no doubt that Boisen shows an astonishing vitality and creativity in the last twenty-five years of his life. Boisen always considered training and research two essentially related aspects of his concern. When his age caused him to put less emphasis on training he gave free rein to his desire to do more research.

Meanwhile, Boisen's contact with the training program had lessened, and he discovered that the movement of which he was considered to be the father had its own momentum. Although he was critical, he was able to let it go in directions which certainly were not his own. His main concern, however, remained to safeguard his basic idea. In this context Boisen found it very important to edit the many cases which he had collected during his work as chaplain in the hope that the case-method would remain central in the training centers. Between 1945 and 1947 Boisen was free to do this job.

In 1950, the Council celebrated its twenty-fifth anniversary. Boisen was at that time no longer chaplain at Elgin, but kept living there at the invitation of the hospital administration. And notwithstanding the many conflicts and "growing pains" of the later years, notwithstanding his distance from the movement and criticism of many of his own students, Boisen was given the place of honor at this celebration, perhaps a little bit to his own surprise. It was on this occasion that Boisen formulated his credo which he considered a summary of the "central convictions which have grown out of my efforts to deal with the problem of mental disorder in myself and others." It was his incapacity to write his credo which had thrown him into the mental hospital in 1920. Now, thirty years later, celebrating the twenty-fifth anniversary of the movement which came out of this experience, he was able to complete his credo and communicate it to his friends. Then he could say:

> I believe that the paramount human need is that for love and that there is a law within which forbids us to be satisfied with any fellowship save that of the best.[24]

Through the courageous understanding of his own case and the continual study of many cases like his own, Boisen's life became the long search for this "fellowship of the best." When he describes in his credo the aim of education: "To lead the growing individual to transfer his loyalty from the finite to the infinite,"[25] we know that this transference has been his lifelong task. In 1935 Alice Batchelder died. In 1936 his first and main work, *The Exploration of the Inner World*, was published, and we see from that moment a continuing flow of creative writing which found its culmination in his autobiography: *Out of the Depths* in 1960.

The last five years of Boisen's life were years of silence. His health was weak and although there were no clearly psychotic episodes his mental condition was on the borderline. At times he was very preoccupied with his own fantasies, and the idea of suicide as an act of self-sacrifice entered his mind occasionally. Vague fears of a world catastrophe, often related to news items about nuclear warfare, haunted him. More than ever he talked about his old friends and students. Visitors meant very much to him and he wanted them to stay as long as possible even when his physical and mental condition could hardly tolerate much conversation. At times he was clear, coherent, and very articulate, with an admirable memory for past events. At other times, however, he was difficult to contact and surrounded by a cloud of preoccupations. With great thankfulness he talked about the hospital where he

---

24. O. D., p. 197.
25. O. D., p. 197.

spent the last thirty-five years of his life. Elgin had become his home, his home as chaplain, but also his home as patient. In the mental hospital he had found his vocation and faithfully he had carried it through. It was there where he wanted to die and to be remembered.

In October 1965, at the age of 89, Boisen died at Elgin. Except for some articles by Seward Hiltner and Thomas Klink, his death drew rather little attention. In a way he was a forgotten man, by many remembered more because of his idiosyncrasies and schizoid personality than for his contributions in the field of the psychology of religion and pastoral psychology. But perhaps there is need for time and distance to be able to see the full stature of the man whose obvious weaknesses obstruct a clearer view of him. It is this feeling that sounds through the meditation of Thomas Klink when he was on his way home after the committal of Boisen's ashes:

> But because he lived and suffered and imposed his always-distant urgency on others, some of the living seem less likely to be scattered as burned out ashes 'back of the hospital' over the shallow waste ground. . . .[26]

---

26. Thomas W. Klink. "Anton T. Boisen, 1976-1965. A remembrance of the committal of his ashes, October 6, 1965." "*Journal of Pastoral Care,*" Vol. XIX, No. 4, Winter 1965, p. 230.

THE BOISEN HERITAGE IN THEOLOGICAL EDUCATION

Ross Snyder

[The following was one of several articles which appeared in the September, 1968 issue of *Pastoral Psychology*, which was devoted to the life and work of Anton Boisen. Ross Snyder was Professor of Religious Education at Chicago Theological Seminary, where Boisen served as adjunct faculty from 1924-1942. Snyder gives a fresh and creative reflection on Boisen's pioneering work from the perspective of a religious educator seeking to define and live the meaning of vital religious experience.]

Let us ask, first of all, how we would "do theology" in a seminary or in a local congregation if we were true to the Boisen heritage. If we ask, "How does one become an adequate theologian?" our answer (if we were with Boisen) would include the advice Jung gave to those who inquired about how to become a good therapist:

> If one wishes to understand the human soul, he need not bother with the experimental psychology of the laboratory which can tell him practically nothing. He would be better advised to take off his academic robes, and wander with open heart through the world, through the horrors of prisons, insane asylums, hospitals, through dirty city dives, through the drawing rooms of elegant society, stock exchanges, socialist meetings, to experience love and hate . . . in his own being.

The most obvious achievement of Boisen's life was that he was the instrument through which clinical training for theological students did become a respected part of theological education for students all over the country. This is true, even though few seminaries think of it as a *necessary* and integral part of the education of all their students, even though the movement was taken over by Freudian or Rogerian view-points about human nature and therapy, *as contrasted with* the views held by Boisen, and even though the clinical experience the student was having, was happening in the absence of expert theological resources.

Boisen must have felt solid satisfaction through the years in seeing the progress being made toward the vision first enunciated by his friend, teacher, and guarantor, Dr. Richard Cabot, who in 1925 had published an article in "*Survey Graphic*" proposing that something radical be done about the need for better prepared pastors. He proposed that *every student for the ministry* be given a kind of clinical training for his pastoral work similar to the clinical training a medical student receives during his internship. Even the most advanced seminaries are still only *trying* to supply this kind of training. This fact is testimony to the hardpan of custom and teaching method idolized for years.

Boisen heartily affirmed for seminary education Whitehead's criticism of education in general:

> We are too exclusively bookish in our scholastic routine. . . . The second-handedness of the learned world is the secret of its mediocrity . . . every intellectual revolution which has ever stirred humanity into greatness has been a passionate protest against inert ideas . . . our goal is to see the immediate events of our lives as instances of our general ideas.

Boisen was frustrated in his many proposals for new designs in theological education made to a faculty, ironically enough, dominated by Whiteheadian theologians.

Interdisciplinary Effort

If we are to do theology well, not only must we keep ourselves in the midst of intense destiny experiencing, but it must be done in an interdisciplinary staff. Through his joint seminars with Cushman McGiffert here at the Seminary, Boisen made clear that the theologizing is an interdisciplinary effort focused upon the lived moments of people desperately struggling to constitute a life world. The critical point is that in theological education theology itself must be an interdisciplinary effort. It cannot be merely a thrashing over of straw which once bore living wheat—the shredding and winnowing of the theologians' books about each other. "God talk" that uses language from other disciplines may be more penetrating and accurately symbolic of God and the religious life than language from the foggy past of an imperialist church, or language formed by world views of a world which never has been and never will be. The old strategem of dismissing every thought about the depths of the human psyche with the contemptuous remark, "That's merely psychology," came to be seen as a puff of evasive wind.

Study Contemporary Religious Experience

The study of lived moments of Christian existence is a necessary part of theological education. Professors and students should be engaged in a study of the varieties of contemporary religious experience, as William James did in his day, and as Boisen did in his hospital chaplaincy and in his study of ecstatic sects during the depression years. If Boisen himself had been in his prime in these last years, we would now have recorded and analyzed the wealth of destiny struggle within America's present transition from a grisly past into freedom for both Negro and white. There would now be articulated deeper insight into the nature of the religious as revealed in this moment of history-making.

We need to look forward to a return to firsthand study of religious experience, contemporary man's experience, both East and West. Who can understand Christianity who has not made such a study? Who is fit to live and lead in this world who has not such a breadth of comprehension? Who can understand his own time without such study?

The time is where when no one will be adequate unless he has tasted the mind that comes from encounter with people in the desperate moments of their lives, with the lived moments that are happening all the time in the thrusts of our common struggle to *be* in the modern world, as well as from a study of man's sensing of fascinating, awesome holiness through all the centuries.

For Boisen, such a study was not just for the sake of being "cultured." He believed rather that in the study of religious experience, you were discovering what enabled man to be human. What enables man to live in the midst of a precarious and broken world is disclosed in religious experience. William James, too, had such a hope. If a young man were to ask Boisen the question put to Jung, "How do I become a good therapist?" Boisen would agree with Jung's answer, but he would add: "Inquire into the living and written documents of people who have *religion at a fever pitch*, for there you will see the elemental questions man faces as he tries to be human. More importantly, you may see the secret of what brings people successfully through such struggle." Boisen was determinedly convinced that the *religious* was the indestructible core, integrating spine, originating genes of *human* life.

Today we might ask the question from an existential and phenomenological point of view: "What *exists* man . . . as courage to become manifest, take on individuated form, as freedom to live in a world that is in danger and utter a 'nevertheless,' as an expressive spontaneity and an intentional project in a world that tries to make him a replaceable thing, as a Self cultured richly with meanings in a civilization imprinted by electronic communications?" Boisen's answer would be: "the religious."

The study of the history of religions in our day has more and more moved toward a phenomenological investigation of religion. One approaches the actual lived moment with a humble openness trying as best one can to establish "what *is here?*" How can I comprehend this on its own terms? Boisen would rejoice with all this. But he had the advantage of going through the experience himself. He had access in a way denied to those who are merely observing. But he also had another advantage. Boisen studied religious experience not only as a participant, but as one ministering to those who were in the midst of such experience. His was not the role of the spectator; he was *within the healing process.* And what *that* is, is what we must discover.

If one is to study religious experience, which is essentially an event of transformation, one must be a *servant* student, one who willingly and skillfully shares in the creating and redeeming which must be brought off. The servant minister could be the most sensitive and accurate research instrument we have. Why then does hardly any minister accept this research function, this culturing into insights and meanings that he is constantly a ministering part of? At least for Boisen, only he who serves, i.e., the therapist, will find out anything deep and important. Could every minister grasp in their uniqueness and richness, at least the lived moments with their documentary meanings of *one* person through the years of his ministry? But the minister must be present as a man of *religious quality* who has himself gone through turmoil and experienced a power not altogether under his own control that is working to make him whole within and whole with all men everywhere. Only a person with this kind of peace can be a researcher in the religious life in the Boisen way.

Theological Students Must Possess Their Own Intense Experiencing

Intense experiencing is the stuff of your one life on earth. It *exists* you. The road to soul-health is to take your own lived moments and experiencing seriously. *Your* experiencing is not to be despised, ignored, covered over, dampened, and trivialized. In its very confusion and crisis, something great is struggling to be born— an actualization of yourself within a universal love of God and fellowman. In theological education we are finding ways to help students possess the depths of their own experiencing in place of trying to live at second hand from books alone.

However vigorous people may become in the justice struggle, we know with Boisen that from time to time there is going to be in each person who participates in such a struggle (and particularly in the leaders), a mysterious upheaval of self-doubt, frenzied running after the destiny of his one life on earth, stark aloneness and alienation. They need someone present as *minister with* them. Teachers cannot be merely sociologists or propagandists, for something is struggling to right itself in them, and fountain out in new expressive acts. Equally important, students must become skilled in existence clarification, else their lives become stuffed with idols and so burnt with hostilities as to prevent their service to God and man. At this point Boisen was exceptionally severe with himself. He believed with the Hebrew prophets that where something went wrong, it was not to be blamed on outside forces ". . . my mother and father, my peer group, my time in history . . . did this to me. They made me what I am today." No. A time of crisis should cause *conscience* work. What can I learn from this? What is my integrity? What repentance on my part will right *me*?

Conscience

Boisen fought all his life for the importance of conscience. Perhaps here is his main idea contribution to the theological study of man. Boisen understood conscience from within the thought system of George Herbert Mead. Conscience is one's interiorization of a Significant Other, and of the significant symbol structure of one's society. This is the way *human* beings are made. This is the way mind, self, society is constituted.

Conscience therefore is primarily a *loyalty* phenomenon. This Boisen learned from Royce. Its basis is caring, trust, in some Significant Otherness that for this person is *the* Significant Otherness. This view is being affirmed by many today. I. A. Richards asserts that "troth"—a choice from which all other choices flow—is not only the necessary base for being a person, but for any important learning. Erikson, modifying the classic Freudian assertion that rebellion and sex are the major tasks of all adolescents, now says that youth's driving hunger is to discover what is true to him, and to what he can be true. And so the discovery and establishment of fidelity is the crucial move if he is to become adult. And Marcel has made memorable the phrase "creative fidelity." A flood-tide of health for youth is beginning.

For Boisen, a sense of guilt was a sense of isolation and estrangement from that which is supreme in our system of loyalties. We have broken the fidelity, violated the troth, done something which is "unspeakable" i.e., that we fear to reveal to the Significant Other. Until we can voice it—and without losing any of its horrors, we discover that the Significant Other is still present to us—we live in harrowing anguish and duplicity.

Our guilt is not to be eased off, but *realized* and worked through. We are to enter into our guilt and feel it in every pore. But not wallow around in guilt feelings, keeping our dark moment to ourselves on the pretense that it is unmentionable. In that way we would stay alienated, increasing our estrangement from others and from trust, since we are living in the depths of distrust of our fellowman, afraid that he will see us in an unguarded moment.

For Boisen, the content of conscience was the Hebrew prophet, who saw each *disaster* as a call to *repentance* on his part; each new era as a call to new existence. He did not blame others; he had enough on his hands if he asked: "What did *I* do that was wrong? Where is my guilt? What is the new possibility, the new transformation God is bringing off? What act *now* on *my* part begins to restore the relationship?" According to Boisen, the Hebrew had a great advantage over all other people—his attention was centered upon a one God whose great concern was that his children should live righteous and holy lives. This relationship was finally the only one that counted for Boisen.

Conscience, for Boisen, was also identification with his fellow-sufferers in the hospital. Conscience was his sense that he had now found his destiny. He had found his habitat, and the meaning of his life on earth. The *place where* his life was in touch with the universally human. With the Redeeming Love and Intelligence that moved all things. These people in their suffering and struggle were his basic society of at least five people who believed in each other, understood together the deep mysteries of life and how one staggered into the open with hitherto undreamed of possibilities.

Conscience was also Josiah Royce's Beloved Community, a communion of people of all times and places who were this *existence*. He belonged to a net of life whose quality was capable of embracing all men, and so becoming universalized. Boisen's religious view would have been sympathetic with that Teilhard vision: that the urge of evolution is the emergence of a world net of thoughtful men, deeply caring about each other, in honest communication with each other, each open to the lure of God to become more than he now is.

This Beloved Community was also a present small society which is an atoning community, atoning not in the sense of demanding a victim, but atoning in the sense set forth by Royce, a community (or its representative) willing to go through the pains of hell alongside a person, so participating in the journey as to transform the evil and the traitorship into possibility of new good that would not have been possible before. Conscience and the religious are seen as the very basis of therapy. A view similar to Boisen's has emerged in Integrity Therapy and in Philip Anderson's thesis that *covenant* is the secret of therapy. For Boisen, conscience was huge, awe-some . . . the place where you could see what constituted a human being. Conscience was the entrance to the religious life, if not indeed identical with it.

Boisen reported that the "drifter" has a low chance of ever getting out of a mental hospital. Only the person who is *not* at ease with himself, the person who is struggling, fighting, erupting inside, will ever get well. Only those deeply disturbed about their alienation from the Beloved Community, and about the defeat of their self-realization will ever become whole. Those who have no "Significant Other" with whom they desperately desire relationship, passionately care about and want to serve . . . have nothing to pull them out of despair; have no destiny because they have no pull of future. They have too inadequate a conscience.

The Breakthrough Community

Boisen was concerned equally with what we usually call the individual and what we usually call society. For him, these were not two things, but two poles of the same reality. He was interested in more than his private breakthrough. During the thirties he also studied what I would call the breakthrough community. How does the breakthrough community happen?

A sensitive man—brooding over the condition of the dispossessed, the lowly of the land whom society apparently has no place for in its economic, social, political structures—feels himself deeply in the same fate, torn, bewildered, passionately aroused. He has a torrential breakthrough of a love of God and fellowman because he feels as never before the love of God pouring out toward him, flowing through him. He shares that experiencing with other people. A group of at least five people begins to believe in him, is caught up in the same passion and vision. A vital religious sect is born. All too soon it will become conventionalized religion, for it will gain adherents who themselves have not had the primal experience out of which the new vision came. It will be something they speak *about*, rather than *out of*. What was once a living religion becomes custom, becomes secondhand, becomes phoniness, becomes something you do as a sort of mild entertainment on Sundays. Such is the fate of a breakthrough community. And often the new life is located up in the skies. This is understandable, for only in a new earth unlike the present social order will love have a chance.

An antropologist, Anthony Wallace, has recently proposed from his study focused on the Seneca Indians, that properly understood, every religious movement is a *revitalization* of a people. And he points out that where so many of our developmental programs for new countries fail, is that they totally concentrate on improving the economic resources, and often in a way that destroys the self-esteem and dignity of the people involved. Instead of a breakout of new love of man and God, of new possibility of esteem, of new vision of a possible future, exactly the opposite happens. No wonder. The essential religiousness of man has been both ignored and violated rather than awakened.

Boisen was interested in the revitalization of a people. As he studied, he came to feel that the churches of his time were almost totally inadequate for this task. They were interested only in individualistic message, sterile prattle, and dogmatic abstractions that never in the world could inflame a people with love and creative furor.

Yet is not every minister to be the originator of a breakthrough community?

Toward a Language Necessary to Express the Religious

Anton Boisen is a continuing strength in the battle against the imperialisms of a positivistic science and crude forms of empiricism. There are depths to man. They are important. They, too, are where man lives, not just in a planned city. Man, if he is human, does not live in a callow secular city, but in his dreams and in his sense of destiny. Today, because of the obvious inability of a language of bare prose to enable us to talk about significant feelings, to talk about conscience, to talk about the religious, we are beginning to realize the centrality of a language of poetry, a language of deep experiences, a language of the religious. A language which enables us to think well about the destiny of man. Boisen was working on such a langauge. This language will partly be a language of images which man can use to think with, decide with, symbolize hopes and visions of greatness in his world. The development of such a language, the study of what image is, the function of vision in the breakthrough of the new, of how symbolic communication takes place is a part of our task, and a part of the heritage of Anton Boisen.

ANTON BOISEN: FIGURE OF THE FUTURE?

David A. Steere

[Writing in the October, 1969 issue of the *Journal of Religion and Health,* David A. Steere, Professor of Pastoral Theology at Louisville Presbyterian Theological Seminary, assesses the continuing relevance of Boisen's work. He notes that Boisen's outline for "A Theological Curriculum for 1950" contained the same principles as the "Theological Curriculum for the 1970's" proposed by the American Association of Theological Schools. Asserting that Boisen's call for an empirical study of theology cannot be ignored in the future, Steere concludes with several challenging questions remaining as part of Boisen's legacy.]

The death of Anton T. Boisen in October of 1965 has occasioned few serious summations of his life and thought.[1] Boisen is generally regarded as the father of clinical pastoral education. His studies in the relationship between religious experience and mental illness reached far beyond his time. It is the purpose of this article to offer an appraisal of his contribution to the psychology of religion and to pose questions concerning its meaning in the future.

Note: The author's name and *op. cit.* are omitted in listing Boisen's works wherever clarity does not require them.

1. See Hiltner, Seward, "The Debt of Clinical Pastoral Education to Anton T. Boisen," *Journal of Pastoral Care,* 1966, 20, 129-135; and Pruyser, Paul W., "Anton T. Boisen and the Psychology of Religion," *Journal of Pastoral Care,* 1967, 21, 209-219. Cf. The Anton Boisen Memorial Issue of *Pastoral Psychology,* 1968, 21, 9-14, 49-63.

Exploration of a Little-known Country

From a family that produced a long line of distinguished educators, Boisen came to the Presbyterian ministry by way of Indiana University, Yale Forestry School, and Union Theological Seminary in New York.[2] When he was forty-four, a series of unfortunate incidents centering around an unsuccessful love affair culminated in an acute psychotic episode. In October of 1920, Boisen began his journey into what he termed "the little-known country" of mental illness. With his illness diagnosed as schizophrenia (dementia praecox) by his physicians at Westboro State Hospital, he remained acutely disturbed for a period of about two weeks, then snapped out of it, and in early November was transferred to the convalescent ward.

Boisen immediately derived several things from this experience. He disagreed with his physicians, who insisted that all mental illness was the result of cerebral damage. While still in the hospital, he wrote his old friend, Fred Eastman, he was convinced that illness like his can occur when there is no organic difficulty at all. The problem lay in some disorganization of the patient's world that had upset the foundations on which ordinary reasoning processes are based.[3] This idea met with little support among his doctors. In December of 1920, his attending physician refused him a week-end visit with the Eastmans on the ground that his idea that he had no mental illness (cerebral disease) provided sufficient evidence that he was not yet well enough.[4]

A second conclusion was that his upheaval was inherently purposive in character, not meaningless. The flood of ideas that rushed in upon him should merit careful examination. The fundamental fallacy among the mentally ill was that these ideas carry authority because of the way in which they come. Some of them were both distorted and destructive. But some of them were fertile in suggestions and may stand the test of time.[5] In December, Boisen read Freud's *Introductory Lectures*, which he felt corroborated his own understandings. Mental illness (neurosis) roots in deep-seated conflict between subconscious forces, and the cure is to be found not in the suppression of symptoms but in resolution of the conflict.[6]

Intuitively, Boisen reached beyond these two initial conclusions for a third one that was to become the central concern of his life. If he had recovered from his psychotic episode as he thought he had, it could be ascribed to the curative forces of religion, which were largely responsible for the disturbed condition in the first

---

2. The writer is drawing upon Anton T. Boisen's autobiography, *Out of the Depths*. New York, Harper & Bros., 1960.

3. *Ibid.*, p. 97.

4. *Ibid.*, p. 112.

5. *Ibid.*, p. 199.

6. *Ibid.*, p. 103.

place.[7] He had studied the psychology of religion under George A. Coe at Union Theological Seminary, where attention was given to the mystical experiences of St. Teresa, Madam Guyon, Heinrich Suso, George Fox, the apostle Paul, and others. To Boisen there was no line of separation between these religious experiences and the abnormal mental state he had experienced. All had alternating exaltation and depression, heard voices, saw visions, and received inspirations and automisms similar to his. These had their origin in inner conflict and struggle. And they had an organizing function: their end was the unification of the personality. The distinguishing feature between religious geniuses and the insane was the constructive outcome to the experiences through which they passed.[8] The crisis of emotional disturbance should be seen as an opportunity to explore the inner world that bore the potential for a higher integration of life on the one hand, or for its destruction on the other. Many forms of mental illness must be seen as religious problems that cannot be successfully treated until they are so recognized.[9]

The Neglect of Liberal Theology

One of Boisen's first moves was to challenge what he felt to be the neglect of liberal Protestantism in his day. The "social gospel" was in its hey-day. The church mobilized its efforts to reform social institutions with a fervor not unlike the growing impulse of our own time to effect social change among the larger client-structures of politics, economics, education, etc. Boisen was for all this. But he was alarmed by a concomitant failure to meet individual needs. Even before his psychotic episode, he had published an article attributing the decline of the church's influence to its failure to compel the attention and allegiance of the individual following the breakdown of its old appeal to fear of a future hell.[10] The church should address itself to the hell of wrong habit, of diseased will, of misused opportunity, and of guilty conscience. These need to be made as vivid to the individual as the hell pictured by Jonathan Edwards.

Emerging from his illness, Boisen had an interesting response to the famous Scopes trial in Dayton, Tennessee, over teaching evolution in the schools. He wrote an article entitled "In Defense of Mr. Bryan: A Personal Confession by a Liberal Clergyman" in May of 1925.[11] His point was a simple but penetrating one. The

7. *Ibid.*, p. 199.
8. *Ibid.*, pp. 135-136.
9. *Ibid.*, p. 113.
10. Boisen, "Factors Which Have to Do with the Decline of the Country Church," *American Journal of Sociology*, 1916, 22, 177-192.
11. *American Review*, 1925, 3, 323-330. Cf. "Evangelism in the Light of Psychiatry," *Journal of Religion*, 1927, 7, 76-80.

liberals had surrendered the authoritative message of salvation. The fundamentalist group for which William Jennings Bryan spoke, in spite of its obvious perversions of scientific truth, was still mainly concerned with the problem of healing the sick soul. It at least presented an authoritative message of personal salvation, while the liberal group concerned itself primarily with programs of religious education and social reform. True, the fundamentalists treated the sick soul without diagnosis, but the liberals neither treated nor diagnosed the human soul in health or disease. Boisen's original title for the article was "In Defense of Mr. Bryan by a Disciple of Dr. Fosdick." However, when he submitted the paper to Harry Emerson Fosdick, the latter replied it would be published under that title only over his dead body.[12]

Boisen was convinced that the church must give attention to a ministry in the personal crises of life. Here we encounter the two central thrusts of his thought. First, there was a conviction that empirical study of certain types of mental illness would yield new understandings of the nature of religious experience and open avenues to an informed ministry of pastoral care. Second there was a belief that such studies would inevitably reinforce the fundamental structures of traditional theology as bearing an authoritative message for the sin-sick soul.

Clinical Training and Theological Education

The logical place for Boisen to follow his interests was a mental institution. In 1924, Dr. Richard C. Cabot arranged for his appointment as chaplain at Worcester State Hospital. Boisen's relationship to the well-known physician and teacher at Harvard Medical School was an interesting one. Although Cabot denied to his death the existence of psychogenic factors in the origin or treatment of mental illness, he continually solicited funds for Boisen's work. Cabot had a famous lecture entitled "The Wisdom of the Body" in which he outlined the marvelous devices the body employs in maintaining and restoring health.[13] Boisen suggested once, after its delivery in New York, that he was interested in searching for analogous processes in the human mind. Cabot shook his head emphatically and replied he believed thoroughly in the wisdom of the body, but not in that of the mind.[14]

During the summer of 1925, Boisen brought four theological students to Worcester in what was probably the first program of clinical pastoral training as we know it today. The students had regular contact with patients, kept records of their observations, read in the psychology of religion, attended interdisciplinary staff

---

12. *Out of the Depths*, p. 152.
13. This was based on a title by Walter B. Cannon; its substance is found in Cabot, Richard C., and Dicks, Russell L., *The Art of Ministering to the Sick*. New York, The Macmillan Co., 1936, Chapter IX.
14. *Ibid.*, pp. 175-176.

meetings, and held seminars in the interrelationship between religion and mental disorders. The following year brought the publication of his famous article in *Christian Work*, "The Challenge to our Seminaries," pleading for a clinical year of such studies as a standard part of theological education.[15] To Boisen, the recognition of psychogenic factors in mental illness left the church in a truly remarkable situation. Through absenting itself from the treatment of emotional disorders, it was ignoring precisely the type of case where it is impossible to tell where the domain of the medical worker leaves off and that of the religious worker begins.

Boisen's suggestions for the theological school were visionary. The seminary curriculum must admit the actual raw material of life to its subject matter. Students should learn how to read *living human documents* as well as the traditional documents of the church's faith.[16] The study of human personality in health and disease could lead to the discovery of the great motive forces governing life and lay the foundations for a whole new area of theology.[17] For when we recognize in mental illness exaggerated forms of tendencies present in everyone, we have opened a new avenue for understanding the normal and gained a means of studying the struggle of sin and salvation in bold relief.

Theological training in the future should be a continuous affair, with the parish as the laboratory and the person in difficulty as the main concern. The seminary would be a clearing-house of information and the supervisor of methods. Theological studies need concrete material about human life to which classroom teaching can address itself.[18] Two quarters of clinical training in the midst of academic studies were envisioned with the faculty co-ordinating classroom and clinical procedures, working in each setting. Boisen's unpublished monograph entitled *A Theological Curriculum for 1950* embodied many of the principles of the recent "Theological Curriculum for the 1970's" produced by a study committee for the American Association of Theological Schools, e.g., seminar groups focusing on contemporary human problems, the use of case study materials, and supervised experience in specific areas of ministry.[19]

An Empirical Approach to Theology

Even more important to Boisen than training good pastors was his lifelong interest in developing research in the psychology of religion within his profession.

---

15. Reprinted in *Journal of Pastoral Care*, 1951, 5, 8-12.

16. "Theological Education Via the Clinic," *Religious Education*, March, 1930. (Reprint)

17. "The Challenge to Our Seminaries," *op. cit.* (note 15), p. 12.

18. "Clinical Training for Theological Students," *Chicago Theological Seminary Register*, 1945, 35, 16.

19. *Theological Education*, 1968, 4, 671-712.

His hope was to strengthen the body of theology through a systematic inquiry into the origin, meaning, and consequences of religious beliefs. He was critical of contemporary empirical approaches to theology by Macintosh and Horton because of their reliance upon secondhand data and their failure to practice empirical methods seriously.[20]

In 1936 Boisen published *The Exploration of the Inner World*, which drew together the major strands of his thinking.[21] It was an effort to substantiate the relationship between religious experience and mental illness. First, he presented a series of case histories of patients at Worcester State Hospital in which he identified three types of reaction patterns: *drifting*, with a marked tendency toward deterioration; *delusional misinterpretation*, in an effort to "save face"; and *panic*, an acute emotional disturbance that Boisen described as analogous to fever, indicating attempts at cure and reorganization.[22] Boisen immediately sensed the relatively better prognosis of this latter type, which roughly corresponds to the catatonic schizophrenic reaction. Its results are sometimes constructive. Its regressive features are attempts to assimilate hitherto unassimilated masses of life experience. The sense of peril may represent the seriousness of personal struggle elevated to cosmic proportions; the ideas of self-importance, a heightened sense of personal responsibility. All these things represent the person's efforts to reorganize life on a different basis.

Next, Boisen presented the personal histories of selected religious leaders, derived from scripture, biography, and autobiography. They included Paul, George Fox, John Bunyan, Emmanuel Swedenborg, Ezekiel, Jeremiah, etc.[23] Their ideas and conflicts were analogous to those held by patients of the *panic* type. Common to both groups was the dynamic and purposive character of their experiences. Their upheavals came at times of personal crisis when questions of identity and mission rush in with a compelling sense of immediacy. They represented an effort to solve problems of personal destiny. Both groups were attempting to raise their values to the level of the cosmic and the universal, to establish and maintain a right relationship with all that is represented in the idea of God.

---

20. "Cooperative Inquiry in Religion," *Religious Education*, 1945, 30, 291-292. Boisen charged that Douglas C. Macintosh in his *Theology as an Empirical Science* (New York, The Macmillan Co., 1927) concerned himself chiefly with the problem of religious knowledge and nowhere studied the religious experience of actual men. Neither did Walter M. Horton in *The Psychological Approach to Theology* (New York and London, Harper & Bros., 1931) base his conclusions upon the direct observation of psychological data, but upon material gleaned from the writings of Freud, Janet, Hadfield, and others.

21. *The Exploration of the Inner World.* Chicago and New York, Willett, Clark & Co., 1936.

22. *Ibid.*, pp. 15-56.

23. *Ibid.*, pp. 57-82.

Pruyser has pointed to Boisen's lasting preoccupation, if not obsession, with his typology of schizophrenia and to some of the serious inadequacies of his thesis.[24] For one thing, Boisen comfortably divided mental illnesses into distinct groups of organic and functional disorders, remaining oblivious to the emerging holistic understandings of the organism even in his own day. The simple equation of constructive resolutions of the catatonic state with mystical experience is open to quarrel from both medical and religious perspectives. From the standpoint of the theologian, to make mysticism the paradigm for all religious experience is a dubious assumption at best. No doubt, Boisen was driven in all these things by the unique struggles of his own personal life. He was a deeply religious man, and his illness was replete with religious symbolism. He was not content to dismiss the entire experience under the "secular" rubric of "illness" and leave it devoid of the meaning it took on for him.

We must not let the limitations of Boisen's own particular findings blur the significance of what he was undertaking. He saw in mental illness the opportunity to study the function of theological beliefs in periods of intense personal crisis. These empirical studies of theology differed markedly from the usual systematic inquiry in terms of the propriety, exactness, and logical consistency of beliefs. Instead, the focus was upon the actual operation of these beliefs in the person's life situation. In what do they result: in life or in death? Do they serve to aid the person in reorganizing his life, providing a center of integration about unified efforts, goals, and values? Or do they function to bring about further disorganization and deterioration?[25]

Boisen described the case of a patient who, after being unfaithful to his wife, organized his entire life around her in something approximating religious devotion. But this was not sufficient. Finding it impossible to submit to her in all things, the patient felt a pressing need for a higher level of adjustment that produced illness. The particular ideation of his sickness was that God desired him to take his own life by giving it up for his wife. The patient literally acted out what he was attempting to do with his life, signaling the inadequacy of its present organization and attempting to break its hold upon him with finality. In this case the idea of God functioned to express the thrust of the patient's life to transfer loyalty from the finite to the infinite. Autonomy is impossible for the person organizing his life about that which is less than ultimate. The idea of the sovereignty of God can function to render the patient independent of the changes and dangers of his present situation.[26]

Through the process of recording the religious ideas of patients, Boisen made some clinical observations about the way beliefs functioned. The idea of God serves

---

24. Pruyser, "Anton T. Boisen and the Psychology of Religion," *op. cit.* (note 1), 213-216.
25. *Exploration of the Inner World*, p. 191.
26. "Theology in the Light of Psychiatric Experience." *The Crozer Quarterly*, 1941, 18, 47-67.

as a symbol of that which is supreme in the individual and his social system of loyalties.[27] It represents what the individual deems to be abiding and universal. It is associated symbolically with the thought of those whom the person counts most worthy of love and honor. The idea of God also represents the larger fellowship in which the individual seeks identification, taking on a system of values that are a function of the relationships he seeks. And it assumes the task of symbolizing judgment whereby the individual measures his efforts at entering into these relationships through self-judgment.[28] Something like the idea of God is either explicitly or implicitly operative in the lives of all people, whether they call themselves religious or not.

Boisen's method of inquiry was a rather primitive form of phenomenological investigation through participant observation of the mentally ill. He practiced the essentials of the method as Herbert Spiegelberg outlines them: 1) investigating a particular phenomenon and its general essences; 2) apprehending the essential relationships among these essences; 3) observing the modes in which the phenomenon appears and its constitution in the consciousness; 4) suspending belief (or systematic metaphysics); and 5) interpreting the meaning of the phenomenon as it becomes operative in the life situation.[29] Whether we accept his particular findings or not, Boisen opened a door to the empirical study of theology that we can ill afford to ignore in the future. If the idea of God does not function this way, how does it? We have recently been told by the death-of-God theologians that the idea of God inevitably serves a repressive function in the psyche and that man will be truly human only when he has dispensed with it. Serious phenomenological investigation in the vein Boisen began may offer invaluable empirical data to this issue.

Boisen's breadth of interest makes it extremely difficult to classify him within a given discipline. His second major work, *Religion in Crisis and Custom*, extended his empirical studies into the province he described as a "sociological and psychological study of religion."[30] It was basically an expansion of his thesis in *Exploration*, showing in American Protestantism the tendency of religious experience to arise spontaneously in times of social crises among religious groups and movements. He addressed *Problems in Religion and Life* to the parish minister, encouraging a pattern of research involving sociological analysis of the community and an elaborate set of records concerning each family within the congregation, together with individual case studies.[31] Throughout, Boisen's passion for initiating research dominated his

---

27. *Exploration of the Inner World*, p. 47.

28. *Ibid.*, pp. 176-178.

29. Spiegelberg, Herbert, *The Phenomenological Movement*, Vol. II. The Hague, Martinus Nijhoff, 1960, pp. 653-701.

30. *Religion in Crisis and Custom*. New York, Harper & Bros., 1945, p. xiii.

31. *Problems in Religion and Life*. New York and Nashville, Abingdon-Cokesbury Press, 1946.

writing. He lamented the fact that there were no journals in the field of religion in his day that could claim scientific standing.[32] He saw the empirical study of religion as the means of uniting medicine and religion and of reinstating theology to the position from which it had been dethroned as the queen of the sciences.[33] Even in clinical training, his concern was more with understanding the patient through the empirical study of case histories than upon specific methods or techniques in pastoral care.[34]

A Theology of Crisis

Boisen's own particular theological constructs deserve closer attention than they have received. In electing to discuss the functional dimensions of mental illness as a struggle of sin and salvation, he was not unmindful of the disfavor into which the word "sin" had fallen. But none of the proposed substitutes expressed so exactly what was the real evil. For the word "sin" implied the rupture of one's supreme loyalties, the idea of moral failure and the thorough-going seriousness of the absence of right relationships with that which is represented by the idea of God. Boisen expressed no objection to the substitution of new words for old ones, an inevitable part of the growth of language and culture. But such substitutes as "maladjustment," "immaturity," or "mental disease" lacked the dimensions of meaning he encountered in the ideas of acutely disturbed persons.[35]

By phenomenological observation, he identified a certain constellation of traditional doctrines that seemed to come to the fore in personal crises.

1) *Total Depravity* corresponds to the great reservoir of unacceptable, instinctual cravings blocking the way to higher potentialities among the mentally ill with the possibility of engulfing and destroying them. No philosophy of life that fails to take account of the possibility of disintegration or damnation is really facing the facts.[36]

2) *Sin and Guilt* are synonymous. Sin involves not so much an infraction of moral law as a breach of trust regarding ultimate loyalties. Its essential evil is the sense of estrangement and isolation resulting from the presence of something "unspeakable" in one's life that he is afraid to tell for fear of condemnation.[37]

---

32. "Cooperative Inquiry in Religion," *op. cit.* (note 20), p. 290.

33. *Exploration of the Inner World*, p. 191.

34. "The Present Status of William James' Psychology of Religion," *Journal of Pastoral Care* 1953, 7, 155-157. Cf. *Out of the Depths*, pp. 189-190.

35. *Exploration of the Inner World*, pp. 209-211.

36. *Ibid.*, p. 193.

37. "Theology in the Light of Psychiatric Experience." *op. cit.* (note 26), p. 60; "The Problem of Sin and Salvation in the Light of Psychopathology," *Journal of Religion*, 1942, 22, 292.

3) *Confession and Forgiveness* are modes of release from this sense of isolation. In psychotherapy, the patient lays bare to the physician his inner difficulties, thus placing himself at the bar of judgment. If he is not condemned, he experiences restoration and the opening of relationship with those whose love is necessary.[38] All psychotherapy resolves itself into a matter of confession and forgiveness. The distinctive task of the minister is to break through this sense of isolation and estrangement due to guilt. Whatever the human instrumentality, there is a sense of being forgiven directly by God.[39]

4) *Repentance* is the conviction of sin and the first step toward salvation. It is a mistake to attempt to lower the conscience threshold in order to eliminate moral conflict. Even severe emotional disturbances are frequently manifestations of nature's power to heal. A breach of trust must be followed by the experience of reconciliation marked, on the one side, by the acknowledgment of wrongdoing and, on the other, by the capacity to understand and the willingness to resume friendly relations.[40]

5) *Sacrifice.* There is much to substantiate the value of the doctrine of self-sacrifice as seen in the cross. The need of the individual to pay the price of full commitment and devotion is a central problem to most mental sufferers. Strivings to eliminate the unacceptable in their lives and discover a new center for their personality are frequently associated with ideas of death and rebirth. Efforts at self-punishment are often attempts at self-discipline and self-control. Christ's death on the cross was a bold declaration that self-realization comes through self-sacrifice for the group. Paul discovered this in his doctrine of the spirit as opposed to the law. It represented a shift in his thinking from a static morality to a dynamic morality that found the good life not in outward correctness but in self-forgetful devotion to the best. To the man overwhelmed by his sins it presents the offer of a new chance.[41]

6) *Atonement.* Doctrines of vicarious atonement are to be dispraised. The view of Jesus' death as the payment of a price to satisfy the demands of judgment is commonly misconstrued as something that permits one to escape the responsibility for his own life. It becomes just another means of evading genuine personal commitment through self-sacrifice. It often functions to divert efforts at genuine rebirth and reorganization of life.[42]

7) *Salvation* is the re-establishment of right relationship with what is supreme in the individual's system of loyalties. It involves emergence from a static to a

---

38. *Exploration of the Inner World,* pp. 161-162.

39. *Ibid.,* pp. 267, 268; "The Problem of Sin and Salvation in the Light of Psychopathology," pp. 300, 301.

40. "Theology in the Light of Psychiatric Experience," *op. cit.* (note 26), pp. 60, 61.

41. *Exploration of the Inner World,* pp. 204-205.

42. *Ibid.*

dynamic morality based on this relationship, the progressive unification of life around its accepted loyalties and standards, and the type of transformation of personality the physician calls maturity. It is equivalent to mental health or cure, and its progressive character is akin to the old theological idea of sanctification.[43]

8) *The Church* is a group of imperfect persons united on the basis of the ideal they are seeking to realize in their own lives and in the social order. Salvation is both individual and social and is found by entering into that fellowship with others from which to be cut off brings isolation, destruction, and death.[44]

9) *Inspiration.* The tendency to ascribe to a superhuman source ideas that flash into the mind is as old as the human race and has some justification. Whether we classify recipients as paranoiac or recognize them as religious geniuses depends entirely upon the value of their message and of their social achievement.[45] Most patients in paranoid states make a distinction between the voices they hear and those they hear with their ears. In verbal automatism, ideas or thought formations dart so vividly into consciousness that they are ascribed to a superhuman source. The same mechanism is common to poets, inventors, and creative scientists and should be linked with what is usually regarded as insight.[46] Religious experience in times of crisis may serve to validate religious beliefs that have long been familiar but are not yet assimilated into personality structure or to synthesize new insights favorable to the reorganization of personality. Its most pronounced characteristic is the abeyance of the logical faculties in favor of the intuitive.[47]

Boisen's adoption of the "sin" rubric in connection with emotional disorders has recently led O. H. Mowrer to claim him as a predecessor to behavior or "reality" therapy, in which the patient is helped to discard the "excuses" attached to "being sick."[48] Boisen never discussed the matter this way, nor did he deal with the problem of neurotic guilt as opposed to real guilt. For him, the issue was not whether you can hold the person accountable for his sin but not for his sickness. Sin was a matter of broken relationships to be restored. And whether we describe these experiences as sin or sickness, the person must finally assume responsibility for making restoration and getting well. Perhaps the strong resolve with which Boisen fought his lifelong struggle with psychosis is evident in his omission of any real discussion of grace.

---

43. *Ibid.*, p. 61; pp. 209-211.

44. *Ibid.*, pp. 289-293.

45. "Inspiration in the Light of Psychopathology," *Pastoral Psychology*, 1960, 11, 10-18; *Religion in Crisis and Custom, op. cit.* (note 30), pp. 90-112.

46. "Inspiration in the Light of Psychopathology," pp. 15, 16.

47. *Religion in Crisis and Custom*, p. 112.

48. Mowrer, O.H., *The Crisis in Psychiatry and Religion*. Princeton, D. Van Nostrand Co., Inc., 1961, pp. 60-80.

Probably no one reading these theological-clinical constructs will find himself in agreement with all of them. Perhaps they are not so important as the question Boisen poses through them. Are the phenomena described by theological rubrics and those reported from empirical observations in psychology the same or different phenomena? If they are the same, as Boisen believed them to be, then the doors are opened to future exploration of the inner world as a source of one knowledge, both theological and psychological. For the theologian there is a wealth of information about the way his ideas function. For the psychotherapist there is a wealth of data in religious experience and its symbolization as one arena where the curative and destructive forces of life are operative. For the discipline of the psychology of religion there is the opportunity for full-scale empirical studies in the meeting of theological and psychological symbols to describe the actual processes of life.

The Future

Whether history renders Anton Boisen a passing pundit or a figure of the future depends upon the way the shifting times respond to his legacy. It is a legacy more of questions than of answers, an invitation to explore.

1) What is the relationship between a medical view of the human struggle, seen from the therapeutic standpoint as a battle with illness (both psychological and physiological) and a religious view of the same struggle seen from the theological standpoint as man's search for a meaningful relationship to his universe?

2) Beyond Boisen's consuming interest in personal crises (and medicine's in pathology), what are the religious and psychological dimensions of normative, routine, or mundane human experience in their similarity and dissimilarity to those experiences Boisen studied?

3) Can the theologian emerge to find co-operation among the professions in a joint and serious study of living human documents through co-ordinated research in the psychology of religion?

4) Can theological education develop clinical experience for its students in co-operation with other helping disciplines in order to equip pastors to join efforts toward community mental health with competent treatment of the sick soul?

On the evening in 1920 when Boisen was taken to the hospital with his psychotic episode, he announced to his family that the problem of insanity was important and he had decided to investigate it.[49] During the period of confusion that followed, the idea kept recurring that it was his job to break down the wall between religion and medicine.[50] Later, he knew these thoughts that came surging in upon him might be considered by many as "Prophetenwahn," but he insisted that the

---

49. *Out of the Depths*, p. 86.
50. *Exploration of the Inner World*, p. 115; *Out of the Depths*, p. 86.

idea he had been following out with some measure of success was given to him by an Intelligence beyond his own.[51] At the conclusion of his autobiography he wrote:

> I am profoundly convinced of the purposive nature of the searching experiences through which I have passed. I am equally convinced that there is involved something more than blind striving, or *Çlan vitale*. For these beliefs my own experience furnishes evidence to me. I can hardly expect it to do so for others.[52]

---

51. *Exploration of the Inner world,* p. 115.
52. *Out of the Depths,* p. 201.

◧ ◧ ◧

THE CASE STUDY METHOD OF
ANTON T. BOISEN

Glenn H. Asquith, Jr.

[In the June, 1980 issue of *The Journal of Pastoral Care*, Asquith used previously
unpublished materials from Boisen's files at Chicago Theological Seminary to outline
the extensive detail of Boisen's case study approach. The forms cited were likely used in
Boisen's research of the 173 cases at Worcester State Hospital which formed the basis
of *The Exploration of the Inner World* and some of which were also developed for teaching purposes. This comprehensive assessment has contemporary relevance in assisting
both the parish pastor and the pastoral counselor to gain a theological perspective on
pastoral encounters.]

Earlier issues of this journal have frequently cited the contributions of Anton Boisen
as the founder of Clinical Pastoral Education. Indeed, his desire to supplement
classroom experience with a reading of the "living human documents" led him to
recruit four theological students for the first summer program of clinical training at
Worcester State Hospital in 1925. However, it is important to note that Boisen did
not design this program simply to introduce a new form of theological education.
He was also—and perhaps primarily—looking for colleagues in research.[1]

As Paul Pruyser points out, nearly all of Boisen's writings are "intensely autobiographical."[2] Following his first major psychotic episode in 1920 and subsequent

---

1. Edward E. Thornton, *Professional Education for Ministry* (Nashville, TN: Abingdon Press,
1970), pp. 56, 58.
2. Paul W. Pruyser, "Anton T. Boisen and the Psychology of Religion," *The Journal of
Pastoral Care*, 1967, Vol. 21, No. 4, p. 209.

hospitalization, Boisen became engaged in a life-long search for meaning, understanding, and validation of his own experience. He was convinced that the type of
mental illness which he experienced was a *religious* experience because of its curative, problem-solving nature. He believed that "many forms of insanity are religious
rather than medical problems and that they cannot be successfully treated until they
are so recognized."[3]

Because of this, one might say that Anton Boisen was a pioneer of pastoral
assessment. His own training and background had taught him that one way to deal
with a problem is to study it carefully. In *The Exploration of the Inner World*, Boisen
defines theology as the *study* of religious belief—the "spiritual forces" which operate
within us—rather than as a systematic *statement* of belief. In reference to the
psychiatric patients which he and his students interviewed, Boisen said, "We have
sought to determine the origin and meaning of these beliefs, their function in the
individual's life, and their implications for a general system of values."[4]

In order to do this, Boisen developed an elaborate and thorough case study
method. The best and most complete example of this method is found in Boisen's
autobiography, *Out of the Depths*, which he labels as "my own case record."[5]
However, the reader of that volume cannot fully grasp the philosophy or methodology behind the method. The purpose of this article is to describe Boisen's case study
method as an historical precedent to contemporary approaches to pastoral
assessment.

History

The case study method did not begin with Anton Boisen. As Brooks Holifield
has pointed out, Harvard Law School began substituting case studies for classroom
lectures as early as 1871.[6] Boisen first became acquainted with the case study
method while studying with George Albert Coe at Union Theological Seminary in
New York in 1909-1910. In Coe's seminar on mysticism, Boisen read Delacroix's
careful case analyses of the experiences of Saint Teresa, Madame Guyon, and
Heinrich Suso.[7]

Another major influence on Boisen's method was Richard C. Cabot, M.D.,
with whom Boisen studied social ethics at Harvard Divinity School following his

---

3. Anton T. Boisen, *Out of the Depths* (New York, NY: Harper and Brothers, 1960), p. 113.
4. Anton T. Boisen, *The Exploration of the Inner World* (Philadelphia, PA: University of
Pennsylvania Press, 1971), p. 306.
5. Boisen, *Out of the Depths*, p. 9.
6. E. Brooks Holifield, "Ethical Assumptions of Clinical Pastoral Education," *The Journal of
Pastoral Care*, 1980, Vol. 34, No. 1, p. 42.
7. Boisen, *Out of the Depths*, p. 129.

first hospitalization. When Boisen was asked which of Cabot's publications had been most important to him, he did not mention any of Cabot's works on social ethics but rather his best known medical work, *Differential Diagnosis*.[8] These two volumes were published as a result of Cabot's work in his Clinical Pathological Conferences at Harvard Medical School. In these conferences, Cabot and his students would each make a diagnosis of the case being discussed and then consult with the pathologist to determine what had been the actual diagnosis. Importantly for Boisen's method, this educational procedure used in medical school pointed to diagnosis on the basis of known facts as the most important part of learning from the "human documents."

Cabot's social ethics seminar on the preparation of case records for teaching purposes, which Boisen took at Harvard in 1922-23, also had a profound influence upon Boisen's method. In this seminar, the case study written by each participant was mimeographed and distributed to all members of the seminar one week in advance of class presentation. When it was then considered by the group, the time was spent in exchanging views on material which had been read and in many cases commented on in writing before the class meeting.[9] An unpublished statement by Boisen to Cabot indicates the reason for Boisen's extensive use of this method:

> I wish to express in the first place my very great appreciation of the method of teaching which is used in this class. I can say without reservation that of all the courses with which I have ever had to do I regard this as the most satisfactory from the pedagogical standpoint in that it supplies concrete material on which to work, it places the stress on what the student does rather than upon what the teacher says, the problems presented are of fundamental interest and importance, and the principles involved are so clearly brought out and summed up as we go along.[10]

The rest of the folder in which this statement is found contains case studies under the heading of the various topics considered by the class.

Finally, Boisen gained further appreciation for this approach while working with Miss Susie Lyons in the Social Service Department at Boston Psychopathic Hospital in 1923-24. In his previous sociological survey work, Boisen found that he could only gather factual information about an individual. Now, by applying case study principles and going into a home as a social worker to help a person in need, he found that he could study "the entire person in his social setting." By so doing,

---

8. Henri J. M. Nouwen, "Anton T. Boisen and the Study of Theology Through Living Human Documents," unpublished manuscript, Yale Divinity School, n.d. [c 1968]), p. 63. (Later published in part in *Pastoral Psychology*, Vol. 19, (September, 1968), pp. 49-63).

9. Boisen, *Out of the Depths*, p. 147.

10. Anton T. Boisen, "What I have Gained from the Course Thus Far," unpublished memo to Richard C. Cabot, c1923, file 5, drawer 1, Boisen Files, Chicago Theological Seminary.

he could deal with more significant factors such as motives, values, and religious experience.[11]

Theory

A careful reading of Boisen's work indicates that he had a two-fold objective for his case study method. He said, "I have sought to begin not with the ready-made formulations contained in books but with the living human documents *and with actual social conditions in all their complexity.*"[12] As Robert C. Powell pointed out, many leaders in CPE picked up on the aspect of the study of individual human experience but forgot that Boisen also sought to study the experiences of groups in society.[13]

The Search for an Empirical Theology. As clinical training developed from that first unit in 1925, Boisen began to define more clearly his overall objective for both aspects of his method. He was convinced that the study of human experience could enable a theological student to form his or her own theology. For Boisen, clinical training was an ideal opportunity for this, and he often voiced his disapproval at clinical training centers which focused upon the teaching of counseling skills and the study of psychoanalytic thought.[14] A clear statement of Boisen's objective, both for his method and for clinical training, is found at the beginning of his "Types of Mental Illness: A Beginning Course," a manual he wrote for use in clinical training centers in 1946:

> This course is far less concerned with the consideration of techniques and skills than with the effort to discover the forces involved in the spiritual life and the laws by which they operate. It seeks to lay a foundation for the co-operative attempt to organize and test religious experience and to build a theology on the basis of a careful scrutiny of religious beliefs...[15]

Living Human Documents. Following this basic objective, Boisen then lists four more specific objectives for the use of his case study method in clinical training

---

11. Boisen, *Out of the Depths,* pp. 148-49.

12. Boisen, *The Exploration of the Inner World,* p. 185.

13. Robert C. Powell, "Questions from the Past (on the future of Clinical Pastoral Education)," speech given at the 1975 annual conference of the Association for Clinical Pastoral Education, Inc., October 17, 1975, p. 4.

14. In an unpublished letter to Ralph Bonacker, dated December 15, 1944, Boisen wrote, "Please do not misunderstand me. I do not for a minute propose to leave Freud and Jung and Adler out of account. I merely insist that they be recognized as secondary sources and used to help interpret actual experience" (file 4, drawer 4, Boisen Files, Chicago Theological Seminary.)

15. Anton T. Boisen, "Types of Mental Illness: A Beginning Course for Use in the Training Centers of the Council for Clinical Training of Theological Students," Vol. 1, unpublished mimeographed book, 1946, p. 2.

experiences. These objectives are also found in his "Beginning Course" manual, which contained many of his collected case studies and their analyses under a variety of headings.

1. To arouse an intelligent interest in the experiences of the mentally ill, acquainting the student with the achievements of psychiatrists, psychologists and social workers but raising questions and bringing to bear insights which are germane to his own special province.

2. To train the student in those methods of co-operative inquiry which are essential to the building up of a body of organized and tested knowledge pertaining to the experiences of the mentally ill and the means of helping them.

3. To explore the interrelationship between mental illnesses of the functional type and religious experiences which are recognized as valid.

4. To discover the forces and formulate the laws of the spiritual life, revealed in the disturbed conditions, which apply to human nature in general.[16]

Boisen's assumption in these goals is that the individual experiences of mentally ill persons will have general application to the student's understanding of the religious lives of "normal" persons, thus enhancing the student's ability to function as a minister.

Actual Social conditions. In addition to the pastoral assessment of individual experiences, Boisen also applied his method to study social groups. One example of this is his study of the religious beliefs in his home town of Bloomington, Indiana. In this paper it was his objective

to study the history of a particular middle western county with special reference to a pattern which appears to be recurrent in the development of organized religion and the forces which are operative in determining this pattern.[17]

The similarity in language between this and objectives cited for individual studies indicates that Boisen simply shifted his efforts to a social setting while maintaining the same method. This was true in his first survey for Arthur Holt of the Roxbury section of Boston[18] and his later studies of the Holy Rollers.[19]

All three of these studies were combined with others in Boisen's book, *Religion in Crisis and Custom*, first published in 1955. In the Preface to this volume, Seward Hiltner states that it was Boisen's methodological objective to apply the rigorous but imaginative methods of science to religious phenomena, whether in the study of

16. *Ibid.*

17. Anton T. Boisen, "Dividend Protestantism in a Midwest County: A Study in the Natural History of Organized Religion," *The Journal of Religion*, 1940, Vol. 20, No. 4, p. 359.

18. Boisen, *Out of the Depths*, p. 149.

19. Anton T. Boisen, "Religion and Hard Times," *Social Action* 1939, Vol. 5, No. 3.

religion in persons or in groups. Hiltner noted that Boisen "attempted with remarkable success to bring the results of these studies together into an integrated theory."[20]

Boisen also combines both aspects of his two-fold objective in another book, *Problems in Religion and Life*, published in 1946. He describes this as "a manual for pastors with outlines for the co-operative study of personal experience in social situations."[21] In his autobiography, Boisen notes that this book exemplifies the methods he has employed.[22] It is perhaps the most comprehensive and most practical application of his case study method to the work of the pastor. It contains outlines and bibliographies designed to assist the pastor in researching a variety of pastoral situations—again, with a purpose: to gain greater theological understanding of the issues involved and thus enhance the pastor's functioning.

Scientific Principles. In his case study method, Boisen sought to use the best-known scientific principles of his day. Even though he did much of his work during the time of the "Fundamentalist-Modernist" controversy in American religion, Boisen saw no conflict between the areas of religion and science. He believed that religion could learn much more from science, and that in fact theology was "The Queen of the Sciences."[23] In much of his work, Boisen refers to John Dewey's five-step process of reflective thinking as an explanation of the weaknesses of previous scientific methods. In new areas of exploration, hard-and-fast conclusions cannot always be reached. However, the "distinguishing characteristic of modern science" is Dewey's fifth step: "Observation and experimentation to test by empirical fact the suggested solutions in the light of their consequences."[24]

In much of his published and unpublished work, Boisen repeatedly lists seven scientific principles which are important to his method: Empiricism, Objectivity, Continuity, Particularity, Universality, Economy, and Disinterestedness. The principle of Empiricism seems to be most important to his method. He defines this as "the raw material of experience in all its complexity," which is taken as the starting point. He calls for the inductive method, saying that the researcher may be guided by generalizations and "hunches," but actual experience gives him his primary sources and his final authority.[25]

---

20. Anton T. Boisen, *Religion in Crisis and Custom* (New York, NY: Harper and Brothers, 1955), p. xi.

21. Anton T. Boisen, *Problems in Religion and Life* (Nashville, TN: Abingdon-Cokesbury Press, 1946), p. 3.

22. Boisen, *Out of the Depths*, p. 189.

23. Boisen, *The Exploration of the Inner World*, pp. 181-215.

24. Anton T. Boisen, "The Task and the Methods of Theology," unpublished mimeographed paper, n.d., file 4, drawer 3, Boisen Files, Chicago Theological Seminary.

25. *Ibid.*

The concept of Disinterestedness is also very significant to Boisen's method. He believed that the good scientific worker, in his desire to find the truth, must be able to "recognize and discount personal bias."[26] In discussing this principle in *The Exploration of the Inner World*, Boisen said that while his own experience gave him the ideas of what to look for, he sought to remain objective by excluding his experience from the field of inquiry.[27]

Forms

In keeping with the above theory and objectives, Boisen's case study method followed a general pattern of fact-finding, presentation and analysis of data, and discussion of generalizations or implications. In order to have standardized, reliable instruments with which to gather data in empirical fashion, Boisen developed several case analysis forms. The forms discussed in this section are those which were used to study the individual experiences of patients in psychiatric hospitals—the "living human documents." To my knowledge, these forms do not appear in detail in any of Boisen's published works. On the other hand, a detailed methodology for his study of social groups is apparent in his later publications.[28] Therefore, the rest of this article will be devoted to a discussion of the method used to study individual experience.

Form A. What I shall call "Form A" was apparently used frequently by Boisen throughout his career. It appears in many different places in his personal files which are maintained in the Hammond Library at Chicago Theological Seminary. It was reproduced in his "Beginning Course" manual which he distributed to clinical training centers and which is dated 1946. Since this manual contains many cases from Worcester State Hospital, one may assume that Boisen used this form in the late 1920's while he was employed at Worcester. At the end of the form, Boisen gives reference to an unpublished "Syllabus of Examination for Psychiatric Cases" by Adolf Meyer, indicating that this may have provided a basic structure for Boisen's form.

I shall list the basic categories of inquiry which appear in this form. Many detailed questions appear under each category, but space does not allow their inclusion in this article.

I. Preliminary Orientation

   [A brief description of the patient, including age, sex, and previous admissions to the hospital.]

---

26. *Ibid.*, p. 2.

27. Boisen, *The Exploration of the Inner World*, pp. 184-85.

28. For example, see "Questions for the Study of a Religious Cult," in Boisen, *Problems in Religion and Life*, pp. 124-25.

II. Social and Religious Background

[The outstanding features of the patient's heredity and environment, including the social, economic, and religious status of parents, grandparents, and other family members.]

III. Personal History (Previous to Illness)

   A. Early Childhood

       1. Pre-natal Influences

       2. Birth Conditions

       3. Disposition

       4. Walking, Talking, Weaning (if breast-fed), Sphincter-control

       5. Physical Health and Vigor

   B. School Years

       1. Studies

       2. Special Abilities and Disabilities

       3. Health

       4. Social Relationships

          a. With members of the home group

          b. With teachers

          c. With school-mates

          d. With pets

       5. Work and Play

          a. Leisure time

          b. Chores and duties at home

       6. Personality

   C. Adolescence and Maturity

       1. Social Adjustments

          a. Primary Loyalties [with parents and other groups]

          b. Social Contacts

          c. Accomplishments

          d. Recreations and Satisfactions

          e. Religion [church affiliation, attendance, attitudes]

          f. Personality [12 characteristics listed]

       2. Sex Adjustments

          a. Childhood and Adolescent Difficulties

          b. Attitude toward the Same or toward Opposite Sex

          c. Special Attachment or Antagonism toward Either Parent or Other Member of Family

          d. Love Affairs and Disappointments

          e. Sex Irregularities Before and After Marriage

          f. Marriage [facts concerning courtship, wife, children]

       3. Vocational Adjustments

          a. Plans and Ambitions

          b. Industrial Record

          c. Attitude toward Work

          d. Relationship with Employers and Fellow Workers

          e. Opportunity for Self-expression

      4.   Physical Condition and Health

  D. Later Years

     An examination of any major changes in the person's life situation and current health condition.

IV. History of Present Illness (previous to present admission)

    Includes symptoms, changes in behavior, religious concern, attitudes of family toward illness.

V. Characteristics of the Disorder (during period of observation in hospital)

  A. Changes in condition

  B. General Appearance and Behavior

  C. Intellectual Functions

  D. Content of Thought

      1.   Sense of the Mysterious and Uncanny

      2.   Sense of Peril

      3.   Personal Responsibility

      4.   Erotic Involvement

      5.   Philosophy of Life

      6.   Plans and Ambitions

VI. Diagnostic Impressions

  A. An appraisal of the Life Situation

  B. An Analysis of the Reaction Patterns

  C. An Analysis of the Personality Organization

  D. A Consideration of the Clinical Label

  E. A Forecast of the Outcome

  F. A Plan of Treatment

VII. Interpretation

    The diagnostic impression is a consideration of the patient's problem in light of his previous history and of our knowledge of other cases of mental disorder. It is directed specifically toward the problems of classification, prognosis and treatment and it seeks to do this as concisely as possible. From the standpoint of our general problem it is of great value to follow this with an attempt to relate our findings to the experiences of normal persons and to constructive religious experience. More important still is the attempt to review the patient's experience in the light of certain general hypotheses to see how far these hypotheses will explain the phenomena. In any such attempt it is hardly worth while to begin with any fixed categories. The question before us is, What is there in this man's particular experience which becomes intelligible when we consider it in the light of certain leads or theories? What light does this case throw upon the laws of the spiritual life with which we are all concerned?

VIII. Observations and Progress Notes

    Good case records append the primary data upon which the case record has been based. Such data should include the daily notes and observations both before and after the case has been written up and the diagnostic summary made.

    After the completion of the report the daily or weekly notes and observations should from time to time be supplemented by diagnostic and interpretive comments.

Form B. Another instrument found in Boisen's files follows essentially the same format as Form A but is much more detailed in some areas. Most of the questions are spaced about an inch apart, indicating that this form could be filled out by the researcher while interviewing the patient. This form differs in two major areas from Form A. The first is a section labeled "Religious Concern" which appears under "Characteristics of the Disorder" (segment V in Form A). It reads as follows:

Religious Concern
Degree of concern about vital issues
Forces upon which he conceives himself to be dependent—personal or impersonal? human
    or superhuman? friendly or unfriendly? monistic or dualistic?
Practice of prayer, Bible reading, attendance at religious services
Self estimate—exalted or self-depreciative?
Ideas of—communication with God
        conflict with evil spirits
        remorse over sins
        expiation
        cosmic identification
        rebirth
        previous incarnation
        prophetic mission

The second section of Form B which does not appear in Form A is one labeled "Religious Attitude and Orientation." It is a separate section following one labeled "Present Condition" and before the Diagnostic Summary. It reads as follows:

RELIGIOUS ATTITUDE AND ORIENTATION

Present Concern about Vital Issues
His Interpretation of the Disturbance
Attendance at—church services
        mental health conferences
Practice of Prayer
        of Bible reading
Reasons given for Attendance or Non-attendance at Church
His concept of the Bible
His idea of the chief end of life
His concept of God
His concept of the cross

Form C. Form C is worthy of note because it appears to be that which Boisen used to gather data for the 173 cases summarized in Part I of *The Exploration of the Inner World.* Before discussion of these data he wrote,

> I have also interviewed most of the patients with the aid of a list of questions based
> upon the analysis of the thought content found in the first eighty cases [possibly with

the use of Form A]. These questions have proved most helpful in gaining access to the mind of the patient and revealing his significant ideas.[29]

This questionnaire was developed in cooperation with Dr. Helen Flanders Dunbar, who came to Worcester State Hospital in the spring of 1927 in order to research the symbolism found in acutely disturbed patients.[30] Entitled "Schizophrenic Thinking," it contains 34 detailed questions under the six categories found in section V.D. of Form A plus a section labeled "Religious Concern." The "Philosophy of Life" and "Religious Concern" sections are reproduced below. Note the interest in symbolic thinking in uestion 29.

PHILOSOPHY OF LIFE

26. How much serious thinking do you do? What is your idea of what we are in the world for?
27. What is your idea of God? What reason do you have for believing in God? Have you ever seen him? heard him? What is your attitude toward him? his attitude toward you? How do you think we can please God most?
28. Do you believe in other superhuman beings besides God? (If the answer is, Yes, inquire into the reasons for such a belief, searching particularly for any special experiences which may have led to such belief.)
29. What is your idea of this universe in which we live? What do you think of when you see (a) the sun? b) the moon? c) the stars? d) water? e) fire? f) flowers? g) trees? h) rocks?

(In case of particular ideas inquire into their possible origin, as in previous reading, early teachings, etc.)

RELIGIOUS CONCERN

30. What does church mean to you? Have you been accustomed to attending it? To what church do you belong? How often do you go to the services here? What is your reason for going, or not going?
31. What does prayer mean to you? Has it given you any special comfort or help? Have you received any special answers to prayer? For what kind of things should one pray?
32. What does the Bible mean to you?
33. What ups and downs have you had in your religious life? What attempts have you made to turn over a new leaf? Have you had any periods of marked awakening? of back-sliding? When you were at your best?

---

29. Boisen, *The Exploration of the Inner World*, p. 17.
30. *Ibid.*, p. 17n c.f. Boisen, *Out of the Depths*, p. 160.

Evaluation and Implications

The forms cited above may appear to be too tedious and complex to be used as general instruments of pastoral assessment. However, they were intended to point out major areas of concern for the person seeking to understand another individual's experience. In the introductory statements to both forms A and C, Boisen warned against their use in a systematic or mechanical way. They were designed to help Boisen and his students identify the central problems and difficulties which would then lead the researcher into specific areas which needed further study. Boisen also noted that in the preparation of case records for teaching purposes the researcher may depart from the suggested plan of organization in order to highlight significant findings. This is indeed the way in which Boisen prepared many of his cases for use in clinical training groups.

At the same time, it is perhaps the thoroughness and exhaustiveness of Boisen's case study method which is its primary strength. Indeed, as I noted at the beginning of this discussion, Boisen had a *reason* to be thorough—he was engaged in a search for meaning and understanding of his own experience. This helped him to know which questions to ask in making a pastoral assessment. Nevertheless, as Paul Pruyser notes, Boisen was never satisfied with "one-shot impressions" in the write-up of his cases.[31] He was careful not to place too much emphasis on the precipitating factor of a disturbance, because he was convinced that acute disorders were the result of the *accumulation* of inner stresses throughout a person's developmental history. It was only through the careful gathering of these developmental data that Boisen could obtain a longitudinal view of "the ups and downs, the contradictions and inconsistencies, the morbid fantasies or the healthy reality testing which one patient would manifest over a stretch of time."[32] For this reason, Boisen insisted on adequate information in order to make an accurate assessment. In keeping with his theory, he also often included bibliographic references in his case analyses, indicating that he usually sought to make use of written research available on the subjects being considered.

Therefore, there are at least two points at which Anton Boisen's case study method can have relevance to contemporary efforts at pastoral assessment. First of all, a common dilemma of the "busy pastor" is to be forced to make superficial judgements based on inadequate information. The extra investment of time spent in learning the details and the background of the parishioner's situation will enable the pastor to be more prescriptive, and therefore more effective, in his or her pastoral care and counseling. For example, many of the questions listed under the "Religious Concerns" sections of Forms B and C above would enable the pastor to

---

31. Pruyser, *op. cit.*, p. 215.
32. *Ibid.*

have a more complete understanding of the parishioner's religious history and theological understanding, thus facilitating communication on issues of deep spiritual concern to the parishioner.

This leads to a second important implication of Boisen's method. As stated earlier, a basic goal of Boisen's method was to study and understand religious experience as well as to stimulate the formation of the student's own theology. As part of his case discussions, Boisen prepared many questions which forced students to think theologically about human experience. The ability to think theologically about human situations is a stated goal in many educational experiences (including CPE) for seminarians and pastors. Indeed, it is a very worthwhile goal, but it is very hard to achieve. In my experiences in teaching and supervision thus far, I have found both students and professors often fail at the point of being able to make significant theological assessments of pastoral situations. Until this is done, the pastor is unable to minister to the whole person. The legacy of Anton T. Boisen to the art of pastoral assessment may well be the insight that one must take the time and the discipline to ask the right questions in order to obtain a more complete theological perspective on human situations.

◈ ◈ ◈

THE PSYCHIATRIC DIAGNOSIS OF ANTON BOISEN: FROM SCHIZOPHRENIA TO BIPOLAR AFFECTIVE DISORDER

Carol North and William M. Clements

[These authors noted in the December, 1981 issue of *The Journal of Pastoral Care* that there has apparently been no published study which focused solely on Boisen's psychiatric diagnosis. Using Boisen's own approach of empirical investigation, North and Clements carefully applied the DSM-III criteria for schizophrenia, depression, and mania to Boisen's description of his symptoms in his autobiography, *Out of the Depths*. As they admit, this is by no means equal to a personal interview; nor is the issue of his diagnosis of primary importance in assessing his work. Nevertheless, the authors make a very plausible case that, according to current psychiatric understanding, Boisen's mental illness was likely to have been bipolar affective disorder rather than schizophrenia.]

The life and work of Anton T. Boisen hardly need an introduction for many readers of this journal, so significant was his personal and professional experience in the earliest days of the movement which later became known as clinical pastoral education.[1] Boisen was a remarkable person in many respects. Nearly fifty years of professional activity separated his graduation from Union Theological Seminary, in 1911 at age 35, and his last publication, the widely read autobiography *Out of the Depths* published in 1960 when he was 84. Other commentators have aptly noted the

---

1. Edward E. Thornton, *Professional Education for Ministry: A History of Clinical Pastoral Education* (Nashville, TN: Abingdon, 1970), pp. 55-71.

intense autobiographical flavor found in many of Boisen's studies[2] and the fact that more than two-thirds of his publications occurred after his sixtieth year,[3] when many people are anticipating retirement from professional life. The chronology of Boisen's professional career, which never quite fit the mold of normative expectations, was really no more unusual than other aspects of his life. He remains a unique person to this day.

In a memorial editorial published shortly after Boisen's death in 1965, Seward Hiltner organized his contributions into six broad categories: theology through living human documents; mental illness as attempted re-adaptation; clinical pastoral education; psychology of religion; pastoral psychology; and personal aspects.[4] This list communicates something of the breadth of Boisen's interests. However, only direct familiarity with his more than 80 publications, including articles in the leading theological, pastoral, sociological, and psychiatric journals of his day, can adequately communicate the depth of his work. Understandably, this body of published material has continued to attract the attention of theorists and practitioners alike.

During the more than sixty years since Boisen's first psychiatric hospitalization, medicine, like the rest of the world, has experienced advances in knowledge leading to greater precision in clinical descriptions and predictions of outcome. In practical terms this means that diagnoses such as "consumption," for example, which were common in 1920, have been replaced by more precise categories like chronic bronchitis, carcinoma of the lung, or tuberculosis. As knowledge advances, broad categories either become more restricted in their application, or they simply disappear. Psychiatric diagnoses have gone through significant revolutions during this period of time as well. One has merely to refer to the various editions of the *Diagnostic and Statistical Manual* used by practicing psychiatrists to observe this phenomenon.[5]

---

2. Paul W. Pruyser, "Anton T. Boisen and the Psychology of Religion," *The Journal of Pastoral Care*, 1967 vol. 21, p. 209.

3. Thornton, *op. cit.*, p. 58.

4. Seward Hiltner, "The Heritage of Anton T. Boisen," *Pastoral Psychology*, 1965, vol. 16, pp. 6-9.

5. American Psychiatric Association, Task Force on Nomenclature and Statistics, *Diagnostic and Statistical Manual of Mental Disorders*, 3rd ed. (Washington, DC: American Psychiatric Association, 1980). The first and second editions, prepared by the Committee on Nomenclature and Statistics, were published in 1952 and 1968. These manuals evolved from the various editions of the *Statistical Manual for the Use of Hospitals for Mental Diseases* published in the 1920s, 1930s, and 1940s. The earliest such manual appears to be the *Statistical Manual for the Use of Institutions for the Insane* published in 1918 by the Committee on Statistics of the American Medico-psychological Association.

Recently, when a variety of first person accounts of mental illness were reviewed for another project,[6] interesting questions arose in regard to the psychiatric diagnosis which has hovered around the Boisen material. Our original question was framed in this way: "How could a person with schizophrenia write and function so coherently during the majority of his professional life?" The contrast between Boisen's writing and a recent first person account of schizophrenia appearing in *Pilgrimage*,[7] for example, could not be more dramatic. Even a casual reading of Boisen's autobiography leaves the reader familiar with contemporary psychiatric nomenclature with the feeling that somehow his "schizophrenia" is an anachronism.

Over the years many outstanding students of personality and religion have carefully delved into Boisen's writings for a variety of informative purposes. Almost invariably, however, when reading these works one finds Boisen referred to as "schizophrenic,"[8] the term he himself used when speaking of his own diagnosis in *Out of the Depths*.[9] Undoubtedly, the diagnostic category of schizophrenia could have, and very likely did, refer to Boisen's condition in 1920 when his first psychiatric hospitalization took place. However, what was schizophrenia in 1920 is not necessarily schizophrenia today.

Apparently, investigators have frequently accepted the "schizophrenic" aspect of Boisen's self concept, thereby perpetuating this terminology. Without a rigorous examination of the evidence, with psychiatric diagnosis as the prime concern, Boisen might easily be referred to uncritically as schizophrenic for yet another half century. Perhaps he was, but then again, perhaps he wasn't.

We do not, of course, challenge Anton Boisen's accuracy as an historian of his own condition. We do challenge the accuracy of this diagnosis *as it is understood in contemporary psychiatry* and applied retrospectively to the clinical condition detailed by Boisen in his autobiography.

Similarly, our investigation does not intend to devalue, or even critique, the main conclusions advanced by others in regard to Boisen. In those cases with which we are familiar, Boisen's actual psychiatric diagnosis was secondary to the authors' central purposes in their respective writings. Stated bluntly, we, too, believe that the psychiatric *diagnosis* of Boisen is not one of the more significant issues in his life; the presence of psychiatric symptoms, however, is. Boisen's mental disorder—how he brilliantly recorded it, explicated it, and found it existentially purposeful—is

---

6. Carol North, Remi J. Cadoret, "Diagnostic Discrepancy in Personal Accounts of Patients with 'Schizophrenia'," *Archives of General Psychiatry*, in press.

7. Elizabeth L. Farr, "Diary of a Schizophrenic," *Pilgrimage*, 1980, vol. 8, pp. 6-19.

8. Pruyser, *op.cit.*, p. 214; Brian Grant, *Schizophrenia: A Source of Social Insight* (Philadelphia, PA: Westminster Press, 1975), pp. 210-213, Lucy Bregman, "Anton Boisen Revisited," *Journal of Religion and Health*, 1979, vol. 18, pp. 213-229; Carroll A. Wise, *Pastoral Psychotherapy: Theory and Practice* (New York, NY: Jason Aronson, 1980), pp. 250-251, 255.

9. Anton T. Boisen, *Out of the Depths* (New York: Harper & Brothers, 1960).

certainly more important than the secondary organization of his symptoms into a factual diagnosis.

Although no claims are advanced for exhaustive thoroughness, we have found no study in which the primary concern is the psychiatric diagnosis of Boisen. The purpose of this study, therefore, is to help fill a gap in the literature by examining Boisen's life from *current* diagnostic perspectives. Our hope is that this effort will contribute in a small way to a greater understanding of Anton Theophilus Boisen, whom we have grown to respect even more as a result of this investigation.

Methodology

Symptom descriptions used to establish Boisen's diagnosis were obtained from his autobiographical account, *Out of the Depths*. This book was examined carefully for any frank psychiatric symptoms or descriptions of experiences which might be considered symptomatic within the context of other psychiatric manifestations. These symptoms and possible symptomatic experiences were first recorded on a primary symptom list. Then they were rearranged and assigned to appropriate diagnostic categories as described in the third edition of the *Diagnostic and Statistical Manual* (DSM-III), which has only recently become available. To be listed under a particular diagnostic category from DSM-III a symptom had to be more than just inferred; it had to be described without equivocation.

The three diagnostic categories that emerge with particular relevance for this study are *schizophrenia, mania,* and *depression.* Enough symptomatic experiences described by Boisen fell into each of these categories to warrant careful consideration for diagnosis. (Other categories contained so few criteria matching Boisen's description that they were discarded early in the study.) Once all of the symptoms were accounted for, the three diagnostic categories were carefully assessed to determine whether the symptom picture described by Boisen met diagnostic criteria for schizophrenia, mania, or depression.

The method utilized in this study—sifting psychiatric details from the context of an autobiography—is no substitute for a careful first person interview conducted within a positive therapeutic atmosphere of mutual give-and-take. Nor is it a substitute for a review of Boisen's actual case records. Short of these ideal conditions, however, our approach appears to hold the promise of yielding the best obtainable information.

A second, and potentially more serious, qualification is the likelihood that Boisen inadvertently omitted relevant symptoms from his autobiography, especially since his graduate training was in language and theology, not psychiatry. Undoubtedly, a personal selection factor also influenced the inclusion of particular symptoms and the omission of others, despite his strenuous efforts for veracity and completeness. These concerns are, however, ones about which nothing can be done in an historical investigation with no recourse to the "living document."

The actual question of psychiatric diagnosis and symptomatology is not one which Boisen ignores, or even minimizes, in his own story. In fact, as his life unfolds he carefully presents these symptoms in their chronological order of occurrence. Later he labels them and cites the page numbers on which they may be found.[10] For those readers who might have ignored their presence and significance on a first reading, he provides an index, if you please—not the style of one who abhors psychiatric diagnosis or withdraws in horror when words like "psychosis" or "schizophrenia" are used in reference to his experience. The present study, therefore, does not appear to risk violating the spirit of one who used his own experience as important data in the study of the psychology of religion.

Results

I. Schizophrenia

As a major psychotic illness, schizophrenia is defined by the presence of six specific conditions (A-F), each of which must be met for the diagnosis to be made.

A. For a positive diagnosis the patient must meet one or more of the following conditions:

1. Delusions of control or delusions of thought broadcasting, insertion, or withdrawal. Boisen records no delusions of this type.

2. Somatic, grandiose, religious, nihilistic, or other delusions in the absence of persecutory or jealous content.

Example of a grandiose delusion:

> Something terrible was about to happen. This world of ours was to have become a brilliant star; but something had gone wrong, and it was now to become a Milky Way. I was, it seemed, or should have been, a very important person; and my failure was chiefly responsible for the impending catastrophe . . . (p. 170).

Example of a religious delusion:

> . . . I came upon a horse-blanket within which was wrapped up some peculiar white linen fabric. These it seemed were some most scared relics. They were connected with the search for the Holy Grail and represented the profoundest spiritual struggle of the centuries. Then I found

---

10. *Ibid.*, p. 202.

that by lying flat on the floor near the ventilator shaft, I could hear the most beautiful voice I had ever heard. It was the celebration of the Last Supper . . . (p.93).

Example of nihilistic delusion:

I was too much absorbed in my own thoughts, particularly those regarding the approaching end of the world and those responsible for the use of force and for the charge homicidal intent . . . (p. 88).

What prevents these bizarre nihilistic, grandiose, and religious delusions from carrying full weight toward a schizophrenic diagnosis is their temporal connection to Boisen's mood. Examples of such delusions were noted only when Boisen was either excited or depressed.

3. Persecutory or jealous delusions with hallucinations.

Example of a persecutory delusion:

A little later he brought me food, an unusually generous portion, but I refused to eat it, because I thought it was drugged. I remember also some voices going through a ritualistic service in a sing song fashion which was distasteful to me and sounded insincere. . . (p. 93).

It is not clear in the text whether the voices were a part of the delusion of drugged food, but since they seem unrelated to the content of that delusion, they cannot be indisputably considered to fulfill the criterion of a persecutory hallucination.

4. Voices: commentary on patient's behavior or conversing with each other. Boisen's voices were not of this nature.

5. Mood-incongruent voices.

All voices described by Boisen occurred in the context of mood disturbances such as depression or elation.

6. Incoherence, loose associations, illogical speech, or poverty of speech in the presence of inappropriate affect, delusions or hallucinations, or catatonic or disorganized behavior.

Example of illogical speech:

I took his suggestion [the attendant told him to go back to bed] and began to raise a disturbance, calling out at the top of my lungs the first and craziest thing that came into my head. This happened to be, "I've got to go insane in order to get married" (p. 89).

Example of incoherence: Boisen's statement of belief—

> I believe in the immortality of the human soul and in the survival of the personality. I believe that life consists of two cycles, one in the flesh and one in the embryonic condition. These cycles consist of strong-weak and perfect-imperfect combination, in which the strong is mated with the weak and the perfect with the imperfect. I believe that a reversal of this combination would secure a better race. This would come through the refusal of the weak and the imperfect to accept their claim of pity and of need. I believe that such a refusal will alone release the divine from its prison-house and enable it to overcome the world. This should do away with death and establish communication throughout the world (p. 80).

Boisen's periods of incoherence and illogical speech can probably be interpreted most accurately as behaviors associated with his elevated mood and general over-excitement. He does not cite examples where illogical or incoherent speech occur apart from such conditions.

B. The symptoms in Category A must also be associated with significant deterioration in functioning in at least two major life areas.

Examples of impairment:

a) self-care—Boisen was hospitalized on three separate occasions due to his inability to maintain himself adequately outside the hospital environment:

b) work—Boisen's career suffered intermittently from psychotic episodes in which he ceased to function effectively.

This dysfunction is eloquently described in the following passage:

> Throughout this period I was in a violent delirium and I spent most of the time reposing in cold packs or locked up in one of the small rooms in Ward 2, often pounding on the door and singing . . . (p.87).

C. Symptoms must last continuously for at least six months in order to make a diagnosis of schizophrenia.

It appears from our examination that no episode lasted longer than about five months, so Boisen does not fulfill the requirement for chronicity.

D. Any affective symptoms are either brief or occur after the schizophrenic psychosis.

In each of Boisen's psychotic episodes clear affective symptoms were part of the experience; in fact, the affective symptoms are described as the central feature of the psychotic experience.

E. Onset of schizophrenic symptoms must occur prior to 45 years of age. Boisen meets this requirement; his first psychiatric symptoms appeared in 1905 at age 29 and his first psychiatric hospitalization occurred in 1920 at age 44.

F. Organic causation must be ruled out in making a diagnosis of schizophrenia.

There is no evidence of an organic basis (i.e., drug ingestion, organic brain problems, as with some epilepsies, or metabolic syndromes such as porphyria) for any of Boisen's psychotic episodes.

In summary, Boisen might possibly have met three criterion symptoms (from Category A); he met Category B by showing clear deterioration in functioning; he also met Category E, onset prior to 45 years of age, and Category F, freedom from organicity. He cannot, however, be definitively diagnosed as schizophrenic according to DSM-III criteria for the following reasons: his criterion symptoms (from Category A) were either not clear enough or they occurred as part of an affective disturbance (i.e., mania or depression); his psychotic episodes were not a sufficient duration (Category C); and his affective symptoms were central to his psychotic episodes (Category D).

Table A
Schizophrenia

A. Meets one or more of the following:
   1. delusions of control; thought broadcasting, insertion, withdrawal .... No
   2. somatic, grandiose, religious, nihilistic, or other delusions in the absence of persecutory or jealous content ...... Possible
   3. persecutory or jealous delusions with hallucinations .... Possible
   4. voices: commentary on patient's behavior or conversing with each other .... No
   5. mood-incongruent voices .... No
   6. incoherence, loose association, illogical speech, or poverty of speech in the presence of inappropriate affect, delusions..... Possible
B. Deterioration in functioning .... Yes
C. 6-month duration .... No
D. Any affective symptoms are either brief or occur after psychosis .... No
E. Onset before 45 years of age .... Yes
F. Not organically based .... Yes

Can make diagnosis of schizophrenia? .... No

II. Depression.

Depression is defined by DSM-III as an affective illness with five criterion categories necessary for diagnosis.

   A. For a positive diagnosis of depression the patient must experience low mood for a least two weeks.

   Boisen indicates he experienced low mood in several instances, for example:

   > It was a beautiful day, but there was no sunshine for me, and no beauty—nothing but black despair (p. 47).

   B. For a positive diagnosis the patient must meet at least four of the following symptoms continuously for a period of at least two weeks:

   1. Poor appetite or weight loss.

   This is not mentioned in Boisen's account.

   2. Sleep problem.

   This was a major complaint during Boisen's periods of low mood; for example:

> Because of the tense and suggestible state of mind I was in that morning, this sermon [about obedience to God's will] could hardly have failed to have a profound effect. I took it as a message to me. It was followed by several sleepless nights (p. 54).

3. Agitation or retardation.

Boisen describes having experienced a trancelike state on at least two occasions. His thinking at these times exhibited strong depressive tendencies. The following example may represent the retardation (or slowed functioning) of depression, or possibly a confusional state or a kind of depersonalization more characteristic of schizophreniform illnesses.

> I was dazed. It seemed an impossible ending. But I did not give way to the reaction of weakness, as in the earlier rebuffs. For several days I remained in Chicago, pleading with her. Then there came upon me a trancelike state similar to the one in Washington in 1908, and with many of the same ideas (p. 74).

4. Loss of interest, pleasure, or sex drive.

Example of loss of pleasure:

> It was a beautiful day, but there was no sunshine for me, and no beauty—nothing but black despair (p. 47).

5. Low energy; fatigue.

Boisen does not complain of this symptom.

6. Guilt or worthless feelings.

Expressions characteristic of depressive thinking were a central feature of several of Boisen's psychotic episodes. Example:

> I felt stripped of self-respect and burdened with a heavy sense of failure and guilt (p. 46).

7. Slowed thinking, decreased concentration, or indecisiveness.

Example of decreased concentration:

> I found myself unable to do the routine classwork. Only what was related to my dominant interests could hold my attention (p. 47).

8. Death or suicide thoughts; suicide attempts.

Boisen describes none of these. It seems likely that he would have mentioned them had they been present.

C. For a diagnosis of depression there must be no bizarre behavior or mood-incongruent delusions or hallucinations in the absence of depressive symptoms.

All of Boisen's psychotic behaviors occurred within the context of mood perturbation.

D. The depressive symptoms must not be superimposed on a schizophrenic or paranoid disorder.

Schizophrenia has already been ruled out. Paranoid features were secondary to affective disorders and cleared when these symptoms abated.

E. The depressive symptoms must not be organically based.

Boisen presents no evidence to support an organic causation for his depression.

In summary, then, Boisen appears to meet DSM-III criteria for at least one episode of depression. He meets the low mood requirement (from Category A); he meets at least six criterion symptoms from Category B; his psychotic behaviors were all mood-congruent (Category C); his depressive symptoms were not part of some other psychiatric disorder (Category D); and he also meets the requirement of freedom from organicity (Category E).

Table B
Depression

A.	Low mood	Yes
B.	One or more of the following for two or more weeks:	Yes (4)
	1. poor appetite or weight loss	No
	2. sleep problem	Yes
	3. agitation or retardation	Possible
	4. loss of interest, pleasure, or sex drive	Yes
	5. low energy, fatigue	No
	6. guilt or worthless feeling	Yes
	7. slowed thinking, decreased concentration, or indecisiveness	Yes
	8. death or suicide thoughts; suicide attempts	No
C.	No bizarre behavior or mood-incongruent delusions or hallucinations in the absence of affective symptoms	Yes
D.	Not superimposed on schizophrenic or paranoid disorder	Yes
E.	Not organically based	Yes
	Can make diagnosis of depression?	Yes

III.Mania.

Mania is described by DSM-III as an affective illness with five criterion categories necessary for diagnosis.

A. For a positive diagnosis of mania the patient must experience an elevated or irritable mood for a period of at least one week. Boisen describes an elevated mood as a dominant feature of several psychotic episodes, for example:

> I was tremendously excited. In some way, I could not tell how, I felt myself joined onto some superhuman course of strength. The idea came, 'Your friends are coming to help you.' I seemed to feel new life pulsing all through me. And it seemed that a lot of new worlds were forming (p. 89).

B. For a positive diagnosis the patient must meet at least three (four, if mood is irritable rather than elevated) of the following symptoms continuously for a period of at least one week.

1. Increased activity.

Boisen not only took to writing intensely during his period of elevated mood, but he experienced derangement of his behavior in a generally excited and overactive fashion, for example:

> I threw myself into the task, became intensely absorbed in it, so much so that I lay awake at night letting ideas take shape of themselves. This was for me nothing new. Writing has never been easy for me, and it is only under strong feeling and concentrated attention that ideas begin to come. I was therefore merely following what I regarded as a necessary and, for me, normal method of work. This time, however, the absorption went beyond the ordinary. I was no longer interested in anything else, and I spent all the time possible in my room writing (p.78-79).

2. Pressure of speech.

Boisen was not observant about this aspect of his behavior, at least partially because the nature of his illness did not allow him the perspective of a third-person observer. We do not know if he demonstrated pressure of speech; however, we do have evidence of pressure of writing in lengthy statements written during his psychotic periods. In addition, he gives an account of his sense that ideas were coming too fast, a phenomenon which is likely to be manifested in the form of pressure of speech.

3. Flight of ideas or racing thoughts.

Boisen's writings during his psychotic periods demonstrate a problem with flight of ideas. To a certain extent he recognized this difficulty.

Example:

> . . . strange ideas came surging into my mind, ideas of my own suspected importance. With them began the frank psychosis . . . (p. 79).

4. Grandiosity.

Boisen admitted to "delusions of grandeur" (p. 92). For example, he thought he was a very important person (p. 79) and once he thought he was at the Last Supper (p. 93).

Example:

> While working one day on the Statement of Belief—I think it was Wednesday, October 6— some strange ideas came surging into my mind, ideas of doom, ideas of my own unsuspected importance (p. 79).

5. Decreased sleep needs.

Boisen described extended periods during which he did not sleep anywhere from one or two nights (pp. 78, 115) to ten weeks (p. 120).

Example:

> It was my job to defeat the plans of those whom I regarded as enemies, some of whom, it seemed, were representatives of the devil himself. This required constant watchfulness, and throughout those ten weeks I scarcely dared to sleep (p. 120).

6. Distractability.

Example:

> But I kept getting more and more excited. I was invited to play checkers and started doing so, but I could not go on. I was too much absorbed in my own thoughts . . . (p.88).

7. Excessive activities with potentially painful consequences.

Boisen does not describe this type of behavior.

C. For a diagnosis of mania there must be no bizarre or mood-incongruent delusions or hallucinations in the absence of manic symptoms.

All of Boisen's psychotic behaviors occurred within the context of mood perturbation.

D. The manic symptoms must not be superimposed on a schizophrenic or paranoid disorder.

This has already been determined.

E. The manic symptoms must not be organically based.

Boisen gives no evidence that there was an organic cause for his mania.

In summary, then, Boisen appears to meet DSM-III criteria for at least one manic episode, and probably several such episodes. He meets the elevated mood requirement (Category A); he meets at least five criterion symptoms from category B; his psychotic behaviors were all mood-congruent (Category C); his manic symptoms were not part of some other psychiatric disorder (Category D); and he meets the requirement of freedom from organicity (Category C).

Table C
Mania

A. Elevated or irritable mood .... Yes

B. Three or more of the following for one or more weeks: .... Yes(5)

     1. increased activity .... Yes

     2. pressure of speech... Possible

     3. flight of ideas or racing thoughts .... Yes

     4. gradiosity.. Yes

     5. decreased sleep needs... Yes

     6. distractibility .... Yes

     7. excessive activities with potentially painful consequences.............. No

C. No bizarre behavior or mood-incongruent delusions or hallucinations in the absence of affective symptoms............................ Yes

D. Not superimposed on schizophrenic or paranoid disorder .... Yes

E. Not organically based .... Yes

Can make diagnosis of mania? .... Yes

Discussion

Schizophrenia is by contemporary definition a chronic and unremitting illness. The typical picture is one of insidious onset and continuous life-long disturbance, often with steady deterioration. Boisen, in contrast, did not show the insidious onset of psychosis typical of schizophrenia. He himself recognized that he had five distinct psychotic episodes, and possibly five additional episodes that came and departed very quickly—for example, "Then I snapped out of it, much as one awakens out of a bad dream . . ." (p. 95). For long periods in between these episodes Boisen was free from psychiatric symptomatology. Each of his psychotic episodes was triggered by a specific environmental event, particularly by times when his friend Alice, whom he loved, rejected him. The combination of rapid onset and departure of psychotic episodes with relatively normal functioning between the episodes, and the central role of affective symptomatology in the descriptions of his psychotic states are more suggestive of affective disorder than of schizophrenia.

Boisen's history is one of an acute onset of affective symptoms leading quickly to a floridly psychotic state lasting only a few weeks or months and remitting rapidly, with long periods of relatively good mental health. Current DSM-III standards reveal the dominance of manic and depressive symptoms during his psychotic periods, thus effectively ruling out schizophrenia as a diagnosis. This does not discount the severity of Boisen's illness, nor does it deny Boisen's psychosis; it merely recategorizes his illness into a different major psychiatric syndrome—bipolar affective disorder. Instead of describing Boisen's problems as schizophrenic, future investigators might refer to them as a bipolar disorder with a greater likelihood of being accurate in terms of current standards of diagnosis and nomenclature.

Conclusion

Persons with professional training in theology have often documented the distortions and inaccuracies found in the writing of psychiatrists and psychologists who attempt to interpret religious phenomena. (Perhaps the earliest example is the Rev. Oskar Pfister's *The Illusion of a Future*, written in response to Sigmund Freud's *The Future of an Illusion*.[11]) Now, the time has come for investigators within the cognate fields of the psychology of religion to insure that when diagnostic categories from psychiatry are employed, only the highest standards, reflecting the best of modern clinical practice be used as guidelines. In the case of Anton T. Boisen this procedure has led to a challenge of the "traditional" diagnosis employed in pastoral

---

11. Sigmund Freud, *The Future of an Illusion*, trans. by W. D. Robson-Scott (New York: Liveright and the Institute for Psychoanalysis, 1928) and Oskar Pfister, "Die Illusion einer Zukunft" (The Illusion of a Future), *Imago*, Bd. 14, 1928.

literature and the proposal of a new diagnosis—bipolar affective disorder—more in keeping with his clinical picture of a rapidly developing affective psychosis which clears with equal rapidity and is followed by significant periods of professional functioning on a high level. As knowledge continues to develop, this diagnosis, too, will in all likelihood become dated and need to be revised. For the time being, however, it appears to be the most accurate.

◈ ◈ ◈

ENCOUNTERING LIVING HUMAN DOCUMENTS: BOISEN AND CLINICAL PASTORAL EDUCATION

Glenn H. Asquith, Jr.

[Boisen has been criticized for the lack of a pastoral emphasis in his approach to clinical pastoral education (CPE). This article argues that there were indeed pastoral dimensions in Boisen's goals for CPE and that his basic theory and approach have continuing relevance to the contemporary practice of CPE. The first sections of this article, detailing Boisen's personal history, were incorporated into the Introduction to this book. The following is excerpted from the latter half of the article, which appeared in the Summer, 1988 issue of the *Journal of Psychology and Christianity*.]

The Goals of CPE

Boisen was convinced that the study of human experience would enable a theological student to form his or her own theology. In 1946, he produced a mimeographed manual and distributed it to all the centers that he visited. Entitled "Types of Mental Illness: A Beginning Course. . . ," the manual contained many of his favorite case studies along with his interpretation of them. It also contained a clear statement of his overall goal and objectives for CPE:

> This course is far less concerned with the consideration of techniques and skills than with the effort to discover the forces involved in the spiritual life and the laws by which they operate. It seeks to lay a foundation for the co-operative attempt to organize and

test religious experience and to build a theology on the basis of a careful scrutiny of religious beliefs.[1]

Following this statement, Boisen summarized the objectives of his training program.

1. To arouse an intelligent interest in the experiences of the mentally ill, acquainting the student with the achievements of psychiatrists, psychologists, and social workers but raising questions and bringing to bear insights which are germane to his own special province.

2. To train the student in those methods of co-operative inquiry which are essential to the building up of a body of organized and tested knowledge pertaining to the experiences of the mentally ill and the means of helping them.

3. To explore the interrelationship between mental illnesses of the functional type and religious experiences which are recognized as valid.

4. To discover the forces and formulate the laws of the spiritual life, revealed in the disturbed conditions, which apply to human nature in general.[2]

There are several notable emphases in these objectives. The first emphasis has to do with *pastoral identity*. From his own experience, Boisen knew that the patient suffered when a trained pastor was not present to help him or her interpret the meaning of his or her illness. Boisen did not intend to make "junior psychologists" out of his students; he wanted them to understand their own unique place in ministry to the mentally ill. This explains why he was concerned when he saw CPE centers placing psychoanalytic thought and practice at the center of their training process.

A second emphasis has to do with *knowledge and ministry*, a dual emphasis that Boisen saw as inseparable when it comes to pastoral care of the mentally ill. He stressed method and knowledge, but he also made a place for the learning of pastoral skills in CPE when he spoke of "the means of helping them."

A third emphasis had to do with Boisen's affirmation of the long-debated axiom that certain forms of "craziness" may actually be a sign of *religious insight* and experience. He had his students reading the case histories of George Fox, John Bunyan, Emmanual Swedenborg, and other noted religious leaders along with Biblical figures such as Ezekial, Jeremiah, and Saul of Tarsus. Boisen labeled these persons as "successful explorers" in the sense that, while they passed through periods

---

1. Anton T. Boisen, *Types of Mental Illness: A Beginning Course for Use in the Training Centers of the Council for the Clinical Training of Theological Students.* Vol. 1 (Unpublished mimeographed booklet, 1946), 2.

2. Ibid.

of severe emotional disturbance, their experience brought socially valued insight and significant achievement.[3]

The final emphasis maintains that study in a mental hospital will have *general application* to the religious life of normal persons in a parish setting. Theological and spiritual concepts may be tested as the student examines the experiences of the mentally ill. This study assists students in shaping their own theology and understanding of life, and this growth has general application to ministry. The latter point, which is the genius of CPE, is still often missed in contemporary practice. It may also be the reason why Boisen placed secondary importance on skill and practice and primary importance on identity, knowledge, and understanding. To be sure, Boisen's pastoral exploration was designed to assist mental patients, but it was also intended to enable theological students to become better pastors in any setting. This benefit of CPE should be realized regardless of the context of training, whether general hospital, psychiatric hospital, parish, prison, or street ministry. If the emphasis in training is only upon learning a particular skill, the student will miss the important wider application of constructing a pastoral theology.

All in all, Boisen's vision for CPE provided a new source of authority for the ministry of the church, which would be grounded in a disciplined study of human experience as an important supplement to doctrine and tradition. In an article promoting the cause of CPE, Boisen said,

> The theological training of the future will be a continuous affair, with the parish as the laboratory, and the person in difficulty as the main concern, and the seminary as the clearing house of information and the supervisor of methods. The attention will be shifted from the past to the present; from books to the raw material of life.[4]

Continuing Relevance

The prophetic statement above is a reflection of the way in which Boisen's thought is of continuing relevance to theological education and to CPE. In this concluding section, we will consider the contemporary implications of Boisen's views on the standards of CPE (the Clinical), on the role of worship (the Pastoral), and on the methodology of CPE (the Education).

---

3. Anton T. Boisen, *The Exploration of the Inner World: A Study of Mental Disorder and Religious Experience* Philadelphia: University of Pennslyvania Press, 1971 [1936]), 58-82; c.f. Brian W. Grant, *Schizophrenia: A Source of Social Insight* (Philadelphia: Westminster Press, 1975) which cites Boisen as a prime example of one whose illness brought social insight.

4. Anton T. Boisen, "The Challenge to Our Seminaries," *Christian Work* 120:4 (January 23, 1926), 11-12.

The Standards of CPE

As an organization grows, governing standards are necessary in order to maintain its integrity. Thornton's history of CPE tells the story of the struggles which developed among the early leaders in CPE to establish a set of standards. In 1967, forty-two years after the first unit of clinical training, four differing factions finally united and agreed on one set of standards which are updated annually.[5] These standards are intended to guarantee that any program of CPE, wherever offered, will meet certain clinical and educational requirements. An important part of the standards deal with and govern the certification of supervisors and the accreditation of training centers.

Unfortunately, the need for uniformity can inhibit the creativity and originality which often characterizes an organization's beginning. Boisen studied and understood this phenomenon in relationship to organized religion. He noted that religion arises out of human need but that it can lose its original fervor and meaning as it becomes organized.[6] Nevertheless, Boisen disagreed heartily with the concept of enforcing standards for the supervision and teaching of CPE.

It is ironic that two important figures in the development of CPE were rejected according to the standards created by that organization. Boisen himself was found to be unqualified as a supervisor by the Council for Clinical Training in 1945.[7] Wayne Oates, who studied with Boisen and who was the primary source for the acceptance of CPE among Southern Baptists, was also found unfit as a supervisor by the Council in 1946, even though he had met the standards then in vogue.[8] In a letter to Oates following this rejection, Boisen said, "As I see it, the function of the Council is far less to determine and enforce standards than to make possible collaboration on the part of those who are working in this field for the furtherance of their common objective."[9]

While the standards of the Association of Clinical Pastoral Education (ACPE) have served the important function of giving CPE credibility in clinical settings as well as in theological education, Boisen's view may still have relevance for the way these standards are used and enforced. It has been the experience of many in the recent past that the certification process for supervisors has focused more upon the *clinical* competence and interpersonal skills of the supervisor and less upon the candidate's *theological* competence and preparation. The multi-dimensional nature of CPE implies that academic ability, theological acumen, and skill as an educator are

---

5. Edward E. Thornton, *Professional Education for Ministry* (Nashville: Abingdon Press, 1970), 172-196.

6. Boisen, *The Exploration of the Inner World*, 214.

7. Thornton, *Professional Education for Ministry*, 63.

8. Ibid., 154.

9. Letter to Wayne Oates, June 18, 1946, Boisen Files, Chicago Theological Seminary.

just as important as the candidate's self-awareness and skill in giving the "right" spontaneous answers to examiners.

A further implication is that true clinical learning, as with meaningful religion, takes place on the edge of creative awareness. Boisen's thought gives testimony to the fact that those who may be regarded as "misfits" are often in the midst of significant growth and socially important insight. The early leaders of CPE were creative mavericks who were dissatisfied with the status quo. In the interest of standards, CPE cannot afford to lose the contemporary leadership of such persons, lest it become "at ease in Zion" and lose its place on the cutting edge of both pastoral care and theological education. Anton Boisen's cane, which is passed to the presidents of ACPE, is more than an artifact. It is a symbol of the prophetic origin of a movement which is still in need of "Pappy's" original ideas.

The Role of Worship

The lesser known but important aspect of Boisen's pastoral exploration is his belief in the importance of corporate worship. He saw the church as "no mere body of doctrine or ceremonies but a fellowship, and its central task is the perpetuation and re-creation of religious faith from mood to mood and from generation to generation."[10] In order to accomplish this task, the church must have leaders, symbols, practices, and creeds by which faith can be kept alive and vigorous.[11] Boisen was concerned not only for the relevance of theological tradition but also for the vitality and strength of the church.

Because of this, Boisen placed strong emphasis on the role of worship in ministry to the mentally ill. Early in his ministry at Worcester State Hospital he found that the hymnals that were available were weak theologically and dangerous psychologically. He noted that some of the hymns referred to enemies and could easily evoke hallucinations; others promoted the doctrine of the vacarious atonement and thus offered "an escape device rather than a summons to the sacrificial way of life."[12]

To address this problem, Boisen completed his own hymnal in 1926 and entitled it *Lift Up Your Hearts*. He revised it three times, with the last edition being published in 1950 under the title *Hymns of Hope and Courage*. It contained a suggested liturgy along with carefully selected hymns, prayers, and responsive scriptural readings with attention to their literary quality, doctrinal validity, and therapeutic effect. Boisen was convinced that

---

10. Anton T. Boisen, *Religion in Crisis and Custom* (New York: Harper & Brothers, 1955), 210.

11. Ibid., 212.

12. Anton T. Boisen, *Out of the Depths: An Autobiographical Study of Mental Disorder and Religious Experience.* (New York: Harper & Brothers, 1960), 155.

words do count and that religious belief is more likely to be affected by the hymns than by the sermons. For mental patients who are grappling desperately with what is for them Ultimate Reality, it is therefore of the utmost importance that the religious service should bring suggestions which are wholesome and constructive.[13]

Boisen was interested in more than just the therapeutic value of worship. Because of its religious and theological significance in the practice of faith, Boisen saw its leadership as an important part of his role as chaplain. He expected his students to give worship the same priority.[14] Boisen's emphasis on worship is significant for at least two reasons. First, it describes a major pastoral dimension of his work with patients. He was not engaged simply in detached, scientific study of their experiences but sought to address the meaning of their experience as well as to provide for worship which would be relevant to, and give inspiration in, the midst of their struggle. In his approach to worship he combined theological and psychological knowledge with a strong sense of pastoral identity, and he sought to pass this on to his students.

Second, Boisen's emphasis is a reminder to contemporary programs of CPE to continue the stress on worship as a part of ministry. Thomas Oden questions the validity of specialized pastoral counseling which is devoid of any liturgical or sacramental context.[15] Likewise, attention to worship as part of clinical pastoral education will not only strengthen the student's ministry to others but also provide another important forum for the testing and reflection of one's pastoral theology.

The Methodology of CPE

As noted earlier, one of Boisen's concerns in the development of CPE was a growing emphasis on "technique" as opposed to "understanding." An alternative to Boisen's case study approach in clinical training was developed by Russell Dicks in the form of the verbatim report. This method emerged out of necessity in Dicks' practice in general hospitals where students did not have long-term access to patients as they did in psychiatric hospitals. Further, it came in the context of Dicks' association with Cabot, whose interest in clinical training stressed the profes-

---

13. Ibid., 155-156.

14. On a mimeographed sheet entitled "Suggestions for Theological Students" given to students entering his clinical program at Elgin State Hospital in 1932, Boisen gave the following instructions: "Do not forget that you are here as a group of religious workers. As such you are expected to be loyal to the religious services of this institution. Attendance at services is indeed not required, but it is felt that unless you are out of town or on duty elsewhere your place on Sunday mornings is at the service which stands as the one weekly expression in this institution of the loyalty which we recognize as supreme." (Boisen Files, Chicago Theological Seminary).

15. Thomas C. Oden, *Pastoral Theology: Essentials of Ministry* (San Francisco: Harper & Row, 1983), 4.

sional functioning of the pastor in the face of human need.[16] Cabot and Dicks' collaboration on this issue resulted in the publication of the classic text *The Art of Ministering to the Sick* (1936).

The verbatim has been an important tool for the supervision of students in clinical settings where professional skill and self-awareness are important issues. Boisen himself saw it as an important contribution. He remained concerned, however, that its widespread use would result in a lessening of interest in the basic *understanding* of the experiences involved.[17] A heavy reliance on the verbatim has led CPE methodologically toward a greater focus on professional skill, making serious theological reflection a secondary concern. In 1975, Seward Hiltner observed that "the basic theological concern from which Boisen began has continued to occupy, at best, only a secondary position in most training centers."[18] Likewise, theologian Jenny Yates Hammett expressed the belief that "the original CPE concern to develop an empirical theology has over the years been retranslated as empirical psychology" and that CPE has not changed its "basic liberal orientation of scientific method over theological content."[19]

Several recent efforts have been made to restore theological reflection to the central place which Boisen advocated. In his approach to verbatims, William Arnold suggests that, before the student evaluates his or her performance in a pastoral encounter, he or she should do some systematic reflection on the theological issues involved. These include evidence of grace, mutual gifts, sense of hope, limitations, distortions, and possible future developments of the relationship.[20]

Paul Pruyser suggests that pastors employ a new definition for the old word "diagnosis." Instead of thinking in the categories of behavioral science, the minister should assess the person's situation in theological terms, including awareness of the holy, providence (and capacity to trust), faith, grace or gratefulness, repentence, communion, and sense of vocation.[21] Assessing case material in these kinds of categories will have a theological effect on the pastor's operational stance in relation to the person.

Charles Gerkin employs Boisen's image of the living human document as a paradigm for his hermeneutical theory of pastoral counseling. This theory integrates the language of psychology and theology in such a way as to shift the operational

---

16. Thornton, *Professional Education for Ministry*, 52-53.

17. Boisen, *Out of the Depths*, 185.

18. Seward Hiltner, "Fifty Years of CPE," *The Journal of Pastoral Care* 29:2 (June, 1975), 92.

19. Jenny Yates Hammett, "A Second Drink at the Well: Theological and Philosophical Context of CPE Origins," *The Journal of Pastoral Care* 29:2 (June, 1975), 89.

20. William V. Arnold, *Introduction to Pastoral Care* (Philadelphia: Westminster Press, 1982), 34.

21. Paul W. Pruyser, *The Minister as Diagnostician: Personal Problems in Pastoral Perspective* (Philadelphia: Westminster Press, 1976), 39, 60-79.

stance of the pastoral counselor to a *fundamentally* theological position—that of enabling clients to reinterpret the meaning of their experience in the light of the Judeo-Christian tradition. This shift will restore the discipline of pastoral care and counseling to the theologically-centered identity that Boisen sought. It will also prevent theological reflection on pastoral work from becoming "like the bumper sticker slapped on the bus as it is pulling out of the parking lot on its way to a psychologically determined destination."[22]

A careful study and reexamination of Boisen's thought can address the theological bankruptcy which characterizes much of clinical pastoral training. A simple nod to theological language in the evaluation of a verbatim usually does not change one's pastoral identity or approach in the relationship itself. Building on Boisen, Gerkin's hermeneutical approach provides one key. First of all, the autobiographical base of Boisen's work may be considered an important pastoral asset rather than a liability. It is impossible for a pastor to meet fully human beings at the point of their growth and pain unless that pastor has done some serious reflection on the meaning of his or her own experience. Inevitably, the experience of others touches our own experience, and unless pastors have come to terms with the meaning of their personal history, their ability to help others is limited. Indeed, Boisen may not have been fully aware of his own depths,[23] but his honest struggle to validate the meaning of his experience gave him a deep and significant meeting point in his ministry to the mentally ill.

Secondly, Boisen's in-depth case study method, with attention to theological issues, has the potential of *increasing* the pastor's skill in relation to others. Frequently, pastors can make a superficial or incorrect approach to a person on the basis of inadequate information. Taking the time and the discipline to make a careful study of another's experience will enable the pastor to be more effective in intervention and care, based on the more complete theological perspective which results from this method.

The testimony of some of Boisen's students at Elgin provides support for his approach to CPE. One student said, "My chief benefit was from a theological viewpoint. I think I see that theology was more important than I had thought."[24] Another student wrote, "I have been forced to rethink many of my own religious

---

22. Charles V. Gerkin, *The Living Human Document: Re-visioning Pastoral Counseling in a Hermeneutical Mode* (Nashville: Abingdon Press, 1984), 17-22.

23. See Ernest Becker, *The Revolution in Psychiatry: The New Understanding of Man* (New York, The Free Press, 1964), 81.

24. Charles E. S. Kramer, Letter to Anton T. Boisen, September 17, 1935 (Boisen Files, Chicago Theological Seminary).

ideas as we studied the spiritual conflicts of Bunyan and Fox and Saul of Tarsus."[25] A third observed:

> Because of the experience of the summer, the techniques of religion assume a new and deeper significance. Prayer, worship, confession, salvation, sin, death, life and the accompanying symbols; all these become more than words. No one who has spent a summer as a theological intern in a state hospital can again let these vital expressions slip easily off his tongue. The uses and devices of religion reveal themselves as the essential instruments of man's attempt to come face to face with reality.[26]

Boisen's pastoral exploration leaves a foundational legacy which has continuing critical importance for the methodology of CPE. After over sixty years, CPE is still challenged to maintain the dynamic, dialogical balance between the insights of living human experience and the truths of theological doctrine. Such a position is not static and therefore, like Boisen's life-long search itself, may never be fully achieved. Nevertheless, his clinical method of theological inquiry may be held up as both a standard and a point of reference in the conduct of clinical learning.

Conclusion

Boisen is a figure of the past, the present, and the future. His voice was sometimes muted by his own illness and by those who dismissed him because of it. In spite of this, he had an urgent message which continues to be of value to anyone courageous enough to explore his inner world. Psychology of religion, theological education, and CPE should all be grateful to Boisen for his personal belief that "the end of life is to solve important problems and to contribute in some way to human welfare, and if there is even a chance that such an end could best be accomplished by going through Hell for awhile, no man worthy of the name would hesitate for an instant."[27]

---

25. Robert N. Stretch, "Religion in Mental Health," (Unpublished paper, Summer, 1935, Boisen Files, Chicago Theological Seminary).

26. Ouelette, "A Theological Student Spends a Summer as an 'Interne' at Elgin," *Collected and Contributed Papers* Vol. 2 (Elgin IL: Elgin State Hospital, 1936), 257.

27. Boisen, *Out of the Depths*, 132.

SUBJECT INDEX

NAME INDEX